Bloomsbury Recalled

Bloomsbury Recalled

QUENTIN BELL

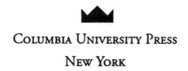

COLUMBIA UNIVERSITY PRESS

NEW YORK

A portion of the costs of publishing this book has been
borne by a Centennial gift from Andrew and Janet Neilly.

First published in the United Kingdom under
the title *Elders and Betters* by John Murray (Publishers) Ltd.,
50 Albemarle Street, London, W1X 4BD

First published in the United States by Columbia University Press,
562 West 113th Street, New York, NY 10025

Library of Congress Cataloging-in-Publication Data

Bell, Quentin.
    [Elders and betters]
    Bloomsbury recalled / Quentin Bell.
      p. cm.
    Originally published: Elders and betters. London : J. Murray,
1995.
    Includes index.
    ISBN 0-231-10564-9 (acid-free paper)   PA ISBN 0-231-10565-7
      1. Bloomsbury (London, England)—Intellectual life—20th century.
2. Authors, English—England—London—Biography.   3. Intellectuals—
England—London—Biography.   4. Artist—England—London—
Biography.   5. Bell, Quentin—Family.   6. Bloomsbury group.
I. Title.
DA685. B65B45 1996
942.1'42—dc20   95-45907

Casebound editions of Columbia University Press books
are printed on permanent and durable acid-free paper.

Printed in the United States of America

c 10 9 8 7 6 5 4
p 10 9 8 7 6 5 4 3 2 1

Contents

Illustrations follow page vi

1. Pig in the Middle	1
2. Clive Bell	22
3. Vanessa Bell	43
4. Duncan Grant	59
5. David Garnett	71
6. Maynard Keynes	85
7. Roger Fry	106
8. Leonard Woolf	116
9. The MacCarthys	129
10. Meetings with Morgan	140
11. The Stracheys	147
12. Ottoline Morrell	161
13. Ethel Smyth	169
14. Claude Rogers and Lawrence Gowing	176
15. Robert Medley and Mary Butts	193
16. Anthony Blunt	203

Appendix I	*A Room of One's Own and Three Guineas*	212
Appendix II	*Maynard Keynes and His Early Beliefs*	221
Index		227

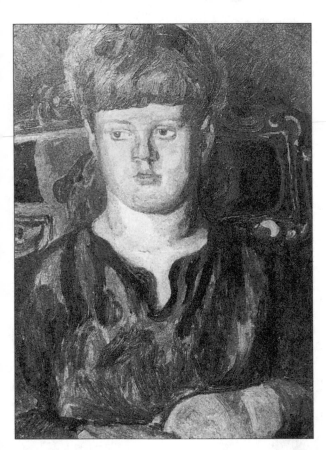

1. The author
by Duncan Grant,
1922

2. Clive Bell by
Henry Lamb,
1911

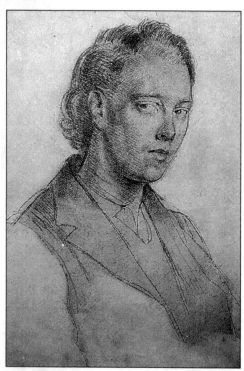

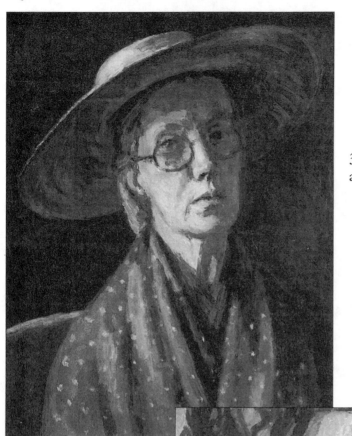

3. Vanessa Bell,
a self-portrait, 1958

4. Duncan Grant,
a self-portrait,
c. 1926

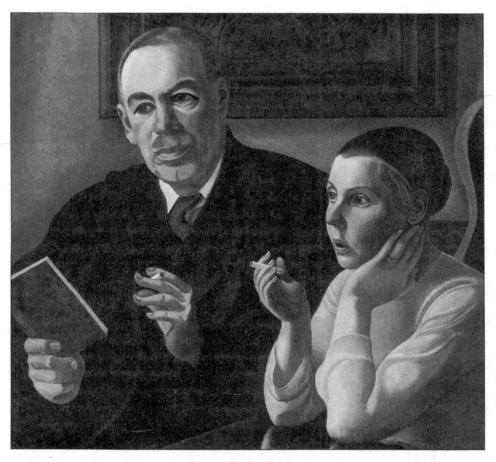

5. Maynard and Lydia Keynes by William Roberts, *c.* 1932

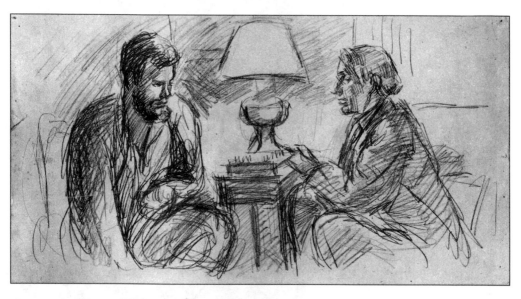

6. Julian Bell and Roger Fry playing chess, study for an oil painting
by Vanessa Bell, *c.* 1930

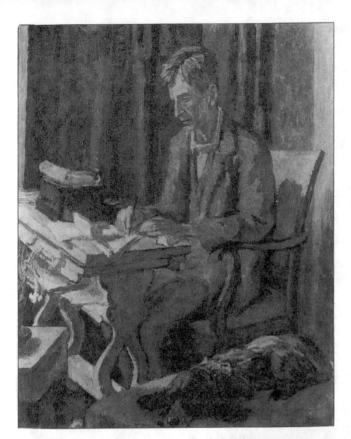

7. Leonard Woolf
by Vanessa Bell,
1940

8. Desmond MacCarthy
by Duncan Grant,
c. 1942

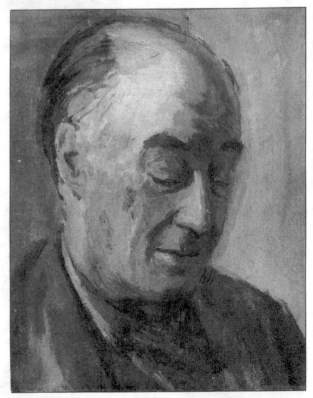

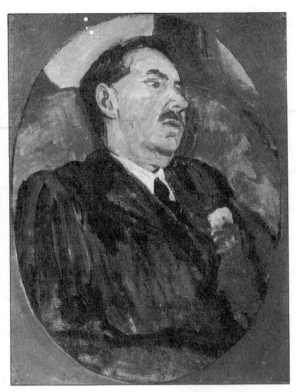

9. E.M.Forster
by Vanessa Bell,
1940

10. Lytton Strachey
by Vanessa Bell,
1912

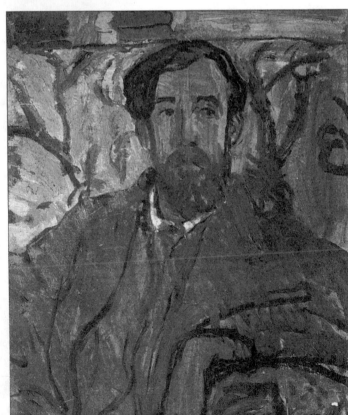

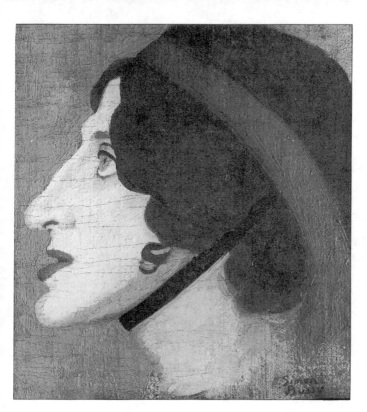

11. Lady Ottoline Morrell
by Simon Bussy,
c. 1920

12. Ethel Smyth,
a sketch by Quentin Bell,
from an undated photograph

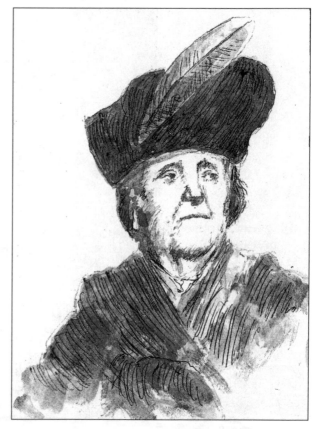

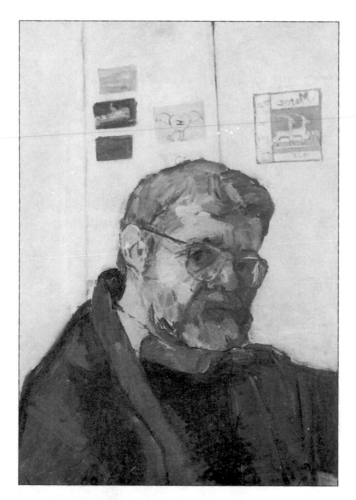

13. Claude Rogers, a self-portrait, 1975

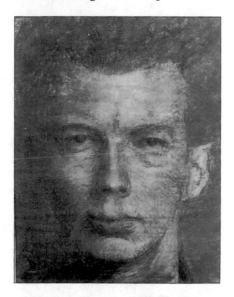

14. Lawrence Gowing, a self-portrait, undated

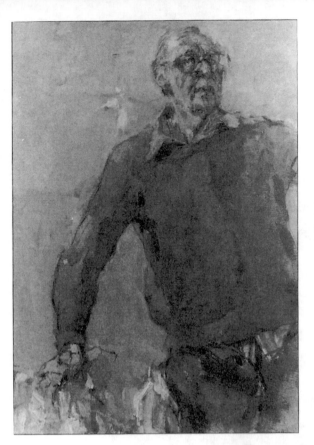

15. Robert Medley,
a self-portrait,
1977

16. Anthony Blunt
by Peter Foldes,
1947

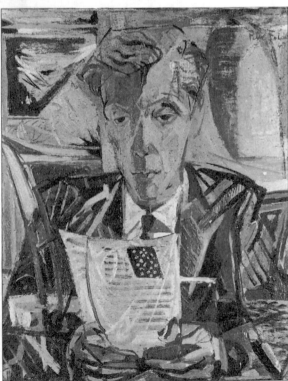

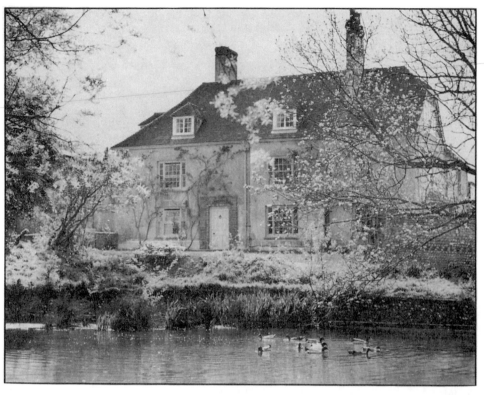

17. Charleston

18. 46 Gordon Square

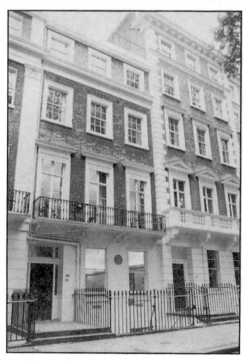

Bloomsbury Recalled

I

Pig in the Middle

THIS BOOK BEGAN as an autobiography. There was a time, not so long ago, when I thought that it would be agreeable to write my own life. After three failures I have changed by mind; therefore the main body of this work is devoted, not to me, but to my elders and betters, a term I have used to describe my parents, their friends and acquaintances. Nevertheless I have found it necessary to say something about myself. My portraits are based largely upon my own observation; the character of my evidence depends upon my qualifications as a witness and the reader is entitled to examine me before hearing my testimony. Like those figures upon the margin of a canvas pointing inwards towards the main subject of the picture, I need not stand in an important position, but I must be present, for the visible spectator provides a human scale and may also establish the period of the whole.

The definition of the period is indeed very important. Nearly all of those persons whom I describe were born before 1890; I was born in 1910. I could not examine my subjects intimately before they were middle-aged and before that time (say, 1920) they had known a world at peace and thereafter had witnessed horrors – war, famine and revolution – an age of violence and insecurity that is still with us today. I grew up amongst people who, because they were older than I, were less able to enjoy the novelties of life and were more sensible to the distresses of the age than we, their children.

Of those people whose portraits I have attempted, the majority were artists or patrons of the arts, that is to say of the visual or literary arts, and were described, perhaps rather loosely described, as

Bloomsbury. I saw Bloomsbury at close quarters in what I consider to be its final period, a period which ended when the Second World War began. This also was the end of my rather long nonage.

The period that I shall now try to discuss is therefore not very long, and later I shall not stay within its limits, but it seems worth describing for there are few people who had the same kind of experience and are alive today.

I was born at 46 Gordon Square, Bloomsbury. The doors of No. 45, No. 47, and indeed of all the other houses in the square, were black, or if not black, dark grey or a funereal blue. The door of No. 46 was a startling bright vermilion. The colour had been chosen by my mother, Vanessa; she also decorated the interior of the house, making use of equally startling colours. My father, Clive Bell, was in those days a left-wing radical. From an early age I knew that we were odd.

I and my brother Julian, two and a half years my senior, went together to be educated in a school on the other side of the square; it catered for very small boys and for girls of all sizes and offered prayers of a non-denominational kind every morning. Julian made friends with a little boy, the son of a Nonconformist clergyman who lived nearby in Taviton Street. Our nurses took us together to Regent's Park; there my brother and his friend held discussions which usually went above my head but in one of them I learnt that some day I must die.

When we visited our friend's home I was amazed and impressed: everything was so smart and clean and highly polished. I admired the lincrusta wallpaper, the photographs framed and mounted in velvet, the polished brassware and above all the elephant's tusk, wonderfully carved to resemble a steadily diminishing procession of little elephants. It was all new and splendid.

Then one day we learnt that our friend was forbidden to speak to us. We were rejected, not on account of our parents' taste in interior decoration, but because Julian had ventured to cast doubts upon the historical accuracy of the book of Genesis.

It was we who were nonconformist. We – that is the Bell children – might fail to believe in the story of Noah's Ark and no great harm would come of it; there were only a few people who felt deeply on the subject. But everyone – so it seemed – was agreed that the Germans were inhuman beasts, everyone that is, except our parents.

We had a nurse and a nursemaid, Mabel Selwood, whom I loved and who had succeeded a certain Elsie whom I dreaded and detested. Mabel had a lover, a non-commissioned officer in the Coldstream Guards. Mabel was enthusiastically patriotic and infected me with her enthusiasm. Sometimes at night I would see the angry, terrible face of the Kaiser glaring at me out of the darkness. After tea, in the drawing-room, I played at being a gramophone scratching a chalk in circles upon the drawing room floor and bawling out the most atrocious abuse of the enemy. My uncle, Leonard Woolf, who was both musical and a socialist, found these exhibitions noisy, vulgar and disgusting. He and Virginia learned not to call at No. 46 at times when they might expect a recital from me.

I had as one may say 'known about the war' from the beginning, but I do not think that I understood that the war could affect me or my family. At first it was something at once distant yet terrifying but which also engaged my enthusiasm. There was, in those early days, no rationing and among my parents' friends no one who seemed in danger. But in 1915 something did happen which struck my imagination forcibly.

In Fitzroy Street a short walk from where we lived there was an excellent baker called Zeller who made the best bread and buns in our neighbourhood. In 1915, when the *Lusitania* was sunk by a German submarine, a band of 'patriots' marched upon Mr Zeller's shop and smashed its windows. It transpired that Mr Zeller was not responsible for sinking the *Lusitania* and was in fact Swiss. I hope that he was properly compensated; certainly his windows were replaced and decorated with the arms of that German family which now called itself Windsor.

I heard of this incident at a time when I was becoming aware that my family and many of the friends of my family did not share those patriotic feelings which prevailed in the nursery and in our school. Was it not possible, if the Germans should be so disobliging as to sink another ship, that the crowd would batter down our bright red door in Gordon Square?

In 1916 the Government, having failed to defeat the enemy with an army of volunteers, and that army having sustained a great many casualties, it was decided to impose compulsory military service. My father and many of his friends were faced by the need to serve in what seemed to them a foolish and unnecessary quarrel, or to go to prison. There were however means of escape: men engaged in work of national importance were, if they could satisfy a tribunal, exempted. To this end my father took refuge at Garsington, the home of Lady Ottoline Morrell, and there rode about the estate looking agricultural on a horse. Duncan Grant who, for as long as I could remember, had been practically a part of our household, went to Wissett Lodge in Suffolk. With him went David Garnett who had been serving with the Friends' Ambulance in France. Their plan was to gain exemption from military service by fruit growing. Vanessa, her servants and her children joined them.

Wissett Lodge was a delightful place: there was a big garden and two large ponds, one of which was stocked with a great shoal of goldfish, fish so unsophisticated that a child might catch them in his hands. The garden was a perfect place in which to play and we got into a great deal of mischief. The grown-ups seemed infected by our wild behaviour, so much so that they joined in the war games to which we were addicted. One in particular was to end the delights of Wissett for me. Julian and I having decided to be Athenian soldiers, and having armed ourselves with staves as tall as ourselves went charging across the lawn to vanquish some imaginary Spartans. I fell and struck the razor-sharp edge of a broken flower pot. As I turned towards the house I called out, 'I've cut off my leg, I've cut off my leg, it's only hanging on by the skin'. I was an over-imaginative child, but the wound was undoubtedly severe. I still bear the scar.

The rest of my time at Wissett was spent in bed and I returned to London in a horizontal position. For some reason I found London charming, seen from a back window in Gordon Square. I remember listening with delight to the sound of the muffin man's bell and watching the beams of the searchlights shining up into the night sky.

Although my brother and I did not know it, a tribunal had refused to exempt from active service Duncan and his friend, David Garnett, whom we called Bunny. It was a worrying time for our mother. I remember how one evening at Gordon Square she described Charleston, the new home to which we were going. With a slow deliberate pencil she traced the shape of the house, its walled garden, the pond in front and another pond behind, the paddock, the lawns and the orchard.

In October 1916 two conscientious objectors, either of whom

could have been prosecuted under the Criminal Law Amendment
Act, a woman with two unruly children and no visible husband, one
servant and a dog, were deposited at the gate of Charleston by Mr
Sutton's ancient taxi-cab.

For my part I was disappointed. I had been told that Charleston
was in the south (it is in Sussex). I had recently been taken to the
cinema for the first time and had seen a film of Captain Scott's expedition to the Antarctic. This, like Charleston, lay to the south of 46
Gordon Square and I had hoped for penguins and ice floes. If we had
waited a few weeks I might have been satisfied. I remember during
the cold winter of 1916/17 walking across the field with a bucket to
the only spring in our neighbourhood which had not frozen up.

Even in summer it was a cold house; the only source of hot water
was the kitchen range; cold water had to be pumped up by hand. At
night one took a candle to bed and tried to walk bravely past dark
corners. By day we lived mainly in the dining room; here we learnt
to read and write and speak a few words of French, here I wept over
the difficulties of the seven times table. Here during the March
offensive of 1918 distant gunfire from across the Channel shook our
windows as it was to shake them again in the summer of 1940. Here
we ate our increasingly frugal meals.

The newest thing in that neighbourhood was the railway, and
despite the railway the pace of life was very slow. A few miles from
us at Charleston there was a great chalkpit where, until compara-
tively recently, the chalk had been loaded upon an ox-cart. The ox
carried its load without supervision: it set off alone with a blow to its
rump, making its way down Bo-Peep Lane towards the green lane
that is now the A27 from Brighton to Eastbourne. This it crossed.
Knowing its way it proceeded onwards, turning neither to right nor
left, until it reached the railway station at Berwick. It took a long
time to make the journey for the ox, although immensely strong, is
slow. Those farmers who found it worthwhile to plough downland
still made use of oxen in the early decades of this century; the horse
was too weak to pull a plough through such steep stony ground. It
was not until the tractor arrived that the ox was finally despatched.

The old farm workers were pleased to see the tractor: 'it put the
noses of them fuckin' horses out of joint'. For them, the horse was a
modern intruder.

We children soon found a paradise in the garden and beyond

where military and naval games could be played. The downs were grazed by sheep which cropped the grass to one vast natural lawn, free then of the wire fences of more recent times. Here one might find dewponds and in them great crested newts with orange bellies and even, which was surprising, little fish. The old road which ran along the foot of the downs from Firle to Alfriston was still used by the grocer's van (it is now a cart track), while the 'new' road which found its tortuous way around the fields and on to Lewes, was safe for children on donkeys. In later years I would cycle alone the eight miles into Lewes to purchase gunpowder, ostensibly for use in a muzzle-loader.

It almost seems that Vanessa had her children educated upon homeopathic principles. The school in Gordon Square which taught us to be religious and patriotic, and the nurses who took a very similar view of what was suitable for children, were succeeded by a governess who tempted my brother to repeat his doubts concerning the book of Genesis. She took us first to the Selmeston Church and then to the Charleston pew at Firle. Her views about the war were equally conventional. She had a good deal of trouble with Julian; me, she spoilt. She called herself Mrs Brereton and had a daughter, whom we children liked, also an amiable, rather feeble young man, but there was no visible Mr Brereton. In this she conformed to the mores – if that be the word – of Charleston.

Nevertheless she took a poor view of us and thought us culturally pretentious; she deplored our taste in interior decoration and wrote a satirical novel about us. If this is still in existence and some scholar were to find it he would have, at least, a literary curiosity – one of the very first satires on Bloomsbury and, who knows, perhaps a master-piece. As I have said Mrs Brereton spoilt me and I was devoted to her. She taught me a certain amount of history, a subject on which she was entertaining though not reliable.

Mrs Brereton had a friend in the War Office who convinced us that we were winning even when it seemed that we were not. In the end we did win. Peace, but not plenty, arrived and was followed by a baby sister and a time of what seemed even greater hardship than we had known during the war. We boys became an unbearable nuisance at Charleston. We were sent off to the Woolfs at Asham, a few miles away, which was a treat, then we were at Hogarth House, Richmond, until Leonard took us back to 46 Gordon Square which at that time contained a mixed population consisting of Clive, Maynard Keynes, Harry Norton the mathematician, J.T. Sheppard, who was later to be Provost of King's, and various 'on-withs' such as Mary Hutchinson. Clive did his best to amuse us; we saw the ballet, we made ourselves ill at Buszards' tea rooms, we were taken to the cinema. But in the end we proved too much of a nuisance and were sent back to Charleston.

When I was about eight or nine I had an aesthetic experience which seems worth recording. In the nursery at 46 Gordon Square there had been a gramophone – a large square box with a horn above and a dog on its side. There were also some records of patriotic songs – the only one that I recall dating from the Boer War. This machine came from Gordon Square to Charleston but I do not remember it being used there although there was no other. When I found it, it had been taken to pieces and these were covered with dust. With the machine there was a record and on the record was a label which I could not understand. I was alone but it was not very difficult to reassemble the pieces by myself. I knew there should be a needle and there was none, but by this time I was determined to make the thing work. I took a penknife and walked out into the field in front of the house, there I found a blackthorn and cut off a twig; this supplied me with several needles. I wound-up the machine. At Charleston there was no musician and no musical instrument. What I heard was thus quite unexpected, ghostly faint but very clear and pure. I now realize that it was a partita by Bach, but at the time I had no name for it. It moved me to tears.

The incident has a certain historical interest. Nowadays we are so lavishly supplied with music that it is unlikely to come as a novelty even to a child of eight. The sad thing is that this lovely surprise did not come to a young musician.

The events of the next few years might with care be placed in chronological order but hardly deserve such exact consideration; for a time I was educated by Miss Rose Paul and for a time I was again at school in Gordon Square.

We spent one autumn in St Tropez, at that time a very quiet place where children anticipated the licence of a later age by bathing naked in the sea. But I was unhappy there. I think that Julian and I were both jealous of our sister Angelica, although it was surely natural that the youngest should, in some ways, be preferred and

Vanessa had always wanted a girl. I can speak with some certainty about my own feelings – the feelings of the pig in the middle.

Thus, when I was about ten years old, I wanted to commit murder. I decided to kill Angelica's doll, a rather smart French affair with eyes that opened and shut and an imbecile simper. One afternoon, when there were no witnesses, I flung it down violently upon a stone floor, cracking its skull; it was made of some tough composite material, and its foolish smile remained intact so that it seemed to have defeated me. I remember the deep feeling of guilt with which I concealed evidence of my crime, which in fact was never found out. In later years I did still resent being, as I saw it, the least favoured child and this feeling did not entirely vanish until I became aware that Duncan, not Clive, was Angelica's father.

It was on our return from France that Julian and I discussed the future rather seriously. He was to leave Owen's School in London and go to Leighton Park. I was to go to a preparatory school in Hampstead. Julian had been unhappy at Owen's School, but thought his new school would be more congenial. He was to be miserable, as I too was to be miserable, at Leighton Park, but now for several years I was to be fortunate in my education. Peterborough Lodge was a good school, standards were high thanks to the large influx of boys from Jewish families living in Hampstead and I fell in love, intellectually and perfectly innocently, with a very bright little boy, the son of a Dr Roaf. I have always expected to find that unusual name in some list of distinguished scientists or academics. He soared above me to a higher class and seemed destined for great achievements.

We used to meet in the playground during the mid-morning break and discuss things that were not on the school curriculum: the existence of God, the immortality of the soul, the possibilities of science, the scientific stories of H.G. Wells, the likelihood of a war with the United States, also the political arguments of the moment.

It was a time when I was becoming aware of politics. Julian had come back from school declaring that he was a socialist. I decided that I was a liberal. It was 1924 and Ramsay MacDonald had formed the first Labour government. A memory of that time sheds some light on my mixture of cleverness and simplicity. For some reason, when we were tête-à-tête, one of the masters read me John of Gaunt's patriotic speech from Richard II ('This royal throne of kings, this scepter'd isle' etc.) and asked for my comments. I saw the speech as a piece of party politics. I did not say that John of Gaunt was a humbug or a jingo but I did say that he was 'laying it on a bit thick' or words to that effect: he was denouncing the opposition and courting the favour of the electorate.

I realized at once that I had said the wrong thing. My teacher was moved, not only by Shakespeare's poetry but also by his own patriotic feelings. Did I not share them? I supposed that I did, it was an aspect of the matter that had not occurred to me. He was very annoyed and, as I see now, thought that I was teasing him. If only he had given me a hint of the answer for which he was looking I am sure I should have obliged for he could, and indeed did, make my life unpleasant.

Altogether it was a time when I was learning a good deal for in addition to my studies I was in a way being instructed by Maynard Keynes.

Clive had suggested that I should be sent to live in France rather than go to a public school. The suggestion was made after lunch one day and included all sorts of glamorous and enticing embellishments. I was present and did not know that plans made after lunch should not be taken too seriously. When I discovered my mistake I was in despair. It was Vanessa who mended matters.

An amiable Monsieur Renoir, a nephew of the great Impressionist, had a colleague, Monsieur Pinault, at the Lycée Louis Le Grand in Paris who could house me and teach me and thither I was sent at the age of fourteen in the spring of 1924.

The first few days were horrible; I discovered that I could not understand a word of the language, but Monsieur Pinault was a good teacher and I soon found that I could make myself understood and then that I could understand. Madame Pinault was a kindly woman and a wonderful cook – I became enormously fat.

Monsieur Pinault was one of those Frenchmen whose whole life had been changed by the Affaire Dreyfus. It had made him a passionate enemy of militarism, implacably hostile to the church, a supporter, though not I think a member, of the Communist Party and a trade unionist. He was a cultivated man with a proper respect for the writers of the Grand Siècle, but his real enthusiasm was for Voltaire and the Encyclopaedists, for Victor Hugo, and for Zola; amongst the painters he admired Delacroix and Courbet.

My own opinions had already been affected by Julian's socialism and I found myself able to agree with a good deal of what Pinault had to say. There was a generosity, a decency and an intellectual curiosity about Pinault which made him hard to resist. I did not then know that his taste for good food, good wine and intelligent conversation was surpassed only by his appetite for young women.

After 14 July we left Paris, took the train for Argenton and went thence to Gargilesse, a village in the foothills of the Massif Central, made famous by George Sand. Here the Pinaults had a daughter, a son-in-law and a farm, and there Pinault became a new man, stripping off his ugly, respectable city clothes and prefabricated tie to wear the simplest dress or, occasionally, none at all as when he strode through the turbulent water of the Creuse, muscular, hairy and hellenic, casting his net for fish. I remember him again building stooks of his son-in-law's wheat while I worked behind with the gleaners.

A few months ago I had a letter from M. Renoir reminding me that he had introduced me to Pinault and asking me whether it had been a success. I replied, truthfully, that it had been by far the most valuable part of my education and had enriched my life enormously.

When I arrived at Leighton Park, Reading, in the autumn of 1924 I was terribly fat, bad at games, hopeless at mathematics, very weak in all subjects save scripture (it has always been my forte and was a favourite with Pinault). I was in truth bad at everything, even French, for although I could talk, I could not and still cannot, write French. I learnt very little, I was for a time perfectly miserable, later on I was merely bored. My school life was nasty, brutish and, thank heavens, short. I never even attempted school certificate and after three years, when I was 17, I left.

Shortly afterwards I went to Munich where I suppose I did learn something; the Alte Pinakothek is not only a rich collection but one in which nearly all the great European schools are represented, and a seat in the gallery at the opera only cost 50 pfennig.

The following year I again went to Paris and it was then that I began to paint seriously – my career as an art student is touched on below. In the summer I went to La Bergère, a house which my family in some fashion shared with a retired Colonel Teed who was a vintner and made excellent wine. This was in Cassis, which the Colonel described as the Latin Quarter of Sodom and Gomorrah.

In two successive summers I found myself sharing the house with Clive and as it were playing the part of Leporello to Clive's Don Juan; at times it was difficult and painful, at other times very amusing. At the end of that first summer I took a boat from Marseilles and went to Naples. I spent a frugal and solitary winter in Rome, frugal because I had spent far too much of my allowance on taking and furnishing a studio in the Via Margutta, solitary because in the first place I knew no one and saw no one until the last few months of my tenancy, also because I found that I rather enjoyed solitude.

I returned in the summer of 1929 via Arezzo and Florence to Cassis, where I found Clive trying to maintain a complicated relationship with a young woman.

As before, the complexities of life were interesting but in a new way, for now I myself was involved as the friend, and later the partisan, not only of Clive's inamorata but of Clive's rival, Yvonne Kapp. The alarums and excursions of that triangular affair concern me here only because Yvonne and I became friends and with certain lacunae have remained friends until the present day.

When I fell in love with Yvonne it must have seemed, to adapt a phrase of Jane Austen's, that I did so 'to disoblige my family'. In fact I had no ulterior motive, I just found her voice, her appearance and her mind immensely attractive, as indeed did Clive, but that did nothing to alleviate the situation which indeed was depressing. Yvonne at that time, and perhaps still, disliked almost all the works that Bloomsbury has ever written or painted. Bloomsbury (by which I really mean Clive) was mildly dismissive of Yvonne's writings, but when she became a member of the Communist Party there was no lack of ammunition to throw in her direction. I imagine that both sides enjoyed the exchange of fire, but for the pig in the middle it was no fun at all.

In 1933 Yvonne and I took a holiday in southern Spain. We returned, as we had set out, by sea, and during the voyage I developed a bad cold. When I got back to Charleston it persisted. I began to run a constant high temperature and a cough, my pleura was affected and at one point the doctors emptied it, drawing off about a quart of fluid which looked very like champagne. Dr Chalmers, a celebrated specialist, diagnosed tuberculosis and, acting on his advice, I spent the winter of 1933–4 on the top of a Swiss mountain.

I was not alarmed. I was convinced that I was not really consumptive; also, apart from the cough and high temperature, I did not feel at all ill. I enjoyed some fierce arguments with a clergyman, managed to do a little painting, and embarked upon historical research on the principality of Monaco for which I was totally unqualified. This activity, which had been suggested by Yvonne, was a wonderful medicine. My lack of qualifications forced me to educate myself and, although I never knew enough to get in sight of publication, it kept me cheerful. By the spring my cough was silenced, my temperature was normal and, having grown quite slender at school, I became rather fat.

The following winter I spent in the south of France; still at work on my ludicrous research I had the impertinence to visit the great Monsieur Gabriel Hanoteaux, an eminent historian, a man who once came within an ace of making a war between England and France, who had seen the great charity bazaar fire in 1899 and who now had – what shall we call it? – the generous folly to give me letters of introduction to the *monsignori* who could admit me to the archives of the Vatican. When I consider my ignorance I am astounded by my courage.

I was given a lift to Rome in Vita Nicolson's chauffeur-driven car, it having been lent to Vanessa. Angelica, who came with us, has described that Italian sojourn in her autobiographical work *Deceived with Kindness*. Reading her account I am saddened to discover how many vexations she suffered at a time when I had supposed that she was enjoying herself. She does not reproach me but I feel that I was very insensitive. An excursion which we made southwards via Naples and thence to Paestum and which I found immensely enjoyable was, as she remembers it, a succession of miseries – dirty hotels, filthy lavatories, bugs, heat, bad food and indigestion for which the charm of Caserta and the splendours of the Poseidon Temple failed to console her; it makes melancholy reading.

While we were in Italy many of the masterpieces of Italian painting were being exhibited in France. It was this which decided me to return home a little earlier than my family and to travel via Paris. When I got back to Gordon Square I found Julian and Clive planning a journey to China. Julian had that afternoon been offered a chair in the University of Hankow. Ever since coming down from Cambridge he had been looking for a job.

Julian left for China on 29 August 1935, Angelica left soon afterwards to live in Paris and by mid-September I was alone at Charleston save for Grace, our domestic 'treasure', now a permanent resident in the house. This was lucky for me because I developed a very bad cold with a high temperature. Leonard and Virginia came from Rodmell to cheer me up and keep me in touch with the world. The world was in an interesting condition. Italy was preparing to go to war with Abyssinia and the Labour Party was deciding what it would do if there were a war. The Woolfs, who had been at the Labour Party Conference at Brighton, brought me the Labour view of that debate which set Lansbury the charming pacifist against Bevin the brutal realist. At the time I was fascinated but it did not lower my temperature.

Then letters began to come from someone called Pierre Gerôme; it appeared that he was connected with an organization of French intellectuals opposed to fascism. He was making plans for the economic policy of the Front Populaire which we hoped would be returned to power at the forthcoming elections. Would Mr Keynes be so kind as to look at them?

I asked Grace to take a message to Keynes, who was at Tilton half a mile away. She returned with a note from Maynard. Who was Monsieur Gerôme and was he a crypto-communist? Of course I didn't know. Letters went to and fro, the negotiations became complicated and my health did not improve. Finally it transpired that Monsieur Pierre Gerôme was not a crypto-communist, in fact he was not even Monsieur Pierre Gerôme; that was merely a *nom de guerre* and really he was my friend François Walther under whose roof my sister was living. When all these complications had been resolved Maynard looked at the proposed programme and dismissed it as too reactionary to be taken seriously. Meanwhile my temperature had returned to normal.

While Julian went to China and Angelica to Paris I settled in a less glamorous part of the world – the Five Towns. I had decided to become a potter and it seemed the right destination for me. It must be allowed that at that time what was called 'our fine china' was pretty appalling; this I had expected; I was looking not for beauty but for technical information. Yet I discovered beauty. The inhabitants complained, and not unreasonably, that their wretched muddle of cheap housing and old fashioned 'pot banks' was a disgrace; and so it was, but it was also extremely beautiful.

The old bottle-oven was a lovely thing and when it was belching blue flames into the night sky it was superb. Down by the canal there were great patches of brilliant yellow sulphur. It was a mess but a highly pictorial mess. The Bay of Naples with Vesuvius smoking away was not so exciting as Stoke-on-Trent after a snowfall with all its furnaces alight.

Apart from this scenic beauty there was much to admire in the Five Towns: Burslem School of Art and its principal, that amiable Scot Gordon Forsyth; the art gallery which was splendid although usually deserted; even some of the pottery. Aesthetically then it was attractive, but I was also attracted by something else and here I must retrace my steps.

When I used to visit Cambridge to see Julian and his friends, Anthony Blunt, Guy Burgess, Harry Lintott or Eddie Playfair, I noticed that my brother was considered an eccentric because he took an interest in politics. By the time he came down he was still considered an eccentric, but now it was because he had *not* joined the Communist Party.

I have always felt that if only I knew a little more about the Church of England I could have written an illuminating essay on the Oxford Movement. I have felt so much of what those young men must have felt: the 'fellow travellers' of the English establishment as they moved closer and closer to the Roman Kremlin. On the one hand our smug, comfortable, 'reformist' religious establishment, so tepid, so close to respectable Anglican trade-unionism; on the other the vigorous, heroic, romantically wicked International of Rome and Moscow. The moderate men lacked glamour, but the extremists smelt of mendacity and innocent blood.

Julian and I both remained in the Labour Party but whereas I, distressed by the schism in socialism, the wasted energy of fraternal strife, went as far and perhaps further than our leaders permitted in the struggle for the united front, Julian, who hated the communists, remained adamant in his attitude. Ironically, his death for the Republicans in the Spanish Civil War led even so well informed a politician as Tom Driberg to suppose that he was a communist, a supposition which, in its way, reflects credit on the Communist Party.

The communists whom Julian met were I think almost entirely men and women of the middle classes, and although some of them were intellectually impressive there were a great many converts who made up in enthusiasm for what they lacked in common sense; they were romantic and this, for Julian, was a term of abuse. They compared unfavourably with the practical-minded working men whom he met fighting an uphill battle in our own very conservative constituency.

My own experience was somewhat different. I too learnt to know and value our comrades in darkest Sussex but when I went to Staffordshire I met socialists of a different kind. Here, too, there were young enthusiasts whom I could admire, but I also met others, mainly older men, who had prospered in the Labour Party, climbed out of the ranks and seemed perfectly content to remain in the comfortable positions which they enjoyed. These seemed much more inclined to oppose the communists than to discomfort their Conservative opponents. It had to be admitted that the communists also were ready to use very dirty weapons in their counter-attacks upon the socialist establishment. And yet, amongst them, there were some heroic characters, men living in great poverty but still ready to spend the little that they had in an unselfish and unambitious manner, for what they believed to be the liberation of man.

Newcastle-under-Lyme, the constituency in which I found myself, was peculiar; it was a pocket borough, belonging to that genial but unpredictable character, Colonel Wedgwood. Wedgwood had held the seat since 1906 and had only once had to fight for it, and that was when he was divorced. He now called himself a socialist. In Staffordshire a Wedgwood could call himself anything and still be elected unopposed as the Colonel was sometimes an independent and sometimes a 'single tax man'. (The doctrines of Henry George flourished in the potteries – a peculiar local 'heresy'.)

In these circumstances I did at least come into contact with the industrial workers and with the great army of the unemployed. I was able to learn how to confront and how to talk to hostile, or what was worse, indifferent crowds or even to no crowds at all; to stand up in a market place or at a street corner and to deal with hecklers – sometimes black-shirted – who used their fists. I used to enjoy 'chalking parties' where we would write pungent remarks on public walls, always with a scout who would whistle if the police put in an appearance. I learnt also that I was not much use at canvassing despite the tutelage of a genius who could work miracles on the doorstep, he having sold patent medicines.

All this led me into organizations which were proscribed by the Labour Party and, when I returned to London, I joined another communist-led organization known as the 'Artists' International Association'. I remember complaining to Peggy Angus, who at that time was very active in the movement, that our committee meetings were unbearably long. 'You're a fine one to talk,' she replied, 'you don't have to go to the fraction meeting.' The 'fraction' consisted, so far as I can remember, of the eight communist members of the executive; the 'rest of us', two in all, consisted of Mischa Black and myself. The unhappy comrades who had to attend both meetings must have been in session from about four in the afternoon until midnight when business ended and I drove back in my battered Morris to Charleston.

But despite this unwieldy executive the artists got things done. I was told that our anti-fascist exhibition, from which the police removed a portrait which it was feared might offend Herr Hitler, was assembled and hung in less than a fortnight. When the Germans invaded Czechoslovakia an organization to take care of refugee artists was instantly created. There were several very able officers in this organization, one of the most capable of them was Elizabeth Watson.

I had met her in Paris, in about 1930 in the Atelier Moderne, Rue Notre-Dame-des-Champs. The students there were for the most part well-dressed young women from America. Elizabeth when she spoke, whether in English or French, was clearly British and upper class; she was very attractive, beautifully and delicately made, her eyes were wonderful, particularly when closed, modelled in very high relief. Her dress had the simple, worn-out look of someone who has economized severely except on oil paint.

After she returned to England I saw her from time to time; she got on well with Vanessa and later with Yvonne. Until I returned from Staffordshire, however, I had not known that she was a party member. I suppose that her work for the AIA was what brought me into the movement. Certainly it was through her that I became involved in what proved to be my disastrous dealings with Picasso.

The year 1937 featured the great Paris Exhibition and was the year Julian returned from China and went to Spain. The Spanish Republic had asked Picasso to paint a mural for its pavilion at the exhibition. I do not know whether Vanessa and Duncan were especially interested in this work but they were in Paris for a few days in May and decided to pay him a visit. I accompanied them.

At that time Picasso had a studio in what had once been an embassy of the Dukes of Savoy. It was located on the left bank of the Seine in the VIIth arrondissement; one mounted a splendid flight of stairs and found oneself in a room which, although fairly large, was too narrow for his still unfinished picture of the bombing of Guernica. It therefore stood askew against the far wall. In front of it, on the floor, stood a multitude of small pots each containing liquid paint. How the artist managed to avoid upsetting them as he worked across his great canvas I cannot tell. For some time we gazed silently at Guernica, then Vanessa said '*C'est bien terrifiante*'. I cannot recall what else was said. But I had special reason for wanting to see the master. I had a piece of paper for him.

'What's it for?'

'For your signature please.'

Picasso signed and I left rejoicing.

At that time General Franco's troops were overrunning Biscaya, refugees fled the country, among them many children; all were destitute and various organizations, including the Artists' International, were trying to raise money for them. A letter to *The Times* was devised, I believe by Eddie Playfair; this was intended to precede a monster meeting at the Albert Hall at which half the intelligentsia of the world would be present. I had been asked, I think by Elizabeth, to secure the signatures of Picasso and Matisse. I had the letter translated by Janie Bussy and François Walther (alias Pierre Gerôme) and it was this which Picasso signed. It only remained to secure the signature of Matisse. But this, I knew, would not be easy. Matisse could be trusted to shy away from anything which was suspected of being inspired by the communists. Again I consulted Janie and François; they knew Matisse far better than I did, and were helpful and sympathetic; they told me it would be fatal to admit that Picasso had signed.

Fearful but determined I went to the Matisse Exhibition in a gallery on the Place Vendôme. It was a splendid exhibition and I had no difficulty in finding pleasant things to say when I met the artist, but when I came to the letter he did not like it. In vain I pointed out that the children whom we were trying to help were far too young to have political opinions, in vain I protested that I was not a communist and that the proposed Albert Hall meeting would be a non-party affair. He was adamant. Finally, when I had lost all hope of moving him, I revealed that Picasso had signed. He started, stared, pulled out his pen and added his name.

I must confess that I was rather pleased with myself. I did not then know that *The Times* would refuse to publish the letter. Meanwhile I was entrusted with another task. Paris at that time was dominated by the exuberant architectural fantasia of 'Expo 37'. At the centre of the exhibition was a vast vulgar tower surmounted by a disagreeable eagle – the German Pavilion – and facing it the even more preposterous Russian Pavilion which was crowned by a male and a female hero of the revolution; both of these were enormous and looked as if they were about to fall off the roof. The Peace Pavilion, which was far from complete, lay modestly outside the boundary of the exhibition proper. Here there were architectural troubles which I was expected to solve, for the AIA was in some way concerned with the building. Knowing nothing of architecture I was of little use, but happily the entire AIA executive together with its wives and lovers arrived at the Hôtel de Londres, Bloomsbury's *pied-à-terre* in Paris, and they took charge of the ailing pavilion. Elizabeth came with them bearing fresh instructions: we were to persuade Picasso and Matisse to come to the Albert Hall.

Matisse was a non-starter I told them, but Picasso might be persuaded. Together we went to see him and he agreed. In retrospect I think it was a mistake to bring Elizabeth with me; clearly Picasso was rather taken by her and if I had been alone I should have received a flat refusal. As it was he agreed, but in such a manner that Elizabeth and I doubted whether, when it came to the point, he would keep his promise.

When the committee in London asked whether Picasso had agreed, we replied that he had, but . . . The committee replied that one either accepts or rejects an invitation. This sounded sensible, but . . . On the appointed day Elizabeth and I arrived at Picasso's door but it would not open. We rang him up. Yes, Monsieur Picasso was there, but after a few minutes he was no longer there. We remained at his door until at last it was certain that he was not coming. Elizabeth asked me to go to London and carry a message from him to the audience in the Albert Hall. I was sufficiently crazy to agree. Fortunately the last aeroplane had departed.

By this time I had stopped feeling pleased with myself. I felt not only that I had mismanaged the business, but that after all Picasso had better things to do than visit the Albert Hall and that it was impertinent of me to plague him. Elizabeth, who remained in Paris, continued to meet him from time to time. He never alluded to the Albert Hall but was in fact perfectly charming to her, so perhaps no great mischief was done.

Meanwhile, I returned to Charleston where I was busy installing a kiln and dealing with other matters connected with pottery. Then, on 20 July, Leonard drove up to the door and told me that Julian had been killed. He took me back to London where we found Vanessa half mad with grief and for a time life became a kind of permanent nightmare.

Later on, when the first dreadful paroxysms were over, there was a long period of convalescence and Vanessa began to plan some kind of monument. She had two ideas and they both came to grief. To begin with she planted a grove of poplars between the garden wall and what is now the car park at Charleston. The trees did not flourish. Her other plan was a memorial volume. I was involved in this work and this too did not live up to expectations. For me it was something new; I had no experience of editing or indeed of publication and I had no control over Vanessa's plans. She wanted someone to say that Julian was a genius, and no one was ready to say more than that he might have become a genius if he had lived longer. Several illustrious people were asked to contribute. Even when they said things that Vanessa did not much like it was hard to reject them and, in the end, although there were some interesting essays and letters by Julian himself, a very interesting essay by Charles Mauron together with contributions by Maynard Keynes, David Garnett and E.M. Forster, the final shape of the book was untidy and disorganized. Altogether we failed to produce anything that could be called monumental.

There was another book which could also be described as a monument to Julian. Virginia Woolf's *Three Guineas* (see Appendix I) is about war and women but it is to some extent also an argument with Julian. But arguing with the dead can be a dangerous occupation; unlike an argument with the living it gives no chance of that dialectical process in which both sides can perhaps arrive at an understanding.

Three Guineas was published in 1938, the year of Munich. I was in France during the crisis that led to that tragic settlement and perceived how anxious the French were not to fight. Earlier in September I had heard Maynard Keynes deliver his Memoir Club paper 'My Early Beliefs'. It was, for me, a depressing experience (see Appendix II).

Then came the Munich Settlement. Our enemies had gained another easy victory at the expense of our allies. We were like Medea who tore her brother to pieces, throwing the dismembered limbs into the sea one by one so as to amuse the enraged father who pursued her, but it seemed that, unlike Medea, we should not escape.

I was with a group of Labour supporters in Newhaven just after the occupation of Czechoslovakia the following March. 'We had better listen to what our Führer has to say,' remarked one of them, so we turned on the radio. Chamberlain was speaking in Birmingham to a loyal audience. What he said was remarkable. He accepted, although he did not say it in so many words, that the policy of appeasement had failed. Now, at last, he was ready to resist the aggressor. He gave a guarantee to Poland and the Poles took him seriously.

War then became practically inevitable and I suggested to Vanessa that she lay in a stock of preserved foods at Charleston. To Alix and James Strachey (Lytton's brother) such precautions must have seemed futile. An irresistible armada of aeroplanes would swoop down upon us and drown us beneath a sea of poison gas; we should be annihilated at once. They were perhaps exceptionally imaginative, but everyone expected that poison gas would be used and when war came the government provided us all with gas masks in little cardboard boxes.

I had been making preparations of a more personal kind, trying but failing to get a clean bill of health from my specialist and then to find some work in which I might make myself useful. In the end I took the easiest way out and that which kept me closest to the family, I went to work on Maynard's farm.

The actual declaration of war came almost as an anticlimax – no fighting on the western front, no gas and, for quite a long time, no bombs. But the declaration was preceded by a political earthquake of enormous dimensions.

The Hitler-Stalin pact was by any standard catastrophic. We had brought it on ourselves; we had shown that we were untrustworthy allies and unlikely to come to the assistance of a power to which we were openly hostile. Nevertheless, to many of us it seemed the copulation of Heaven and Hell, there were a lot of resignations from the Communist Party and much political agony.

And yet that was not the end of the unhappy flirtation of the British intelligentsia with the Soviet Union. When Germany attacked Russia and we discovered that we had an ally who, despite fearful losses, was fierce and unconquerable, there was an enormous revival of support for the Soviet Union which indeed infected many who must have been surprised by their own emotions and even more surprised at the memory of them.

I have transgressed, passing beyond the limits which I set for myself in this brief account of my youth and of the last years of Bloomsbury. But in fact, although the Memoir Club meeting in 1938 may serve as a terminus, I think that my sister's twenty-first birthday party, celebrated at the end of 1939, may provide a more fitting conclusion.

The house was packed and of course there were guests such as our neighbours, the Woolfs at Rodmell and the Keyneses at Tilton. A number of my sister's friends provided an element of youth and beauty. The war had not yet touched us so severely that we could not provide an abundance of food and drink. The party continued for several days. There was music and dancing. Maynard told us the story of how he was mistaken for Duncan, and Duncan for him, to the vast annoyance of Mr Bernard Berenson. Marjorie Strachey provided one of her libidinous performances. Lydia Lopokova danced for the last time. Altogether it made a good end.

2

Clive Bell

I HAVE A distinct memory of 4 August 1914, fifteen days before my fourth birthday. I was at Cleeve House, Seend, in the county of Wiltshire, the home of my grandparents Mr and Mrs William Heward Bell; they had just heard that war had been declared and they were delighted. I and my brother Julian shared the feelings of our grandparents. To make our joy complete we were taken out through the great Gothic front door on to the drive and were shown a wonder. There was a humming noise away to our left; it grew louder and louder and presently we saw a machine which flew through the air. I remember it as moving quite slowly, it seemed not far above the trees which grew before us. As it passed over them it vanished in the direction of Devizes. It was my first aeroplane.

This early memory of an event that was to have such enormous consequences might supply the excuse for a number of very trite observations; here I shall merely record that there was a very marked difference of attitude between our parents and our grandparents. Clive, the younger son, differed from his father on most subjects and I don't think that there was any important topic on which Vanessa agreed with her father or her mother-in-law.

I don't know very much about the history of the Bells. I believe that long ago they were farmers on the Cheviots; at some point someone struck coal and began to make money. My grandfather, who married into the retail side of the industry, worked – if that be the word – mines in Merthyr Tydfil.

According to Clive, who for a short time lived 'on the job', his family owned the entire valley – the mines, the railway, the pubs, the houses, the shops – everything. Every penny that was disbursed as wages came back eventually to the employers, 'and yet', said Clive, 'father could not understand why the men became socialists'.

The business yielded substantial profits which enabled my grandfather to purchase a large house in the village of Seend, to pull most of it down, and to rebuild it. Although it was originally a not very distinguished eighteenth-century house this seemed to Clive a pity. The new buildings erected in 1894, with additions about twenty years later, were strangely impractical. The visitor to Cleeve House was strongly urged not to have a bath, or, if he must bathe, to be content to use very little water: there was a drought at Seend howsoever wet it might be in other places. There were no water closets in the house; instead there were ingenious contrivances which made use of sand. Presently one discovered that for so big a house it had few bedrooms. Space had been sacrificed to accommodate a great hall. From a floor so vast that it resembled a railway terminus during a strike, this huge chamber ascended to the historically suggestive roof-beams of the house. On two sides of the hall was a minstrels' gallery with a balustrade. It must have cost a lot to heat.

The hall was dedicated to an exhibition of the Bell family's prowess. Not that the swords, lances, muskets, battleaxes etc. which were exhibited here had any historical connection with the family, but the innumerable antlers, stuffed heads, stuffed fish and birds in glass cases, the fox brushes, hooves, lion and tiger skins were all, as you might say, 'home killed'. Presiding over the east end of the hall was the gigantic head of a moose; the shape and shine of the creature's nose gave it the appearance of suffering from a perpetual cold in the head. In addition to the moose and other fauna there was also a banner which hung over the balustrade and, if I remember correctly, exhibited upon a field azure three bells argent; there was a belled falcon for crest. Also, that we might have music wherever we went, the pub a few hundred yards up the road was – and still is – called The Bell.

There were hints of blood sport everywhere. Virginia Woolf remembered dipping her pen into an inkwell which had been sunk into the hoof of a favourite hunter. But the hall was the chief repository of dead stock. Livestock in the form of chow dogs, which toned in exactly with the oak panelling of the house, and my grandmother's pack of Skye terriers, created a lasting nuisance.

Art was not excluded: in the morning room a series of pictures by a *Punch* artist explored the funny possibilities of a game of bridge, or it may have been whist; another *Punch* artist, G.D. Armour, who was responsible for a weekly hunting cartoon, had immortalized grandfather Bell mounted and wearing a pink coat. Shannon had painted the girls, not very well it seemed, for his paint had lost its lustre. Vanessa had been asked to restore it and, with the impetuosity of youth, had slapped on Copal varnish with disastrous results. 'It being Seend,' she said, 'nobody noticed.'

As children Julian and I loved Seend; it was excitingly big, the old nurse was kind, we accepted the place at its own valuation. The cooking was good, the cellar was excellent – I still remember the taste of the '96 port. As boys we enjoyed following the hounds under the care of Ovens, the admirable chauffeur. My brother never lost his appetite for shooting and even joined the family when it removed to a Scottish grouse moor. Also there were some of our relations whom it was pleasant to know. But in the end we came to dread the Christmas holidays.

According to his sons Grandfather Bell was an unpleasant character. I think that they were right. He was an angry little man who shouted at people, and a hypocrite who kept up a pretence of religion. Every morning, a gong summoned us to the breakfast room, at one end of which, seated upon leather sofas and armchairs, was the family, while at the other end, seated in a row, were the servants – about six women all spotless in black and white. Grandfather read the 'collect' for the day and a selected passage from the Bible, then with one accord we fell upon our knees and examined the upholstery of our chairs. I was always fascinated by the neat precision with which the servants executed this manoeuvre. They looked like a flotilla of moorhens diving head down into a pond. When the Lord's Prayer had been said they rose and, in the same disciplined fashion, filed out of the room to return with porridge, scrambled eggs, coffee and tea.

Mr and Mrs Bell, a devoted couple, had four children: two sons, Cory and Arthur (later Clive) and two daughters, Lorna and Dorothy; of these only my grandmother took the breakfast religion really seriously, although Lorna was a churchgoer. Perhaps the servants entertained hopes that they might eventually discover a better world. Even my uncle Cory, who was not troubled by a very acute social conscience, was appalled when, surveying the house for the first time, he looked at the servants' bedrooms. The parlourmaid – regarded by my grandmother as a 'treasure' – epitomized her name; it might have been bestowed by a Victorian novelist. She was called Meek.

My eyes were opened to the realities of life at Seend when I was about fifteen, old enough to be allowed to join the grown-ups at dinner, where I found the old Bells, my parents, my uncle Cory, his son and daughter, and Julian. Cory, always a clumsy fellow, managed to break the stopper of a decanter. 'You hog,' roared my grandfather. 'That's what you are, a hog, a hog!' Lieutenant-Colonel Cory Bell (retired), MP, DSO, Croix de Guerre, sat mute and shamefaced while his father shouted at him. It seemed to me something barbarous. Did this, I wondered, happen in other families? Did he sometimes speak to Granny like that?

Cory was Clive's favourite relative; he held the most atrocious opinions but it was impossible to dislike him. He had been a Conservative Member of Parliament after the war and had made friends with some of his Labour opponents who agreed with him in hating Lady Astor. His voice was well suited to one who had to make himself heard amidst the din of an artillery battle. His laugh – he had a strong sense of humour – was like the explosion of a bomb. He would I think have liked to make fun of his father, but one needed more than a DSO for that. He did, however, get a good deal of amusement from antagonizing his two sisters. The eldest, Lorna, was my least favourite aunt; it has to be said that she was unfortunate. When I was about four my brother and I were dressed up in white satin and employed as pages at her wedding – of which I remember nothing. This was followed by a madly extravagant blow-out. The bridegroom was William Acton, said to be the handsomest man in the British Army; later, when I came to know him a little, it seemed to me that if he was no longer the handsomest – and how could he be poor fellow after returning with fearful wounds from the war – he was now certainly the stupidest. I liked and was sorry for their son and daughter. I had met my aunt Lorna in the pages of *Mansfield Park*, but Jane Austen did not commit the cruelty of giving Aunt Norris children.

My aunt Dorothy, the youngest of her generation, was in many ways the most sympathetic. When I first knew her she was still unmarried. In winter she followed the hounds enthusiastically, in summer she had I believe to content herself with tennis. She had also some notion of making herself socially useful, organizing a girls' club in Seend, 'conduct which', according to the local clergyman, 'showed that she was no better than a bolshevik'. Could the club have been as interesting as that? Then, about 1925, she married a gentleman farmer who lived near Marlborough; his name was Henry Honey. Unfortunately one seldom found him at Cleeve House; indeed when one did he seemed out of his element for he was a man with a good and an open mind. He seemed ready to discuss anything; he was far more cultivated, more erudite, more widely travelled than the usual guests at Seend. Dorothy in fact was much more fortunate than her sister.

Perhaps it was this which created the ill-will between them, although I fancy that Lorna made enemies wherever she went. Henry Honey, although not a professional soldier like his brother-in-law, had held a commission, and one day after breakfast at Seend Dorothy remarked that he had been the last man off the Gallipoli Peninsula.

It was an unfortunate thing to say. Lorna at once exploded. Her Billy had been the last man to leave. There was, according to Clive and Cory, the most appalling row between the sisters in which unforgivable things were said on both sides. It never became clear who was in the right. Henry, who spoke Turkish and was an intelligence officer, might have had good reasons for staying with the rearguard. On the other hand, if one were in command of a retreating force it might seem convenient to leave Billy behind. Neither of these heroes was present and the matter remains a mystery. It was left to Cory to sum up: 'Well Clive, I think we are very fortunate in having two brothers-in-law who were both the last man off the Gallipoli Peninsula.'

The virtues of Seend were of the decorous kind: courage, fortitude, patriotism, and a certain bluff good humour. The vices were anger, hypocrisy, muddled thinking and insensitivity. Clive's parents were, so far as we know, models of chaste propriety, and in that generation at all events there was no hint of scandal. The scandal came later and arose not in those places where it might have been expected but in a most unlikely quarter.

My uncle Henry Honey, an ingenious man with a love of technical novelties, had obtained that rare thing, an experimental wireless licence (this was in the early days of broadcasting). His house was a paradise for technologically gifted schoolboys, and he was within easy distance of Marlborough College . . .

The modern reader will not require more information, unlike the outraged parents of the Marlborough boys. The story is commonplace enough, but what is rather astonishing is that my aunt Dorothy was dumbfounded; the mere idea of homosexual love left her astonished. But although ignorant she had the wisdom and charity to behave very well and save her family from disaster.

This is in the main a first-hand account of the Bells at Cleeve House as I saw them in their final years, a time when despite their wealth and status one felt that things were going wrong. The promise of that happy day in 1914 must have seemed remote, the coal industry was in a bad way, agriculture was depressed, Grandfather Bell mourned the 1870s when an English country gentleman was the most fortunate creature on earth.

In 1899 Clive went to Trinity College, Cambridge. 'After all those years of misery at Marlborough,' he said, 'I suddenly found myself treated as a human being.' Nor was that all; he was decidedly fortunate. He arrived in the University with all the apparatus and livestock needed for pursuing the hunt, killing birds, or entertaining actresses. Also fate had landed him on the same staircase as Saxon Sydney Turner and Lytton Strachey. Leonard Woolf was in the same college. Clive must soon have encountered the great intellectual stimulator of that generation at Cambridge, G.E. Moore, the author of *Principia Ethica*, a philosopher with whom the young men fell intellectually in love so that they became infected with a passion which later generations find it hard to understand.

In addition to the immense and quasi-saintly personality of Moore there was in Cambridge a society where young men gifted with a particular kind of unworldy grace might gather in pursuit of truth. It was considered an élite and for this reason tried to shield those who did not quite measure up to its standards from a knowledge of the paradise to which they had no entry. Of these Clive was one; indeed he was a non-starter. The 'Apostles' made a point of being unworldly, and Clive, with his hunting horn and his pretty friends, belonged very much to the temporal world. Another new friend, Thoby Stephen, a much stronger candidate than Clive, was also considered but not elected to the Apostolic Society. He, too, was addicted to the pleasure of the chase and, for all I know, to the pursuit of ladies. He was a jolly, handsome, cheerful giant of a man with a hearty, common-sensical view of the world. It was, however, a rather different kind of common sense than that to which Clive was accustomed at home. My father must have been rather impressed by the intellectual armament of his new friends; they were not dazzling, but they were uncommonly, admirably, deep. There was one matter in which he was I think more alert than they. Lytton might know all Racine by heart, while Saxon read Pindar as you or I would read the morning paper, but I am pretty sure that neither of them could have told a Degas from a Renoir. In fact I doubt whether, when they were at Cambridge, they could have told you anything whatsoever about either of these modern masters.

Clive had a reproduction of a Degas hanging in his rooms at Trinity. If, as I believe but can't prove, Clive brought this with him to Cambridge, we have here an interesting mystery. If he acquired the reproduction when he was at Cambridge there is still something unexplained.

In 1900 there were probably less than a thousand people in the country who had heard of Degas, and large photographic reproductions were still a novelty. Thoby Stephen's sister Vanessa might well have heard of Degas and it is just possible that the reproduction came from her *via* her brother. On the other hand, if Clive came to Cambridge with the reproduction in his luggage along with the hunting horn and the twelve-bore cartridges then there is only one person who might have provided a Degas while he was still at Marlborough.

Amongst the neighbours of the Bells there were at least two *Punch* artists: G.D. Armour and Leonard Raven-Hill. Raven-Hill had hoped to become a painter, but he found a better market for his drawings than for his paintings: *Punch* gave him work and later received him at its Round Table. In 1889 he married Annie Rogers. While he was working in London she remained in Wiltshire and made a number of friends amongst the officers stationed at Devizes. She was Clive's first mistress and, in spite of other commitments, they remained on bedding terms for years.

It is not I hope fanciful to see in Raven-Hill's *Punch* cartoons the work of an artist much influenced by Forain; and it is not a long step from the influence of Forain to the influence of Degas. What more probable than that Clive's first mistress should have given him a reproduction which in a discreet way would have been a reminder of her, and does it not seem natural that a young man who on leaving Cambridge went to Touraine to master the language, and thence to Paris where he was able to enjoy an easy amoral life and new aesthetic excitements, was guided by a mistress who had been there before him?

In 1906 Clive proposed to Thoby Stephen's elder sister and was rejected, but not conclusively dismissed. Vanessa, a virgin of twenty-seven with one unhappy love affair behind her, had found herself at the centre of a group which, greatly daring, had brought the freedoms of apostolic Cambridge into a mixed society. The well-starched inhabitants of Kensington, once the home of the Stephen children, already questioned the propriety of two young women keeping open house at 46 Gordon Square for a party of ill-dressed, unmannerly young men who sat talking and arguing until the small hours. They had perhaps little to fear from Lytton Strachey or indeed from Saxon Sydney-Turner but Clive, when he returned from Paris, was evidently a danger and indeed almost the only eligible bachelor in the group. Also he was the only one who shared Vanessa's interest in painting. But although he was in a sense her natural mate, Clive realized, and perhaps she too realized in part, that he was attempting something of, for him, unprecedented difficulty. To be sure he could bring her material benefits and, as Vanessa's half-brother George Duckworth observed, he had a good seat on a horse and went to a good tailor; but had he really the moral stature, the weight of character, that would entitle him to aspire to the hand of a Miss Stephen? There were two ladies who thought not. One was Beatrice Meinertzhagen (later Mrs Mayor) who was in love with Thoby; the other was Virginia Stephen, Vanessa's younger sister. They both considered Clive a lightweight. But then they were both ready, later on, to yield – in some measure – to his charms. So for that matter did Vanessa. Her marriage in 1907, following closely on the death of Thoby, was an immediate success.

I once asked Vanessa whether Clive was a very handsome man when he married her. 'No,' she said, 'but he was very amusing.' And for a time the amusements at 46 Gordon Square were, according to Lytton, spectacular. But although they may have been prolonged perhaps for a matter of seven or eight years, that unclouded happiness which united the Bells in 1907, although it was certainly enriched by the birth of Julian in 1908, was endangered by the folly of Clive and his sister-in-law.

I have described that sad business in my biography of Virginia; here I would only pause to say that it seems to me the most discreditable incident in their lives; they should have known that no one would get any good of it and everyone, in particular Vanessa, would be made miserable. I think Clive was most to blame. Virginia behaved very badly but was at least moved by a jealous passion for her sister so that 'the thing', as she put it, 'turned a knife in her'. Clive I fear really felt very little; his actions were irresponsible.

And yet this was in its way an admirable period in Clive's life. Like Vanessa he was immensely influenced by his meeting with Roger Fry. This coincided with a general enlargement of Bloomsbury; a slightly younger generation had produced that momentous figure Maynard Keynes. Meanwhile other characters, some of them having little to do with Cambridge – Duncan Grant, Desmond and Molly MacCarthy, Gerald Shove, Ottoline Morrell, appeared on the scene.

Clive became for a time politically active in the struggle between the people and the peerage which centred on the Parliament Bill of 1911. For a while he called himself a radical. At the same time he worked with Roger Fry on the first and, more prominently, on the second Post-Impressionist Exhibition. That tremendous aesthetic upheaval which set the pattern for the development of the fine arts for the rest of the century led Clive to write *Art*, published in 1914, which is surely one of the seminal books of its time. It is a book more quoted than read, and indeed there is much of it which I personally find hard reading. I believe however that in the light of the history of the arts during the past 150 years it is possible at least to venture an opinion concerning the problems with which Clive and his contemporaries had to deal.

The problem for the observer in about 1914 was that for quite a long time he had been asked to look at works of art the content of which was unknown to him. Exotics like Japanese prints and Amerindian sculpture had been coming into Europe and although at first they tended to be considered simply as curiosities, presently they were looked at by artists and critics and admired as works –

sometimes great works – of art. Clearly the 'home market' was getting something different, but the Europeans were nonetheless getting a great deal.

A Chinese scroll carrying a poem in running script, a form of rapid handwriting, must by a Chinese scholar be considered first and foremost as a piece of literature, and it may be that the running script is particularly appropriate from a literary point of view. Nevertheless the residue, that is the shapes created by the brush – what Clive calls the 'significant form' – does exist and may be admired, and it is, in fact, the presence of this formal character which enables us to identify it as a work of visual art. This is not a value judgement: the calligrapher's poem may be a total failure from a visual point of view, but the thing only ceases to be a visual work of art if the poem is recited aloud without the aid of an image of any kind.

The same kind of problem was posed by completely abstract pictures; here the work of art may result from the artist's intention of saying something which might be expressed in a poem – a difficult feat unless some reference is made to the visible world – but whether he succeeds or not in his 'literary' endeavour the artist may still achieve a satisfying result in formal terms.

Any definition of the fine arts must require artefacts to be visible and to some people in some way interesting. That such works must also deliver a 'literary' message of some kind is clearly not the case, for often the message cannot be received.

Clive's argument tended however to be used in an uncompromising manner: formal qualities were regarded as the chief and only virtue in works of visual art and the 'story' was a negligible, or even a regrettable, element in a picture. This perhaps was a reaction against a kind of painting in which the story was in itself absurd and the form correspondingly feeble. It was not long before Roger Fry pointed out that this kind of criticism clearly couldn't apply to Rembrandt, and Clive in his comments on Renoir was ready to discard a form of criticism which amounted to little more than saying that a bad 'story' frequently provided the motif for a bad picture.

In fact the elements that can be found in a picture are so numerous and so hard to disentangle that it is only in those cases where everything except the form is invisible that a formalist approach imposes itself.

In August 1914 Clive, in a conversation with Ottoline and others, gave it as his view that the war would end civilization. At about the same time he wrote a letter to the *Daily News* in which he questioned the assumptions of those who felt that there was an unanswerable moral case for entering the war on the side of France, Serbia and Russia. He thought that an Allied victory would probably lead to another war between the Allies.

His friends took much longer to make up their minds and some of them, Maynard for instance, never really did so; for some, the war was so unexpected and it seemed so improbable that anyone except professional soldiers would fight in it, that at first a definite stand was not called for. But Clive had been sufficiently involved in politics to come to a clear conclusion at once; and in 1915, by which time a swift end to the war had become improbable, Clive launched a pamphlet, *Peace at Once*, in which he called for a negotiated settlement. The decision to do this cannot have been easy; he knew or strongly suspected that his conduct would be condemned by the family at Seend, and the family held the money bags – not I think that it would or could have touched Vanessa's marriage settlement; but he feared enough to be uneasy on this score. On the other hand a public statement – and his pamphlet was publicly burned by the Common Hangman – could not but be noticed. From a practical point of view Clive ran a fairly grave risk of being disowned or disinherited, and for what? If, like Zola, he had relieved his outraged feelings at a moment when there was just enough public discontent for his words to fire a popular movement, then indeed he might have achieved something tremendous: a peace that would have saved millions of lives and the entire social structure of Europe. The prize was so enormous that it might seem worth wagering against the most fearful odds.

But indeed *Peace at Once* now looks like an impossibility. Consider what became of the next important attempt to halt the carnage: this time it came not from an art critic but from a peer who had led the Conservative Party and had been in the War Cabinet. In 1917, following the fruitless assaults of 1915, the Dardanelles fiasco and the hideous disaster on the Somme, Lord Lansdowne, who, like Clive, wanted a negotiated peace, called for a declaration of war aims which a reasonable German could accept. In fact it comes very close to the arguments that Maynard Keynes was to use in *The Economic Consequences of the Peace*. It rejects the peace of revenge and for this reason it was itself rejected, amidst howls of infuriated disgust from patriots in England and in the allied nations generally. Revenge was what they wanted; they would accept no peace that was not inspired by intense and unthinking hatred. 'Though I speak with the tongues of men and of angels, and have not hatred, I am become as sounding brass, or a tinkling cymbal.' Such was the religion of patriots in 1917.

Hatred indeed was one of those 'vulgar passions' which Bloomsbury mistrusted and which undid the sensible proposals of men like Clive and Maynard and Lord Lansdowne; the seeds of hatred so carefully sown and tended were to flourish over a wide territory in Europe for a generation.

Peace at Once was not Clive's last comment on public affairs. When the war was over he published a pamphlet *On British Freedom*. It was better received although hardly more effective, in appearance at all events. I doubt whether Roy Jenkins or any of the other legislators who introduced those measures which have put an end to the persecution of homosexuals, have liberated the stage and remedied all the ills which Clive deplored in the 1920s, ever read *On British Freedom*, but it played I think a useful part in a gradual change in the moral climate of the British nation.

I must return to 1914, for it was then that Clive fell in love with Mrs St John Hutchinson, the wife of an eminent barrister, and began what was I suppose the most important love affair of his life. I cannot claim to know much about the matter; from a child's point of view it had perhaps more importance than one could consciously realize. From 1916 Clive was hardly part of the family; he had his theoretical job as an agricultural labourer at Garsington working for Ottoline and Philip Morrell; every now and then he would come to Charleston, usually bringing Mary Hutchinson with him. He also brought us presents which were particularly welcome in war time. In those years Vanessa and Clive were on friendly terms with each other and nothing more became generally known. Vanessa's affair with Roger Fry (see Chapter 3) had been more or less clandestine; she lived publicly with Duncan, and when that union was blessed with offspring Clive was perfectly ready to play the part of the *mari complaisant* and to play it with some grace.

In the post-war years I think that Clive must have felt a certain self-satisfaction: he had been right about the Post-Impressionists, he had been right – terribly right – about the war; now, in his middle age, he could rest upon his laurels, happy in having found a mistress who – give or take a few infidelities – suited him admirably. He began to venture into what he called the '*beau monde*'; he was reconciled to his family, largely I believe as a result of the bluff diplomacy of his brother Cory who, like some other professional soldiers, had grave doubts about the value of conscription. In politics he became increasingly conservative. At Charleston he would argue with Maynard, whose sentiments were always in a sense pro-German, while he himself became increasingly pro-French, so that on issues like the occupation of the Ruhr, Clive found himself in sympathy with reactionary French politicians.

And yet, when it was decided that I should go for a term to Paris before going to public school, he sent me to a house where I learnt the Carmagnole and the Red Flag. And did Clive change his mind? Not in the least; he was delighted by Monsieur Pinault. French communists, he explained, were different; they were Jacobins really; Pinault was a man who would go to the barricades, a 'man of '48'. And up to a point he was right; Pinault talked a great deal about Voltaire and Victor Hugo, but not much about Marx.

That summer in Paris I not only learnt a lot from Pinault but also from Clive. He stayed for some weeks in Paris and each week there was a treat for me. I remember in particular going on a steamer to St Cloud to visit hospitable Americans who lived in a villa where Gounod had composed. In a beautiful garden I drank my first cocktail and a little man with the most lovely brown eyes played Chinese music on a gramophone. The music consisted of a Chinese woman uttering fearful shrieks; the little man explained that the woman's long fingers were stretched between two tables; as someone broke them with a mallet, each finger produced a shriek. I was not horrified; there was something about the man which made horror an inappropriate emotion. I sensed that he was a person of importance, but it was not until later that I knew for sure it was Picasso.

Clive took a lot of trouble to show me Paris and to make our treats memorable. He was later to do as much for Angelica. Julian was also sent to Pinault – this was after he had left school – while he was taking a course at the Sorbonne. There was therefore no question of taking him out for treats, nor indeed at that time were Clive's treats the kind of thing that Julian enjoyed.

Julian and Clive could talk about English literature (including Surtees), about the French Revolution, and about shooting and that was all. If they approached politics trouble loomed. 'You'll have to write his life one day,' I said. 'I should be too unsympathetic,' was Julian's reply. What made him unsympathetic? *'Civilization'* was the answer.

Clive's essay, published in 1928, was certainly not the kind of work that would please a young socialist, nor for that matter an old one: witness Leonard Woolf's essay on Erasmus, *his* model of a civilized man. It was Leonard's wife, to whom in fact Clive's book was rather elaborately dedicated, who told me that although she thought that Clive had great fun in the opening chapters saying what civilization was not, when it came to a definition, it turned out that civilization was 'a lunch party at No.50 Gordon Square'.

The word 'civilization' can be used in several ways, but one is tied to a very restricted use of the term if, like Clive, one begins by saying that civilization is a means to good states of mind. Having pointed the argument in this direction one can ignore those who think of a civilized society as one which had attained a certain degree of technical and social organization and one certainly cannot use the word civilization of a society which, though highly developed, has left us no literature.

Julian was I think most critical of those passages where Clive sees in Lenin and Mussolini the future saviours of civilization, who will eventually keep the proletariat in its place, its place being to provide comforts for the civilized minority. It is unfair to take such arguments from their context but it can be said that Clive had turned very violently from his democratic ideas of 1910 to a deep mistrust (and at times a hatred) of Demos. After all, it was not unreasonable, after seeing the ease with which the working classes could be persuaded to forget the International and march obediently to war, for a disappointed pacifist to feel that it was wiser to rely upon the good will of those who might best bring the masses to heel.

It is interesting though that Clive could take this view in 1927 when there was a welcome if deceptive calm in Europe. During the next ten years the social and international problems of the world were to worsen in a new and quite horrible way. The period 1927–37 was a sad period for Clive, but for a personal rather than a political reason. The relationship with Mary Hutchinson, which had seemed so delightful and sympathetic, broke down. I do not know the rights and wrongs of the matter nor even whether such terms are applicable in this case. But I saw the effect upon Clive which was saddening. One symptom of his troubles was a kind of desperate womanizing, an impulse to catch hold of and make love to any young woman who came within reach. There were, I gathered, indignant ladies who struggled to escape from passionate advances which they had never in the slightest way encouraged. My own experience, which some-times involved me in the social embarrassments resulting from his conduct, was of a more co-operative type of woman. I, and many others, had to listen to accounts of that Parisian nymph, a star of the world of *haute couture*, whom he proposed at one time to marry. I saw her once: she was elderly and ugly as sin.

There was however one woman, brilliant in mind as she was lovely in person, who rejected his advances but with such gentle address that she became and remained his friend for the rest of his life. When, in about 1931, his eyes gave such trouble that he thought he might lose his sight altogether it was she, Frances Marshall, who kept him amused and sustained his courage. In the end he had to go to Zurich where he was cured. He went entirely on his own, reject-ing my offer to stay with him; indeed, in this crisis he did exhibit a stoic courage.

In a sense Clive's work on civilization was a preface to the more extreme views that he was to express in the 1930s. He was fixed in his opinion that democracy could never provide any protection for the kind of things that he thought really valuable; the only hope lay therefore in autocracy. But as the dictators began to loom large upon the European scene it was hard to believe that they would ever be patrons of culture: the Fascists seemed rather a long way from the Medici; the Third Reich seemed even further from Frederick the Great. Nor did it appear that the dictators were anxious to preserve their power by refraining from embarking upon military adventures as Clive had hoped. Still he could watch the growth of Mussolini's empire and the annexation first of Abyssinia and then of Austria and Czechoslovakia without too much disquiet. What perturbed him was the clamour from the English intelligentsia who were rude to foreign dictators. There were even some English Conservatives who denounced the anti-semitism of the new Germany and flirted – out-rageously as it seemed to Clive – with Soviet Russia (the Soviets were no longer numbered amongst the possible allies of culture). Agitators of this kind were not merely reprehensible in themselves and a public danger, they were also enemies of peace, they would drive us into an alliance with Stalin, they would end by pushing us into war and they should be silenced. There may have been moments when Neville Chamberlain, Clive's favourite prime minister, would have liked to pursue this course, but one may doubt whether any policy of appeasement short of outright surrender would have saved us from war.

War, when it came in earnest in May 1940, brought something of a *volte face*. It was at once touching and funny to see Private Bell and Private Grant of the Home Guard, in khaki and tin helmets, the one shouldering his usual 12-bore hammerless ejector loaded with ball, the other proud of holding an extinct species of rifle, precious because it would accept no known form of ammunition. They (and I) were drilled by an ex-sergeant of the Royal Sussex Regiment and for a time guarded these shores. Clive, now, was silent on the subject of pacifism and began gradually to become reconciled to Churchill for whom he had conceived a strong dislike during the years of appeasement. He was even ready to concede that the Russians had at least certain military virtues. In fact, despite some severe differences of opinion concerning war aims, the period 1939–45 was at Charleston a period of peace. Also it was a period during which Clive was able and willing to perform the outward duties of a married man. In that capacity he had for many years acted the part of the affectionate parent to Duncan's daughter. It was a task which he found easy and indeed congenial, because he was a natural cicerone and one who delighted to entertain and instruct, particularly if the pupil was young, female, beautiful and intelligent. Over and above these qualifications, to all of which Angelica might lay claim, she had another which, though negative, was in Clive's view adorable: she found politics a bore.

Even Virginia had on one occasion attended a Labour Party Congress, and drove around with Leonard in search of voters. Vanessa was even more ignorant of politics than her sister. She did, it is true, go to hear the results of the poll in the 1905 election, but then it was to rejoice at the defeat of her half-brother George Duckworth's Conservative friends. Yet Vanessa, when compared to her daughter, was a veritable Rosa Luxembourg.

It was not simply that Angelica was bored by politics, she actively rejected them. She seemed to have been inoculated with an antibody which made her immune, so that she could venture into the most dangerous plague-spots of discussion and action without ever catching the slightest dose of politics. As a young girl she would listen to the disputes between Julian and his communist friends and feel nothing save mild bewilderment. She lived with – and loved – the Walther family during the critical years when François Walther was mobilizing the French intelligentsia to resist Fascism; and she remained indifferent to the direction and perhaps even the fate of the Republic. At a time when, even in the *beau monde*, you couldn't feel quite sure that a thoroughly 'nice girl' might not start talking about the dialectic of the class struggle, this must have been delightful for Clive and delightful, too, for Angelica, for in such circumstances he could be great fun. I for my part never found Clive great fun after the advent of Hitler. Taking an interest in politics, and feeling, as I do, that the Jews are the salt of the earth, it was too difficult.

But the war, as I have said, did provide a kind of truce; there was a little sparring between us but party politics were for the time being kept on ice. It was after the advent of the Labour Government in 1945 that the trouble started up, and in a big way.

The Labour Government seemed to Clive to be something unnatural and horrible. Since neither Duncan nor Vanessa could really be blamed for it, I found myself in the firing line. I expect that I was utterly exasperating; but unless I were to dissemble it was hard to avoid it.

One amongst many encounters remains clear in my memory. It took place in 1947 at a time when Britain had decided to get out of Palestine. A Commission had been sent by Attlee's government to arrange – or perhaps merely to suggest – which parts of the Holy Land should be Jewish and which Arab. I am not sure whether I then knew that Dick Crossman had been a member of this body and had on the whole favoured the Jews while the others had been pro-Arab. On his return from Palestine Crossman was censured by the Prime Minister for being too favourable towards the Jews.

It was after lunch – it was nearly always after lunch that these disputes occurred. Vanessa and Duncan were drinking coffee, I was reading a newspaper; Clive was talking, ostensibly to Vanessa, but *at* me. The gist of what he said was that the British government was being most unfair to the Arabs; the Jews were getting everything; it was all the fault of Attlee who, of course, was himself a Jew. Only it wasn't anything like so succinct; he went on and on about this Hebrew Attlee, his deceit, his unfairness, his Jewishness, etcetera etcetera.

I went on reading the newspaper, or at least pretending to. I knew that Clive was trying to provoke me into an argument and I knew that in the end he would either force me to intervene or force me out of the room. If he forced me out of the room Vanessa would be upset; if I intervened at least I could expose these foolish untruths, or try to, but then probably everyone would be upset. Finally the goading went too far. I spoke my mind and everyone *was* upset.

There was an odd little postscript when Desmond MacCarthy came to Charleston a few days later, and Clive again complained of the Jewish premier.

'Nonsense,' said Desmond. 'He is not a Jew.'

'Look at his nose,' said Clive.

'It's a typical English lumpy nose.'

And Clive took it like a lamb and shut up – which makes me think that in his mind he was dealing less with Socialist Jewry than with an intolerable child. I fled from Charleston soon afterwards. I was not driven out; indeed I was enticed; but I must confess that one of the many joys of my new life was that I was able to digest my lunch in comfort.

I suppose that it was just before I left Charleston for marriage and the North that Clive entered upon the last of his sentimental adventures. It is not easy to be quite fair or entirely objective about this business, particularly as it shows Bloomsbury in its most unfavourable aspect.

Barbara Hiles had been a Slade student, one of three young women whom Molly MacCarthy termed collectively the 'Bloomsbury Bunnies' and Virginia 'the Cropheads' because of their short haircuts, the others being Alix Sargant-Florence and Dora Carrington. Of these Barbara was the prettiest, neatly made with dark hair and startlingly blue eyes, a practical, sensible little person, very anxious to please and very eager to share in the delights of the cultural life. Virginia, who found her so hard to resist that she was unable to refuse her services as an assistant in the nascent Hogarth Press, certainly had Barbara in mind when she described the 'Bloomsbury Bunnies' as constantly 'feeling their legs to see if they had not turned into hares.' Virginia had a sharp tongue, but as I have suggested, she was so curious that she could not easily keep her doors closed against so eager and so determined a suitor even though Leonard grumbled that, far from helping, she actually made work in the press. Vanessa was a less curious and more forbidding figure; Barbara was not invited to Charleston. Barbara however was as skilful at opening doors as Vanessa was at closing them. Vanessa woke up one day to discover that Barbara and a Mr Bagenal had made a willow cabin at her gate. To be more accurate, they had set up a tent in the rickyard about twenty yards from Charleston farmhouse.

Vanessa considered this a monstrous intrusion, but she couldn't stop Barbara being in and out of the house all day. And of course Barbara *did* make herself useful: the mosaic which still adorns the little pavement outside the studio at the corner of the walled garden is of her making. It was Barbara who went to London and returned with a heavy bag of mosaic tesserae; it was Nick Bagenal (and I) who searched the ploughed fields for flints to be used in making the surround.

Barbara married Nicholas Bagenal, a nice chap who came to know everything that could be known about fruit trees; but she felt she needed a companion who knew about something less *terre-à-terre*, and found him in Saxon Sydney-Turner, who indeed was a brilliant scholar. The affair with him was, I imagine, platonic; but by her husband she had children. Her daughter Judith, about the same age as Angelica, was, amongst other excellent things, a most useful bridge between her mother and Vanessa. Two girls of the same age would naturally be the subject of mutual arrangements by their mothers, and as a result Judith was frequently at Charleston and sometimes at Cassis. As they grew older they tended to move in different directions, but for a time the connection with Charleston made a useful contribution to Barbara's search for the cultural life.

In October 1938, when Barbara was past her first youth, she and her husband made a descent on Charleston where she was a less frequent visitor than she had been. They found the house empty and proceeded, unannounced, to Rodmell. It was a rash act. Virginia, who had been looking forward to a quiet afternoon with Leonard, picked up her pen, wrote to Vanessa and exploded. (Her letter is printed, with discreet omissions, in Virginia's correspondence, Volume VI, No.3454.)

The novelist let her pen run away with her, but it was true in the eyes of Virginia and Vanessa: Barbara did not improve with age. At Charleston she became a joke, and one of the main jokers was Clive, who was at times tempted to reply to those who criticized his smart friends by saying that the dowdy friends of the artists were not much to boast of. 'Little Ba', as she was called at Charleston, was therefore something of a family joke, but not an unkind joke.* No one did or could have hated Barbara – not even the exasperated Virginia – but she was, to quote Leslie Stephen, 'one of those intolerable bores who are the salt of the earth.'

Imagine my feelings when I discovered that Clive and Little Ba were lovers. I met them at an exhibition of pictures. Of course there was no reason why Clive should not escort any lady through an art gallery; nevertheless, the way she clung to his arm, the mixture of complacency and embarrassment with which they greeted me, were eloquent: Clive was, as he would have put it, *'en bonne fortune'*.

It was a little awkward though. It is never easy to make a *volte face* and now it was made more difficult by the fact that Frances Partridge, who made Clive happy by writing amusing letters, wrote him a very amusing one about Barbara. Poor Clive could not allow himself to be amused. Altogether he had to submit to being laughed at. But it was well worth it. Clive needed feminine company and now in his old age he not only needed a woman, he needed a woman who could do things for him; who could buy tickets and make reservations, who could see that he was well dressed and well fed, taken to his club and fetched back again, chauffeured, doctored, reassured and provided with a fair opportunity every day to write a few lines of well-tailored English prose. Barbara could manage it all. Clive, for his part, had something to offer in return.

I don't remember that he ever took her to Charleston, and I doubt whether even Barbara would have wished for that reward, but Clive had better things in his gift: the cultured life of London was in the '50s much more inviting than the dilapidated remains of

---

* Robert Skidelsky, in his admirable life of Maynard Keynes, expresses the view that 'Charleston' would have liked Barbara to have become Mrs Keynes. Homer nods.

Bloomsbury. Better still, Clive could take her to the coast of the Mediterranean, to Nice where Matisse, bedridden but still oracular, was still at work, and best of all to Antibes where Picasso was friendly and there were those who were willing to greet Barbara with enthusiastic affection.

Barbara worked devotedly for Clive in his final years, but the rewards were splendid. I saw her for the last time on the day after he died and tried to thank her for what she had done. I was certainly inadequate, but not insincere.

3

Vanessa Bell

IT IS MUCH more difficult to write about Vanessa than it is to write about Clive; he might be difficult to do but at least he has not been 'done' before. Vanessa has, and sometimes by very competent hands. Inevitably I shall have to repeat things that have been said either by me in my life of Virginia or by others who, as I say, have often managed very well; but not always. Some foolish and some very inaccurate things have been written about Vanessa's youth, and even the far more responsible accounts of her later life do not always present a view which is wholly accurate. There is much which needs to be modified or corrected.

The composition of the family into which Vanessa was born in 1879 is I suppose sufficiently well known. Nevertheless it was so complex and combined elements of such importance to Vanessa and her siblings as to require a brief restatement.

Her father, Leslie Stephen, and her mother, Julia, both married twice. Leslie was the child of a highly intellectual middle-class family. He had been a clergyman at Cambridge who lost his faith, left the University, and married Thackeray's younger daughter Minny, by whom he had a child, Laura. Minny died untimely; her child, who was feeble minded, was still living at home with her father while Vanessa was growing up.

Vanessa's maternal grandmother, Maria Pattle, married John Jackson, a doctor of medicine who practised in Calcutta. He is forgotten and indeed was never celebrated; his son-in-law dismissed him as a nonentity. His wife, although she seems from her letters to have been in no way brilliant, does still enjoy a kind of fame as do her sisters. These women are still remembered for their looks while their husbands are forgotten. They were friendly to the fine arts; they supported Watts, they patronized the pre-Raphaelites. Val Prinsep, Vanessa's cousin, was a painter while her aunt Julia – Mrs Cameron – is remembered for her pioneering photography.

Julia Jackson married Herbert Duckworth. He seems to have been a man of great charm and promise; he died suddenly, leaving his young wife with a son, George, a daughter Stella, and a third child, Gerald, who was born posthumously. Thus when the widowed Mrs Duckworth married the bereaved Mr Stephen they already had four children between them. They begot another four: Vanessa, Thoby, Virginia and Adrian. All eight seem to have inherited something from their forbears: the Duckworths inherited sufficient money and social eminence to put them in a slightly higher rank than the other children. The Stephens had for about a century been writing books and it was soon clear that Virginia would continue the tradition. Thoby and Adrian seemed destined for another Stephen occupation – the law. Poor Laura's condition was surely inherited from her insane grandmother Mrs Thackeray. As for Vanessa, she herself acknowledged the aesthetic influence of her mother's family; but when she addressed herself to the practice of art she did so with a single-minded seriousness which seems to me more Stephen than Pattle.

Another trait resulting naturally from the inheritance of beauty so evident in the Pattle women was a certain awareness of social possibilities. Of Vanessa's great-aunts, one married a director of the East India Company, another married a baronet, a third married an earl; one of her mother's cousins married a duke, another married the son of an earl; this was a total disaster but never mind, the title was genuine. Altogether they did very well for themselves; it was not unnatural for their friends and relations to hope that Virginia and Vanessa would do likewise.

In addition to the eight children there were two parents and about six domestic servants at No.22 Hyde Park Gate – perhaps sixteen inhabitants in that tall, ugly, rather dark house. The full complement was achieved rapidly, between 1879 and 1883, so that at the earliest possible moment Vanessa must have found herself invested with some authority over her juniors. By this I mean that she had to 'look after' her brother Thoby, to whom both girls were devoted, and her sister Virginia, who from the first was difficult and made no easier by displays of precocious brilliance.

Caring for the younger children helped to make Vanessa more grave and more responsible than most girls, and from a very early age she had to deal with her sister's strong and formidable tongue. In a memoir she notes that when enraged Virginia turned a particularly beautiful flame colour, a remark very characteristic of Vanessa.

Life at Hyde Park Gate and at Talland House, St Ives – which latter furnished the happiest days of Vanessa's childhood – centred around Julia Stephen. Leslie, although his writing was done at home, did it behind a study door which was kept firmly closed, and Stella, Julia's oldest daughter and her assistant, was very much her subordinate. When in 1895 Julia died it was not only an emotional disaster, melodramatic in its effect upon the stricken widower, but also a crisis in the domestic arrangements of the family. The unhappy Stella was obliged to run the household and comfort her stepfather as best she might. Vanessa, now a quiet girl of sixteen, became her lieutenant and when, two years later, after an agonising period of uncertainty, Stella married Jack Hills, Vanessa had to take her place. It was no sinecure: she was caught between Sophy, a formidable cook who felt that the family's good name depended upon a proper and no doubt expensive provision of food, and a father who had become insanely anxious about the size of the weekly bills.

A still more agitating source of trouble was the social ambition and more than brotherly love of George Duckworth. George, rich, handsome and generous, moved in high society and wanted his beautiful half-sisters to do likewise. He took Vanessa to parties of his smart friends and tried to launch her into the wider world. Vanessa was bewildered, bored, and a complete failure. She tried to escape from functions which made her miserable, but George persisted in his efforts. It was a sad and a ludicrous business. In the end George gave up and turned his attention to Virginia, who was equally bored and an equal failure but who could retaliate by behaving in a most unseemly fashion.

But George was also a problem in a quite different way. He loved his half-sisters; he loved them enthusiastically; he loved them in altogether too demonstrative a way, kissing, fondling, toying with them and embracing them as if he were not so much a brother as an accepted lover.

Here, because enormous publicity has been given to the story of George's activities and because this publicity has been accompanied by wild speculation, I must pause to state the proven facts of the case.

Gerald, the younger Duckworth boy, inspected Virginia's private parts when she was about five years old. It was a horrid act, but we may doubt whether he was the first schoolboy to do such a thing; it is not a misdemeanour which justifies us in suspecting the offender of anything more serious. There is nothing else at all against Gerald.

George was certainly guilty of stupid and inconsiderate behaviour. Both Virginia and Vanessa suffered from his unwanted attentions, but it remains unclear exactly what happened and when. Undoubtedly his actions could have been a prelude to rape, but for the following reasons we may conclude that they were not.

We have every reason to think that both Vanessa and Virginia were virgins when they married. According to his brother-in-law J.W. Hills George himself was a virgin when he married. In 1904 Sir George Savage, the mental health specialist who treated Virginia, was told by Vanessa about George Duckworth's misbehaviour, and there was an interview with the offender. Sir George was a friend of the family and a public figure of some consequence. If Vanessa had suggested that there was a real danger that George might get his half-sister with child – the scandal would have been colossal – the physician would surely have taken drastic steps; at the very least he would have separated George from Virginia. We can't tell what he did say at that interview, but in fact George proposed to join the Stephen children when they went to live in Gordon Square after their father's death in 1904 and in a moment of weakness his proposal was accepted. It was in fact he who changed his mind. This would seem fantastic if we believe that copulation took place.

One of the difficulties of this research, and one for which I must accept some blame, is that Vanessa, the most reliable witness, kept silent, and in fact it was many years after her death that we children knew anything about the matter. But when she was younger she did tell her cousin Fredegond Shove. A letter from her discussed the business; clearly it had all been very horrible, but wasn't it possible that George himself was unaware of the seriousness of what he was doing? It is possible provided we assume that George did not actually rape his sisters. In her letters to Fredegond Vanessa, our best witness, never said that he attempted this.

Growing up in the house of Leslie Stephen it was natural that a good deal of attention should have been devoted to the education of the children. I have heard it said that the boys got a better education than the girls. On the whole I think that they did; but in fact the girls were better taught.

In the early years of their studies they were all taught by both parents, neither of whom were good teachers. Neither Vanessa nor Virginia could learn any arithmetic which must have exasperated Leslie, who had been a mathematician at University. Someone gave Vanessa enough Latin for her to be able to help my brother Julian when he was about twelve years old, but it is hard to estimate the value of that early instruction.

Thoby and Adrian both went to Evelyns, a preparatory school; later they were educated separately. Thoby went to Clifton, Adrian to Westminster. Both learnt Latin but while Thoby may have acquired a genuine and lasting taste for the classics, for Adrian it was simply a genteel waste of time, a form of conspicuous waste. It was not until they got to Cambridge and could enjoy an exciting exchange of ideas with fellow students that they had advantages denied to their sisters.

Now consider the education of the girls: from an early age it consisted of some teaching of ladylike accomplishments: French which was useful, and the piano, singing and dancing which, for the Miss Stephens, were of doubtful value.* But already they were teaching themselves. Virginia was reading and was writing for a family newspaper.† Vanessa, serious from the first, set herself to tackle those deadly dull and difficult exercises which Ruskin imposes upon the beginner in *Elements of Drawing*. She was as determined to be a painter as Virginia was to be a writer.

And then their father, understanding the girl's needs, came to their assistance. Although it contained some works that Leslie thought unsuitable for a young girl, he opened his library to Virginia. One of the few art teachers who taught children at that time and is still remembered by art educationists, Ebenezer Cook,

---

* When I knew her Virginia neither danced nor sang. Vanessa did sing a little and on one notable occasion danced with great *éclat* but in a manner which would have surprised her teachers (see p. 51).

† The size of her contribution to this journal is uncertain but was clearly important.

was employed to teach Vanessa. She learned art history from a lady who took her and a party of other girls on tours of the National Gallery.

After Julia Stephen's death it fell to Leslie to help Vanessa get an art education. It was not his field; when she returned from art school with a study of an *écorché* he was astounded, having never seen such a thing before. Nevertheless she was able to go to Mr Cope's school which prepared students for the Academy Schools, and these she entered in 1900. Vanessa studied under, and had a great respect for John Singer Sargent. Altogether it seems to me that at that time no British artist could have hoped for a better education.

Like Vanessa, Virginia was given an education which she could use. In addition to a vast amount of reading in English and French she learnt some Greek and attempted to learn German. But Virginia really was disadvantaged: she could have used Cambridge as her sister could not.

This was for Vanessa a time when her happiest hours were spent in front of a plaster cast or, later on, a nude model. This absorbing occupation filled her mornings; in the afternoons, when she would have been much happier with a still-life, there were social duties which a girl must obey, and for which Leslie – by then Sir Leslie – needed an ear-trumpet. They entertained old friends, many of them exceedingly boring, and a sample platoon of the monstrous regiment of relations, who also required tea and conversation. And then in the evening there was George. And George, who continued to live at Hyde Park Gate, was the guardian of morality, or at least of propriety.

When Stella died in 1899, Jack Hills, her newly wedded husband and now a widower, found comfort and kindness in the sympathetic tears of his sisters-in-law and in particular of Vanessa. She was perhaps too sympathetic, so that what had been condolence became something warmer and deeper, something precious but illicit, for the law (as it then was) forbade a man to marry his deceased wife's half-sister. George was upset and the whole army of relations expressed shocked disapproval (shocked disapproval being one of the flourishing home industries of the nineteenth century). In the end virtue was triumphant: Jack Hills was discreet, and Vanessa was miserable. Years later when Hills had gone into politics he met Vanessa to discuss some scheme for having posters designed by artists. Returning from the meeting she remarked that he had been very pleasant and she could well understand why she had been in love with him.

One recollection begets another. I remember a lunch at Charleston: Vanessa, Clive, Duncan, us two boys, perhaps Angelica and one guest, Raymond Mortimer (he came once or twice every summer). Someone began talking about dreams. Vanessa, usually rather silent upon such occasions, remarked that she dreamed that she had committed a murder; the dream was repeated night after night until she realized that she was dreaming about her father's death. 'You see,' she said, 'it was impossible not to be glad. He had been ill for so long, we had for so long been expecting it, and of course it was in many ways convenient. As soon as I realized what I was dreaming about I stopped dreaming.'

'Have you read Freud?' asked Raymond.

'Not at all,' was the reply. 'But I'm sure that it's all great nonsense.'

It is interesting to note that Virginia felt the same contradictory emotions about her father, but in her case with such violence as to result in a complete breakdown. She was more attached than was Vanessa to Leslie and on his death had less to console her. For Vanessa her father's death meant the end of Hyde Park Gate; already there were plans for moving away from the genteel elegance of Kensington, away from the social grandeurs of Duckworths and Fishers, to Bloomsbury, then considered a world of cheap lodging houses and dubious lodgers. But first there was a treat. The sisters went with Gerald to Venice and there, amongst a great many fine things, Vanessa discovered Tintoretto. On the return journey they saw just a little of what was going on in Paris, and here they encountered Thoby's friend Clive Bell.

Although Vanessa had friends and relations, she was also isolated; that is to say she was professionally isolated, much more so than Virginia who could assess the thought not only of the ancients but of modern writers, for it came to her in print from all over the world. Today the same kind of immediate communication is available to visual artists: a drawing made in Los Angeles can be seen in an instant by a critic in Reykjavik or Cairo who has the necessary technology. Like Clive, Vanessa was for many years unable to see an original Impressionist picture; for her, Sargent was modern art. She would, she said, peer at the smudgy black and white illustrations in Camille Mauclair's work on the Impressionists, trying to imagine what the dark approximations of Renoir and Pissarro were really like. In much the same way Duncan Grant at the age of sixteen sat down and painted a landscape hoping that it might look like an Impressionist picture, something that he had never actually seen.

Even when he got to Paris the young enthusiast would see very little of any Impressionist painting unless he knew his way about or had useful friends. By the 1920s a few Impressionists and even a Cézanne had made their way into the Luxembourg Gallery, but in 1904 one had to find the right dealer or private collector. Vanessa's ambition was more modest; she simply needed to meet anyone who was really interested in painting. Her fellow student Margery Snowden was a nice creature but hardly brilliant, and Vanessa seems to have met no one else at the Academy Schools to excite her interest. Thoby so far as I can judge was interested in Greek sculpture, but so far as the fine arts were concerned little else. He had a friend at Cambridge, however, who unlike most of his contemporaries, had an eye both for the girls and for painting. Vanessa was not yet aware that in Lytton Strachey's 'set' both these appetites were thought to be eccentric. But although she kept the man at arm's length, she welcomed the amateur; and when Clive Bell introduced her to young painters in Montmartre and when the ladies were invited to smoke wicked cigarettes in the shameless publicity of cafés and discuss art, or better still, visit Rodin in his studio, she must have been overjoyed.

Later, when they were all back in London and Thoby's Cambridge friendships were renewed in Gordon Square, it was no doubt pleasant to meet Clive again, and also Strachey and Saxon Sydney-Turner. Bloomsbury was coming into existence in 1904. In the following year Clive proposed and was rejected, but he continued to play a role in Vanessa's life, and again it was painting which brought them together. It was Vanessa's object to organize a society which might paint, discuss painting and hold exhibitions, and in the organization of this – the Friday Club – Clive was a fellow worker.

But it was not the pursuit of art which finally brought Vanessa and Clive together. They were united by a common despair. It had been preceded by a visit to Greece. Vanessa had time to notice the great beauty of the manner in which Greek temples were related to the landscape, but for little else. She spent much of her time in bed and returned unwell to London whither Thoby had preceded her. He died – and Clive was accepted. This was only one of the ways in which this tragedy brought his friends together and united a group which soon included Duncan Grant, Maynard Keynes, Desmond MacCarthy and, later, Roger Fry.

Now established at 46 Gordon Square the Bells could express some of their ideas about art. Vanessa had already made a start two years earlier, but now she was married to a husband who would give full range to her ideas, while her sister and her surviving brother, who had ideas of their own, had removed to Fitzroy Square. So, in addition to the bare white walls, with a few isolated pictures (this was a style of interior design learnt from the painter Charles Furse) and the Cameron photographs, 46 Gordon Square now received a big portrait, *Pyramus,* by Augustus John. This was about 1907 and it will be seen that although the Bells were marching with what was then the avant-garde, they still had quite a long way to go.

The years 1907–14 saw some pretty startling changes. Mr Strachey became Lytton and Mr Keynes Maynard; it was common knowledge in Gordon Square that Lytton and Maynard buggered boys. Such things could not even have been talked of in mixed company in 1904. But Vanessa was now a married woman and one who thoroughly enjoyed the matrimonial bed. As yet she had not looked elsewhere for carnal delights, but were such adventures imaginable? By about 1909 I think that they were. Looking at the photographs of Vanessa taken in about 1896 it is hard to imagine that chaste and decorous young lady dancing with such vehemence as to throw off her dress so that she stood up in a crowded room naked to the waist. And yet for Vanessa this was now possible. The idea of 'sleeping around' was to her distasteful, but passion might be crowned by copulation. Where genuine feeling was the motive, the rules of Christian moralists might properly be set aside. Even so, Clive was unfaithful to her long before she was unfaithful to him. Indeed his futile pursuit of Virginia, a misadventure of the heart which wounded everyone concerned, began less than two years after his marriage.

Like her marriage, Vanessa's infidelities were to some extent involved in her art. She had married the only one of Thoby's friends who was deeply interested in painting and then, after four years of wedded life and two children, there came that happy time when, as she put it, 'we stopped talking about "the good" and started talking about Cézanne'. This change of topic (which after years of ethical discussion must have been welcome) was brought about by Roger Fry. His extraordinary energy clearly affected the Bells; they joined forces with him in the immensely exciting discovery of a kind of painting which united observation with a decorative language and which gave discipline and architectural force to art. The genteel timidities which Vanessa now observed in the Friday Club were abandoned, and she began to work with what must have seemed like reckless vigour, painting, not only on canvas and boards, but upon pottery, fabrics and walls.

The period when Vanessa discovered Roger was perhaps the happiest in her life. She was learning and immensely enjoying a new way of painting, she was happily in love, and yet her family life was in no way menaced. She and Roger kept their own homes and enjoyed each other's families.

My earliest distinct memory of her dates from this time: Vanessa, Julian and myself seated on a bench in Gordon Square, Vanessa describing the manner in which children are produced, we children laughing at the odd behaviour of men and women, Vanessa laughing at our amusement. In her later years she was grave as well as sad, but at that time she seemed always to be laughing. She was not what people call 'funny' but she found much to laugh at in life, in her children and her friends. I never heard her describe anyone as an enemy, but those whom she regarded as hopeless bores were also laughed at. Although she certainly was in love with him, she laughed gently at Roger. His fantastic ability to work all day, to discover new elixirs and new miracle workers, amazed and amused her. She laughed, perhaps not so gently, at Clive, and with the mirth of a devoted wife or an indulgent parent, at Duncan.

The years 1914–15 were catastrophic for Vanessa – by which I don't mean that she was deeply distressed by the war; for her it was a distant disaster and a public nuisance until with conscription it became a real menace; it was more of a turning point, a time for momentous decisions and redirections.

One day in 1914 Virginia received a visit from her sister who confessed that she was in love with Duncan, and burst into tears. Virginia found it hard to offer consolation; she had taken it for granted that Duncan would have nothing to do with women. This was an exaggeration, nevertheless at this point it seems that Virginia was right. To fall in love with Duncan and desert Roger, even though Duncan was young, beautiful, and charming, seemed like folly, albeit glorious folly. Also of course it was horribly painful for Roger, and Vanessa could not be indifferent to his grief. But there was another consideration of a different kind. Vanessa always tended to think in terms of art. She had married a critic; then she had found in Roger Fry a critic who was both an art historian and a painter; but now she had found something altogether more exciting – a painter whom she believed to be one of the very great men of the century. With Roger one hated the idea of telling him what one believed to be the truth about his paintings; it was hard to lie to one who valued truth so much. Nevertheless, she valued Roger too highly to lose him altogether and they remained friends for the rest of his life.

Vanessa could offer Duncan an almost maternal devotion and at the same time accept him as a master. It was her natural disposition to adore, to give, to submit, and in Duncan she found a man whom she felt to be worthy of her devotion; always she insisted upon his superiority, and in the worlds of both criticism and creation she found her views confirmed. 'Duncan', said Walter Sickert, 'was born with a crown on his head.' When he began to reach years of discretion Julian, who like me, had regarded him as an eccentric but altogether delightful elder brother, became aware of Duncan's growing stature in the eyes of the world, and suggested to Vanessa that we boys should treat him with rather more respect. Vanessa, of course, pointed out that Duncan wouldn't know what to do with respect even if it were shown to him; but at the same time I am sure that she was pleased.

Once, on a dark winter evening, I was walking with a lighted candle down the passageway at Charleston which leads to Duncan's room, and at that time to mine. The door of his room stood open and there he was kissing Vanessa on the lips. I was not shocked, but I was startled, for I had never seen them kiss in public. So startled in fact that I dropped my candle. In the business of hunting for a light and for the extinguished candle the tiny awkwardness was easily dealt with. But it was surprising; I had never seen such an exchange before.

In the ordinary business of life as I saw it when I had come to years of discretion, Vanessa and Duncan in company were like any other long-married couple, but one felt a peculiarly happy intimacy when they were working side by side – although this was not their general custom. There is though a particular and indescribable charm about the relationship of two people united by love and friendship who work together in the same studio; for Vanessa it was I believe a most valuable experience.

And yet she had to work for it. From the first it must have been clear that Duncan would escape whenever he felt like it into the arms of some man. Duncan had a great many lovers and there were some who, although they excited Vanessa's curiosity, would hardly have been at ease in her presence, for they came not only from the working but from the criminal classes; on the other hand many of his lovers were her friends, or became so. Madame de Sevigné had, we are told, the rare ability to make friends of those who aspired to be her lovers. Vanessa's achievement was more remarkable: those who came as rivals remained as allies.

The exception, so far as I am aware, was George Bergen, who indeed made Vanessa very unhappy. I discuss that miserable business in another place. Apart from this in some ways inexplicable collision with a hostile and potentially fatal intruder who, unlike Duncan's other lovers, could not be tolerantly ignored or kindly entertained, Vanessa's attempt to keep her lover as a constant friend and companion was remarkably successful, as was her management of a household which consisted of herself, Clive and Duncan, a group which received a permanent form in 1939 and endured until – and indeed after – her death.

❊

Julian and I were members of a normal family until 1916; we had a father and a mother who, although they were unfaithful to each other, lived together harmoniously. But from 1916 Clive was at Garsington. For us at Charleston he became a rare though delightful visitor. We liked him when we saw him, but I cannot say that we missed him when he was away. This situation was modified but not drastically changed when peace came. Clive then became a holiday father: he lived at Charleston in August and September; during the rest of the year he and Vanessa lived as neighbours in different houses in Gordon Square. We saw a good deal of him and, when we were grown up, sometimes stayed with him when we couldn't find room elsewhere, but this was occasional. As has been said, Clive, Duncan and Vanessa were not reunited under one roof until 1939.

For us boys there were a number of quasi-paternal figures – Roger, Maynard, Bunny Garnett (see Chapter 5) and Duncan all did something to educate us. However they exerted little or no authority; nor, for that matter, did Clive.

Paradoxically, Clive acted the part of Angelica's father with enthusiasm – indeed, it was not acting, for he loved Duncan and Vanessa's daughter; indeed at times Julian and I were jealous. This situation arose from the fact that the fiction of parenthood really worked altogether too well. Eventually it would have to be uncovered, but I can well understand Vanessa's reluctance to end so satisfactory an arrangement, all the more so because Duncan was not eager to exchange the easy role of friend for the more exacting business of being a father.

Thus we were in one sense a multi-parent family and in another, if not a one-parent family, something like a 75-per-cent-parent family, which meant that most of the work and stress fell upon Vanessa. She once told me, very seriously, that she never envied Virginia her genius for her sister had never known the incredible happiness of having children. I believed her, although I could not empathize sufficiently to understand the kind of joy which could compensate her (she told me this after Julian's death) for the agonies and anxieties which I could too easily imagine.

For us the reassuring comfort of being so well loved had also to be set against the pains of being so fearfully adored. Of the three of us I was the least precious, but in saying this I would not suggest that I did not have as much maternal affection as any one person could cope with. When I was a very young man I had a juvenile love affair which ended badly. I asked for sympathy from Vanessa and got it; indeed I got much more than I could handle and was soon far more grieved by the devastating effects that my avowal had caused in Vanessa's tender heart than in the evanescent hurt which I had sustained. It was difficult to know what best to do; was one to tell all and inflict such dreadful wounds, or keep silent and be accused perhaps of secretive reticence? I held my tongue.

Julian, a more open character, took Vanessa, and indeed everyone, into his confidence. He was a poet, and his instinct was to tell the whole world when he found that he was in love. The fact that Jane to whom he was engaged would hear of his love for Mary even before Mary herself was quite aware of it didn't seem to worry him at all, although Jane might take it rather hard; but then he was the kind of person with whom girls fall in love and, it seemed, the kind of person whom they forgive. What mattered far more was that when he left China and had more or less decided that he must go to Spain and take part in the Civil War, again the whole world knew of his intentions. This would not have mattered so much if it had not meant that his indecisions, which he no doubt found sufficiently agonizing, were hellishly painful for Vanessa.

An incident, absurd in itself but which may help the reader to understand the situation of the Bell family at that time, may just be worth recording. Soon after his return from China and while his plans were still in a state of flux, there was a meal at Charleston eaten by Vanessa, we three children and, I think, Duncan. Vanessa served a pudding; she gave half to Julian, the rest of us divided what remained. Vanessa herself realized that there was something more than a little absurd about this method of displaying affection and said something like: 'You see, I have to.' My own feeling was: 'how hideously embarrassing for Julian'. Luckily he liked the pudding and ate it all up with an unembarrassed grin. He, more than any of us, was able to accept the maternal passion without confusion or irritation. Angelica was the one who suffered most and she was the one who came nearest to angrily shaking off that embarrassing affection. Not that she ever did so; indeed she was the first to find the antidote to the poison that infected the sad years after Julian's death. She presented Vanessa with four grandchildren who did a great deal to make her later years tolerably happy.

I have discussed in another part of this work the events that made the years that followed Julian's death so gloomy. Here I would like to record two curious incidents which occurred during the very worst days of Vanessa's mourning.

The news came to her in her studio at No.8 Fitzroy Street. She collapsed on to a bed and howled like a wounded beast. We – Clive, Duncan, the Woolfs, Angelica and I – gathered around to say and do what we could. There were some more or less tête-à-tête conversations, and on one occasion Vanessa apologized to me for having so completely lost control of herself. I made the obvious noises, but she insisted that there must be many Spanish mothers suffering just as she was, but suffering in stoic silence. That was very much in character.

It was some days before she was well enough to be taken to Charleston. At the end of that period the fires of her first anguish seemed to have burned themselves out and Vanessa was a little – a very little – restored. One afternoon, when Duncan was away, she began to talk about his proletarian lovers, and in particular about those who had 'done time'. Vanessa explained that they always had excuses: 'It always turns out' she said, 'that they have been wronged.' And then, as Clive put it later when we were going back to Gordon Square, 'she did actually smile'. He was childishly delighted and I was touched by his delight. But it was the historical context that fascinated me. Think how the nineteenth century would have recorded that incident.

How could Vanessa's father, how for that matter could Vanessa Stephen, have imagined such an incident: that she should have derived a tiny crumb of amusement from the misdeeds of her lover's perverted minions and that her unfaithful and cuckolded husband should rejoice at this little earnest of returning happiness.

Vanessa's fame, whatever it may amount to, will belong to the history of art; but she also has her place in the history of twentieth-century morality. Reared in a home which, despite Sir Leslie's agnosticism, was not 'advanced' in the Fabian or Shavian sense, she had, as a liberated orphan, defied convention without really endangering what she would still have described as her 'virtue'. Married, she discovered the pleasures of love and in a platonic way espoused the idea of a liberty that would be libertine; but this was not put into practice until she was thirty years old.

Today I suppose there are still women who live chaste, obedient lives and are almost as blinkered, as prudish, as intolerant, as that army of aunts and cousins who maintained the mendacities and the decencies of Hyde Park Gate. But they must be much less numerous and are certainly less powerful. Vanessa was in the advance guard of the army of liberation. To belong to the 'forlorn hope' of any victorious company is perhaps honourable but not wholly enviable. Leaders get wounded, or perhaps merely breathless; they may stumble as they cross the glacis and leap into the trench. I think that this was the case with Vanessa; she had come so far and so fast that at times she needed to rest. Observing those younger women who followed her, she blamed their rashness. Faced by the need to call a cunt a cunt she discovered that she could not quite abandon the proprieties. And we who owed her so much blamed her for growing old.

4

Duncan Grant

DISCUSSING MY PARENTS, I have attempted to write what one might call pocket biographies, briefly mentioning their families and following their lives from early youth. Duncan, whom I knew before I was of an age to remember him, who was my sister's father and for many years an inhabitant of Charleston, seemed a proper subject for similar treatment. But it can't be done. The official biography is in the competent hands of Frances Spalding; she is well qualified to undertake the necessary research. I am not.

Within certain limits I knew Duncan very well, but there were important areas of his life about which I know very little, events which I learnt only from Michael Holroyd's life of Lytton Strachey.*

Holroyd describes a youthful triumvirate, three young sodomites: Lytton Strachey and Maynard Keynes, both from Cambridge, both of them ugly, gifted and in love with Duncan, who was equally gifted and far better looking.

Historically, their situation was interesting:

> . . . Standing apart
> Upon the forehead of the age to come;
> These, these, will give the world another heart,
> And other pulses.

In 'the age to come' – the post-war period – they did indeed play a leading role in the change of atmosphere and the revolution of

---

* *Lytton Strachey*, Chatto & Windus, 1994 (reissue)

morals. They achieved eminence and were themselves changed; they acquired female companions and in Maynard's case sexual conversion. Post-Impressionism, *Eminent Victorians*, and *The Economic Consequences of the Peace* informed our thinking – I have in mind a much wider public than Bloomsbury – during that period of peace and even of optimism which preceded the political agonies of the 'thirties.

To return to the clandestine amours and activities of the pre-war period: Duncan played a leading part; delighting and tormenting his friends, he created what he himself called 'havoc'; he was unpredictable and inconstant and he charmed his way out of the imbroglios that he created. He was invincible when he set himself to charm because in truth he did not need to 'set himself'; he simply *was* himself. One of the most remarkable things I ever saw was Duncan's conquest of Seend. Seend had heard of him and what it had heard was surely scandalous. He was on the face of it exactly the kind of person of whom Seend disapproved. What chance had he with those stuffy but by no means stupid people? But within five minutes he had my aunt Lorna eating out of his hand. It was a wonderful and seemingly effortless performance.

And yet his victorious charm was, as you might say, a by-product; when he took a brush in his hand he was intensely serious and if he still appeared charming the appearance resulted from no conscious effort. He sat there blinking through half-shut eyes, assessing the tonality of his subject, then using the brush with enormous care, leaning back and looking quizzically at nature and at his canvas, a little puzzled but deeply happy, enjoying nature, enjoying his work immensely.

Painting, as J.M.W. Turner remarked, is a rum business. It almost seems that it can be done without conscious thought, or at least that for long periods the kind of intellectual effort which must be made in writing may be abandoned. Duncan, like most other painters, could chatter quite freely with a sitter, or listen quite attentively while Desmond MacCarthy read Henry James aloud, and all the while make a series of careful observations on the shape, texture, and colour of Desmond's face. It was my impression that Duncan, more than most artists, was astonished – whether or not he was pleased – by what appeared on his easel.

There was a time, about 1910, when Duncan was living with his parents and at night would have to take the last tram back to Hampstead, for which purpose he would 'borrow' a penny from Clive. 'Come now, wouldn't it be convenient if you borrowed rather more – say five bob?' But Duncan insisted that a penny was all that he needed.

Duncan was still creating 'havoc' when Clive decided he had gone too far. I was never sure what the nature of his crime might have been but I think he may have opened letters addressed to other people. At all events Clive decided that Duncan should have a good scolding. The only question was how should this be managed? He hit upon the idea of inviting him to dinner so that he and the accused should be tête-à-tête. Accordingly they went to some agreeable restaurant in Charlotte Street. They dined very well. Duncan, who had been forewarned of what was to come, waited for the thunderbolt to fall. The soup came; the entrée came; then the cheese, then some fruit, but no thunder. They had coffees and then a *pousse-café*: still no sign of trouble. Another glass, and Clive began to talk about the sacred nature of correspondence. He seemed to be about to come to the point, but somehow – it had been such a pleasant evening it seemed a shame to spoil it – better to order a third glass of brandy and then, coherent thought difficult, they wandered into the open air. 'Just time to catch my tram,' said Duncan. 'Clive, would you lend me a penny?'

He 'got away with things'. Driving our little car along the Strand, its engine stalled. Duncan got out and cranked it up with the starting handle, not without effect: he just managed to leap out of its way and run alongside as it proceeded slowly down the Strand, its doors shut, finally ramming into a majestic Daimler emerging from the Savoy. The innocent victim was naturally enraged. If the culprit had been you or I this is where the story might become unpleasant. Not for Duncan. The injured party at once became his friend; it is said even that it ended with his giving Duncan a commission for a portrait.

Duncan was the youngest of those who could at the time – about 1910 – be described as Bloomsbury. He was the spoilt child of the group, spoilt because all Bloomsbury succumbed to his charm. Had he then no enemies? He certainly had one in Wyndham Lewis, and perhaps two if we count D.H. Lawrence. Lewis believed himself to be persecuted by Bloomsbury in general and by Duncan in particular. Duncan's alleged crime consisted in taking a theatrical commission which Lewis had wanted for himself. Finding himself walking along the pavement of a narrow street and observing Duncan walking in the same direction on the opposite pavement Lewis spat at his successful rival. 'It was unpleasant,' said Duncan many years later, 'even though he wasn't very good at spitting.' But the annoying thing was that Duncan knew why Lewis was spitting and would have been glad to explain that he had never even attempted to gain the commission of which Lewis fancied he had been robbed.

Duncan made D.H. Lawrence dream of black beetles; he was, according to Lawrence, 'done for for ever'. Lawrence should not perhaps be accounted an enemy but rather, according to his own lights, a candid friend. And no doubt he felt that in telling Duncan that his pictures were bad – hopelessly bad – and worthless because they were 'full of the wrong ideas' – an opinion which he expressed with some violence and at great length – he was in a way doing Duncan a service. As Duncan said, 'this interview was painful to me because I felt that Lawrence was quite unsympathetic to what I was trying to do at that moment.' Although Duncan could not remember to what particular work it was that Lawrence objected, it seems likely that it was the kinetic abstract now in the Tate. Lawrence disapproved of but did not hate Duncan; Wyndham Lewis obviously did, and one may fairly guess that his feelings were returned. In a general way Duncan was not what Cardinal Manning called 'a great hater'. I heard him express dislike for three people: André Gide, Logan Pearsall Smith and Ralph Partridge; what Duncan had against them I do not know.

I cannot remember how or when Duncan came into my life. He was at Wissett in 1915 and came with us when we moved to Charleston in the autumn of 1916. By the end of the war he seemed – although I should have been perplexed to say how – to have become a member of the family and we boys both liked him immensely. We thought of him as a joke, another of the amiable eccentrics by whom we were always surrounded, another member of our colony of pacifists. He and Bunny (David Garnett) rode off on bicycles to Mr Hecks's farm each day where Bunny proved a very competent farm labourer. Duncan I gather was far less useful.

One story of that odd parenthesis in Duncan's life is perhaps worth recording. At that time farming was far less mechanized than it now is; the combine harvester was still unknown, grain was brought back to the farmyard, stacked in sheaves, and left to wait for the itinerant threshing machine. When this arrived the sheaves were thrown into its jaws, while all around an army of men and boys armed with sticks, together with enthusiastic dogs and even a few cats, crouched around and waited for the vast exodus of rats and mice – creatures which had been living happily in amongst the grain. When these emerged they were chased, pounced upon and gobbled up by the carnivores or, when the demands of the flesh had been satisfied, killed in sport. In the evening when the threshing and the killing were over Bunny and Duncan mounted their bicycles and pedalled home, but when they reached the turning to Charleston Duncan dismounted and spoke: 'I suppose I should not be doing this; you may think it wrong', saying which he reached into his shirt and extracted a small live mouse which he placed carefully under the hedge.

At length a day came when Duncan burst into our schoolroom (the dining room at Charleston) saying 'The Kaiser has fled and Germany is a republic', which meant that he could start painting again. An old army hut on which someone had written the words 'Les Miserables' was erected in the Charleston paddock and thither every morning he and Vanessa went to paint. It was not for many years, when I was fourteen or fifteen, that we began to wonder whether he might not be Angelica's father. I personally rather regretted that he was not mine.

Duncan liked painting – that sounds a fairly banal statement, but in fact it is merely a wild understatement. He liked the practice of art so much that he found it very hard to accept that quite a lot of paintings are bad. The mere fact that someone had attempted to paint indicated so great a state of grace that a few faults in execution were pardonable. The most that he would say against a painting was that it was not wholly successful. True, he did once say of an American lady that one had to admit that she lacked talent. Her work, poor woman, was in fact quite horrible.

It is often said that painters know about painting and about nothing else and at times Duncan gave one the impression that this was true of him; he could fill us with amused amazement by his ignorance. Thus for instance he once told Vanessa that he was astonished by the growing popularity of the Liberal Party: he had seen so many cars which bore the letter L. On the other hand we knew perfectly well that although he played no instrument he had a much better musical education than Clive or Vanessa. There were occasions when he took one by surprise. Once in the middle of a conversation about Balzac he began to make remarks that showed in a fairly well-informed company he knew more than everyone. I was surprised because until that moment I had no notion that he ever read Balzac, and this deceptive modesty was typical.

When we were living in London in the early 1920s Julian and I saw a particularly splendid-looking Easter egg in a shop. It was far beyond our means, so we decided to paint a number of pictures and then have a sale of them. Clive, Vanessa, and I think Maynard came to our room and looked at our works. Julian had found a formidable-looking hammer with which to direct the auction, but after selling a couple of pictures the bidding lost energy and enthusiasm; the splendid egg still seemed out of reach. Then Duncan arrived. It was one of those occasions when he adopted a new persona: a crusty, difficult party determined to outbid everyone else. His bids were large; he complained bitterly when anyone else managed to buy anything; he forced prices up and triumphed abominably when he outbid another person. By the end of the sale we had enough and more than enough to make ourselves ill.

Duncan was always capable of taking on a role and playing it with art and conviction. I remember him suddenly transforming himself into Mrs Beerbohm Tree in the role of Lady Macbeth. Virginia also records an occasion when he left her and Leonard weak and helpless with laughter at a performance he gave in the fields behind Charleston; and my own children could testify to his powers as an actor even at an advanced age.

In Charleston orchard there was a clear space not overgrown by nettles, and there we stretched a net over which one threw a rubber quoit. Duncan would sometimes join us. One hot day I took off my shirt. 'Put it on again,' he said, 'you look far too attractive without it.' I was surprised; it was the only time that he ever suggested that I was sexually interesting; and in fact Duncan, who could not but find a pair of growing boys attractive, behaved in an exemplary fashion. Altogether his emotional situation at Charleston must have been rather difficult, or could have been if he had been in any way foolish.

Presently we knew, and in fact everyone knew, that Angelica was his daughter – except for Angelica herself; so far as I could see his attitude was affectionate but never paternal. But of his affection there could be no doubt at all. If I had ever had any doubts on that score they would have been removed when I saw him for a moment on that hideous afternoon when a motor car mounted the pavement of the Tottenham Court Road and, as everyone then thought, left Angelica mortally wounded. But in his day-to-day treatment of her Duncan seemed more like an affectionate uncle than a father. He was perhaps deficient in feelings of an unequivocally masculine and paternal nature; and somehow it did not seem odd that he should surrender this role to Clive who accepted it enthusiastically.

Duncan's strong devotion to Vanessa, a feeling which may without absurdity be classed as a kind of fidelity, a feeling sufficiently powerful to bring him back to her again and again throughout the many years of their association, coexisted with its opposite, viz: a large variety of homosexual adventures. These were of two main kinds, or as one may put it, two social groups: the upper and the lower class. The great majority of the upper-class pederasts – Lytton, Maynard, Adrian, Bunny and, in later years, Angus Davidson, Peter Morris, Edward le Bas etc. etc., were, or became, Vanessa's friends and sometimes seemed more attached to her than they were to him. In addition to this section of the bourgeoisie, there was another group which might be classed as aristocratic or at least as courtiers and, more or less attached to these, a very important figure, the American painter George Bergen. George Bergen came nearer than anyone else to causing a break between Vanessa and Duncan and was for many years the object of a very considerable passion.

To Duncan and to many others George Bergen was an Adonis or perhaps an Apollo: immensely handsome, irresistibly charming, a most gifted painter, a man of wit, perhaps of profundity. The people who described him in these terms were intelligent and sensitive; they saw in him an enormous amount that I could not see. If they were right, I was very wrong indeed.

I think that he did have some gifts as a painter, although his work is very uneven. Physically he was tall, his features always reminded me of the anthropoid apes. I never knew him to be either witty or profound; his remarks concerning his own painting seemed to me pretentious and very stupid. I did not know him very well, but I had one chance to form an opinion of his character and it is this perhaps which has coloured my judgements.

He suggested that I should come and live with him. He made this suggestion in a sufficiently loud voice to be heard by Duncan who was standing nearby. It was perfectly obvious that his only motive in making this suggestion was to be unkind to Duncan. I thought of it and still think of it as one of the nastiest actions I have ever witnessed. I should add that my views concerning Bergen's appearance and attainments were formed before this incident took place.

I also remember one New Year's Eve. Duncan had asked me to join a party; I cannot remember in what terms I was asked nor do I know why Duncan invited me, but I was to go out with him and a group of friends. Duncan and I were with Vanessa in her studio when we heard the party arrive next door where Duncan worked. Vanessa said, 'It's rather melancholy seeing in the New Year by myself.' It was obvious that she was on the verge of tears. Duncan took command: he told me to go and tell his friends that he was unable to join them. I obeyed.

The group in which I now found myself consisted of George Bergen and two companions. I explained the situation – or at least as much of it as needed explanation – and soon found myself with Bergen and his friends in a taxi. I have never been in worse company.

I find it difficult to describe the two men whom George had brought. They were the most unappetizing male tarts I ever saw, filthy with a dirt which was moral rather than physical. One of them made a coarse joke; it was something about Duncan. It is only fair to say that George Bergen rebuked him. I managed to escape.

I hasten to say that these Yahoos were not typical of Duncan's other proletarian friends of whom I saw a small sample. There was a delightful man called H and a harmless lunatic called Tut because he identified himself with Tutankhamun. There was also a very amusing young man who for a time kept a restaurant in Lewes and collected pictures; unfortunately his way of collecting landed him in gaol. There was also an amiable young fellow who helped me in my efforts to make Charleston pond watertight. He tried to involve me in a more ambitious enterprise: the construction and operation of an illicit still in Charleston cellar. 'Only six years' hard,' he remarked with the easy sang-froid of one who has done time. In those days any homosexual could be blackmailed and it must have taken some courage to make love to the criminal classes. Was it danger that made Duncan and so many others find these adventures so tantalizing?

I remember one occasion when Duncan behaved really badly. He was of course drunk, but it was inexcusable. He and Angelica had been invited to a party – it was a musical party in Hampstead at the home of Geoffrey Keynes and his wife. Geoffrey, Maynard's younger brother, was an old friend of Duncan, a brilliant surgeon, a bibliophile, a great admirer of William Blake, with a passion for the music of Vaughan Williams (who was also a friend) – these two I believe might be accounted the lares and penates of the highly respectable and tastefully decorated home to which Duncan and Angelica were bidden that evening. The party was to begin late, so that Duncan was able to go first to a meeting of the Cranium Club in Soho.

I was also at the Cranium and when it ended I returned with Duncan to 8 Fitzroy Street. He was decidedly unsteady, and from time to time found it necessary to cling to the railings of Soho Square or – as a *pis aller* – to me. He was in high spirits and so was I. What with one thing and another we were damnably late when we finally got to the Fitzroy Street studio. Poor Angelica was cross, not unnaturally; she had put on a pretty dress, taken it off again when she got tired of waiting, and was just about to go to bed. She was not impressed when Duncan arrived and told her that there was still plenty of time for the party and objected, when he said he would drive, that he was unfit to do so. I stupidly offered to drive them both, and this being accepted, she got dressed again and we set off.

Unfortunately, Duncan managed to outwit me, got to the driving seat and set off leaving me to clamber into the car when it was already in motion. Duncan, when perfectly sober, drove like a man who believes that a guardian angel will protect him. I have known him turn round and argue with a timid passenger as he rushed through red lights. That night he scared the wits out of me, but I must say that he found his way to Hampstead with unhesitating skill.

When we arrived the party was drawing to a close. There was just one last tribute to the English countryside to be concluded; it was the kind of thing, Duncan said, to make one hate English folk music. Duncan was not half so charitable about musicians as he was about painters and as he approached the piano, which was surrounded by a little group of young people, he said, 'Now let us have some decent music. . . Let's have some Mozart.' The young people, who clearly had decided upon the spot that Duncan was the nicest thing that had happened that evening, were very ready to oblige. I was struck by a horrid fear that 'Uncle Ralph', as Virginia called Vaughan Williams for no very good reason, might be in the room and was appalled, but no one was so much appalled as poor Mrs Keynes. She, after doing her duties as a hostess – which I have no doubt she performed admirably – was just beginning to dish out the coats and say goodbye to her guests, and here was Duncan, who had managed to possess himself not only of the hearts and minds of her guests but also of a half-full bottle of champagne. What made it worse no doubt was the fact that the rebellious young were delighted.

I, who had come uninvited, bringing with me this mischievous guest, could not but feel a certain sense of guilt tempered by irresistible amusement. Angelica was beginning to enjoy herself. I do not think that Duncan prolonged the evening very extensively although he was clearly happy and, drunk as he was, he never misbehaved. He was entirely correct, grateful for what he called 'real music' and ready, finally, to be persuaded to go home.

When we left he had to be helped into the car and it was I who drove. The next morning he was healthy and in good spirits; he had had a lovely evening and his eyes twinkled as he recalled its events.

Perhaps I have made too much of this story, but it may serve to exhibit some of the difficulties which arose from the fact that although one might perceive that he was behaving badly, he could somehow command one's sympathies. This was particularly true if one happened to find the music of Vaughan Williams less enchanting than that of Mozart.

Mozart was indeed his favourite composer and one whom he found more sympathetic than Beethoven, whom he admired but could never love. Although he might hardly have said so in my terms I think it is fair to say that he was shy of *terribilità* and distrusted the use of thunder and lightning in art. He admired humility, distrusted arrogance, violence and cruelty in any of the arts, or at least could accept them only from the hands of genius. In this he was very Bloomsbury, or at least very close to Roger and Vanessa; where he differed from them was in a deep, almost personal, affection for Delacroix.

*

Travelling in France with Duncan, he and Vanessa being in one car, Angelica and I in another, we suffered a minor disaster: the hood of one of the cars blew off and was badly torn. It was beginning to rain, so we made our way to the nearest town. For once France failed us; even if it had not been raining the urban agglomeration at which we stopped would have been uninteresting. A garage would repair the hood for us but we should have to wait three hours for the work to be completed. It was a desolating prospect; three hours can be a long time. 'I think' said Duncan, 'that I shall go to sleep,' with which he curled up in the back of the car, closed his eyes and slept.

Vanessa explained that he could always go to sleep simply by lying down; the pity was that he couldn't manage it while standing up. Duncan seemed to have a magnetic effect on bores: when he entered a crowded room bores, like vultures scenting a wounded beast in the jungle, would gather round him and there was nothing he could do to stop it. I suggested that he might use that other remarkable gift of his which enabled him to command his belly to throw up whenever he felt unwell.

But despite these strong defences Duncan could let himself down in a most disastrous fashion. When he expected a purchaser in his studio he would guard against his own deficiencies as a salesman by boldly chalking what seemed a decent price on the back of his canvases. When the prospective purchaser arrived Duncan would at once decide the price he had asked was exorbitant: three hundred pounds would be reduced to two-fifty, and that to two hundred, which itself would then appear impossibly high and be reduced again. This auction in reverse could end by becoming ludicrous.

This almost quixotic attitude towards money I once heard summarized when Duncan was living almost alone at Charleston and one of his light-fingered boyfriends made off not only with some pictures but also with I know not how much money. Another of his handsome friends, a nice American youth, was anxious to notify the police and recover both the paintings and the cash. Duncan did want the paintings – some of them were unfinished – but for the rest he declared: 'nothing matters less than money'. Not that he wasn't greatly in need of it at that time.

I saw Duncan at several very painful and critical moments in his life but I only once saw him moved to tears, and that was when Vanessa died. I was at Charleston almost by accident; he and I were in the house together and he broke down and wept, accusing himself of 'not having been as kind to her as I should have been'. I did not know what to say or what I should have said if Angelica had not arrived at that moment.

For a time after that Clive and Duncan lived together at Charleston, very peaceably I gather; after all, they had been together for about half a century, laughing gently at each other and their friends.

After Clive's death Charleston was still a social centre. A number of young men discovered the way from the University of Sussex to Charleston. Their arrival marked a change in national taste. From 1939 to about 1960 Duncan together with the rest of Bloomsbury had been under a critical cloud. (It was lightened a little by the young Richard Shone.) Duncan was the only one of the group to live long enough to see the wheel of taste come full circle.

I wish I could say that this reversal of taste made him happy in his last years, but in fact he never remarked to me on the decline in his reputation, nor on its recovery.

5

David Garnett

HE WAS KNOWN to his friends and to an ever wider circle as Bunny. It was a name which he acquired in early youth – I think he owed it to a rabbit-skin hat worn when he was a child; the name stuck to him for the rest of his life, but it did not suit him at all well. Rabbits are small, furry, timid animals; they bolt into burrows; when you shoot them they bowl over; when you eat them they require a copious reinforcement of herbs if they are to taste of anything. David Garnett was large, smooth and, although sometimes a little shy, never timid. He was much more likely to bolt out of a burrow than into it. He was always ready to return fire and if he had been edible he would have had a strong flavour. If he were to be compared to an animal then I should liken him to a bear, a creature with an endearing weakness for berries and honey but also a carnivore. The bunny-hug was warm, but it might break your ribs.

My first memory of him is connected with a coat. It had been left in the hall of 46 Gordon Square and it aroused my curiosity for it was adorned with a splendid decoration, a Maltese Cross, the emblem I think of the Ambulance Service with which he had been serving in France (the year was 1915). But on that occasion I did not meet him in person – not so far as I can remember.

He races swiftly, vigorously, before the mind's eye pursuing a puppy with half a cake in its mouth; they were both going at a tremendous rate. I wonder who won? We shall never know. That was at Wissett Lodge in Suffolk. Thither we had gone to grow fruit. The idea was to avoid conscription. The tribunal which decided these matters of life and death was not impressed; the tribunes, worthy Suffolk farmers, considered soft fruit a frivolous business, and when a witness pointed out that the Garnett family were disciples of Tolstoy and therefore sincerely convinced pacifists, they replied that this was irrelevant. It did not matter whether the Garnett family came from Tolstoy or any other foreign city.

All that summer the carnage was going on in France as never before. The troops were trained and armed and sent off in thousands and tens of thousands to be maimed and slaughtered. The stupid men in command could think of nothing better to do than call for more and more men to be thrown into more and more fruitless offensives. Duncan and Bunny had to try and reverse the judgements of the Suffolk tribunes. They succeeded in keeping out of the war and out of prison, again becoming farmers but growing something less 'frivolous' than fruit.

Vanessa found a house for herself and her children at Charleston, and a job for her men in the neighbourhood. Charleston's walled garden, now bisected by paths, its flowerbeds alternating with ponds and lawns and the place inhabited by a heterogeneous race of statues, was then mainly devoted to the growing of potatoes; but the orchard was full of fruit in summer, and of bees. The interior of the house was littered with the husks of sunflower seeds – you found them everywhere. This was Bunny's doing; he had inherited his physical appearance from his father, together with the long and impressive literary tradition – if that be the word – of the Garnetts; but from his mother he had a no less distinguished but more exotic inheritance. A woman of formidable talents, she was one, and perhaps the most eminent, of those who made the English-speaking public aware of the extraordinary flowering of genius which occurred in Russia during the nineteenth century. At a time when everyone was taking an interest in Russia, Bunny got his Slavs – as you might say – from the horse's mouth. This led to Tolstoy, Dostoevsky, the ballet, and sunflower seeds. It was the sunflower seeds which interested me in the autumn of 1916. The floors of the carriages of Russian railway trains were, so Bunny told us, awash with the husks of innumerable sunflower seeds. I, who was in love with all things Russian, thought that Charleston drawing room would be none the worse for a similar carpet.

In a little room which vanished when the studio was built at Charleston, Bunny sat amidst this glorious debris building what seemed to be wooden toys. They were in fact frames for honey-combs, for Bunny was, among other things, our bee-keeper. I used to visit that little room a good deal. I cannot remember that he ever threw me out. He talked about Russia, he talked about bees, he talked about foxes and stoats, the habits of earthworms and toads, cuckoos and kingfishers. He introduced me and my brother to the work of Richard Jeffries. For many years after he had left us and had become distant and celebrated I hoped that when I grew up I should become a naturalist. This was partly 'good teaching'; Bunny could talk about the behaviour of water beetles in such a way as to make himself interesting and comprehensible, but it was also the result of great good nature.

The Armistice came, Christmas came – and with it my sister. Bunny was moved to prophesy over her cradle that one day he would marry her; but then he vanished, to reappear at long intervals, sometimes driving a car, sometimes an aeroplane. But he remained in my mind, making biology the only science I understood at school and, when *Lady into Fox* fell into my hands, it enchanted me.

But in my salad days – I mean the days when I claimed rather unwisely to be grown up – I found him when we met decidedly unsympathetic; our conversation seemed to develop into a kind of rough teasing. There was never an open quarrel between us but there was a certain unhappy coldness. The reason for this, so he told me later on, was that he thought that I had become a very affected young man. There may have been some truth in it.

Whatever the trouble, it was ended by a very enjoyable visit which I made in 1935 to the Garnetts at Hilton, Huntingdon. There for the first time I saw Bunny surrounded by his family. Bunny himself made an excellent host, obviously enjoyed being a family man, and enjoyed also his success as an author.

I am not sure when I became aware that Bunny was pursuing my sister but I know that when I did I was pleased. She was at that time stage-struck – a pupil of Michel St Denis at the London Theatre Studio. Being out of London most of the time I saw little of the lovers until the summer of 1938, when they suggested that I join them in an expedition to central France. I think that it was some-where in the Tarn – at any rate a pretty country with green valleys and rushing water. It was the rushing water that attracted Bunny.

He was an enthusiast: he enthused over Russia and apiculture, he enthused over girls, he enthused over D.H. Lawrence and T.E. Lawrence; he enthused over aeroplanes, and now he was madly enthusiastic about fly-fishing. He had purchased a book about French trout and the place to which we went contained, it seemed, one of the great trout streams of France. Bunny had equipped himself to do it justice.

He made no sartorial efforts; Bunny it seemed to me had always looked like an angler. Good, old clothes, a shapeless hat which now had flies in it, waders, a big game bag – nothing 'posh'. His rod, however, when it had been carefully assembled, was chic beyond words; one considered it in a spirit of reverence: it was so strong, so supple, so elegant, so generous in the way it spewed out the line which came darting forth like some agile creature armed with wings. Nor was Bunny's manipulation of his equipment unworthy of his exquisitely fashioned apparatus; he walked slowly up the stream, casting and casting again, his fly gliding over the water as though it had been a live insect; his casts were slow, graceful and scientific. The only trouble was that the fish seemed totally uninterested. Back and forth he went, tireless, patient, but futile. I began to fear that we had been defrauded, the guide book had been mendacious: the waters, though lovely to look at, were uninhabited by fish.

But then a little man appeared; he was employed in the kitchen of the hotel. He sat down, took from his pocket a length of string and a lump of bacon fat which he threw into the water at the point where an iron pipe discharged the contents of a ditch into the main stream. After about three minutes he drew out a trout, about 2lbs I should say; within quarter of an hour he had fish enough for the hotel lunch. Bunny regarded him with mixed feelings; he was looking forward to lunch, but was sorry that it had come on the end of a piece of string. The little man for his part appeared deeply puzzled by Bunny. Why did Monsieur go to so much trouble to catch fish which were, manifestly, not to be caught in that fashion? For his part he would most willingly provide the gentleman with string, bacon fat and hook; he would find it a much more efficient method. Would I explain to Monsieur that he would be glad to help?

I translated, although I think that Bunny had understood, and I kept a straight face although the idea of that superbly equipped angler casting his bacon upon the waters was almost too much for me. It was almost too much for Bunny; his face reddened in that alarming fashion which was usual when he was under stress, and for a moment I feared a dreadful explosion. Happily his sense of humour was equal to the occasion and the offer was politely declined, even though it was to be repeated more than once, for Bunny's elegant manoeuvres continued day after day always with the same result.

As an angler he was a failure, but he seemed a most fortunate lover. He and Angelica appeared very happily in love and although I sometimes wondered why on earth they had invited me to join them, it was a pleasure to see them both so happy; and so they remained throughout the entire holiday.

We returned to Paris, and there I remained for some weeks while they went on to London. Presently I followed them; there had been a disaster and now there was the devil to pay. Angelica had been struck by a sudden and alarming illness; she could not be properly looked after at home and Bunny had put her into a nursing home. These arrangements had been made hurriedly and Vanessa had not been told of them – or had been told too late. She hurried up to London to find that her daughter had vanished. She was still in a state of tension following Julian's death and she was enraged. (This at all events was what I gathered, for I arrived late on the scene.)

Julian had once compared Vanessa to Demeter – it was a poetically truthful comparison, and now it was only too apt. Having, in the initial stages, watched Bunny's advances with a fairly tolerant eye, she now saw him as a monstrous Pluto dragging her Persephone into the abyss. Duncan seemed to share her views – I was never sure what he really felt. Taken aside by both parties I was, as always, a go-between, but in fact, like Clive and like the Woolfs, I could not share Vanessa's agony completely and could up to a point sympathize with, and yet deplore, Angelica's irritation at the fuss.

It was the beginning of a difficult and disheartening period which was made additionally unhappy by international events. The phony peace ended in 1939 with the 'phony war', and then, in 1940, with the real and mortal combat. During this period Bunny was consciously or unconsciously transforming a love affair for which there was much to be said into something more momentous – a marriage.

It was this which for a time drew me into the conflict. Angelica had already produced some remarkable paintings at the Euston Road School and did seem to have at last found out what she wanted to do; but she was still very young, only twenty-one, when the war began. It was bad enough that she should at that age have found herself obliged to live in a nation at war, but to adapt herself to accept the habits and friends of an older generation, seemed to me altogether unfair.

'Her mother managed well enough,' said Bunny.

'Her mother married a well-heeled bachelor with wealthy parents and no one else to support.'

It was a long but not unfriendly argument in which I felt and still feel that I was in the right. Old men have no right to prey upon the young. But I was bound to lose in the end; Angelica herself could hardly be expected to know her own mind or, at her age, to oppose so very formidable a character.

But the real agonies of that unhappy period came from my attempts to play pig-in-the-middle. It was a time when Vanessa began to behave in an unprecedented way; she did things that, in her, were unbelievable. When the post came she would intercept a letter addressed to me by Bunny or Angelica and read it before handing it over. And what the devil was I to do? Snatch it back? Or wait, angry and miserable, hoping that she would not find something in the letter that was hurtful?

There was however one adventure of this kind that was not without humour. It was in the summer of 1940; the first air raids were beginning. Bunny and Angelica, who had been living in Sussex, had gone to Yorkshire. The Germans had been so inconsiderate as to drop a bomb somewhere near Hull. Hull is in Yorkshire, *ergo* the Germans were bombing Yorkshire, *ergo* the Garnetts must come back to Sussex, *ergo* I must ring them up and tell them so.

Dismally I agreed (I hate the telephone even at the best of times). I hoped that I might be able to have a word with Bunny, try to persuade him to say something comforting to Vanessa, something perhaps faintly dishonest but kind and reassuring. But for that I needed to speak to him privately and at once I discovered that Vanessa was going to make any such manoeuvre impossible; she planted herself in the embrasure where the telephone was placed in Charleston dining room. She could hear every word I said; probably she would also hear Bunny, who, when he spoke on the telephone, did so very very slowly and distinctly. There was nothing for it, I had to ring up, I had to give the operator the right number, and I got

Bunny himself. I told him that it was painful to hear that there were bombs in his part of the world and said that, at a time of crisis, it seemed to me better that the family should stick together. At least that was the gist of what I said. I suppose that I was unconvincing and very irritating; Bunny left me in no doubt on this point. Slowly and distinctly, he told me that I was a bloody fool. He pointed out that Yorkshire is a very large county; they were in the Dales, many miles from Hull, and in one of the safest spots in England (things that I had already said in a less forceful manner to Vanessa). He also pointed out that we in Sussex were in a particularly dangerous situation; that if there were an invasion – which at that time seemed very probable – Charleston would almost certainly be on the path of the invaders. Surely I had sense enough to see that? He was amazed at my stupidity. He rang off. It was clear that Bunny was angry with me but, needless to say, it took a long time for him to make his feelings of rage and contempt perfectly clear. The comic part came years later when he reminded me of the incident. 'You have no idea' he said, 'how exasperating you were on the telephone. You spoke so absurdly slowly.'

It was about two years after this that Bunny invited me to apply for a job in the Political Warfare Executive where he held a post in the Secretariat and, as I found, was much liked and highly valued. He was on the whole happy there, though sometimes exasperated by things which he regarded as stupidities, and disputes in which it seemed to me that he was usually in the right. But there was now a major complication in the war which made him feel some mixed emotions.

The first intimation that I had of this was when I was cutting a hayfield on Maynard Keynes's farm. It was a lovely summer's day in June 1941; the Garnetts – as I suppose one might then call them – were staying with us at Charleston, and in the middle of the day my sister came out with a basket containing my lunch and an item of news: the Germans had invaded Russia. And, she added, Bunny, who knew more than most people about such things, said that the Russian resistance would collapse in six weeks.

The news which, as may be imagined, was sufficiently interesting in itself, was of particular interest to me because I had just received a book to review from the *New Statesman* called (I think) *The Red Army*. It seemed that a reviewer in such circumstances had to venture a prophecy. Bunny, who knew so much, had given the opinion of his colleagues. Was he right?

Certainly our new ally had a ramshackle look; the purges in the Red Army had been drastic and must have been demoralizing. The Finnish Campaign of 1939–40, in its initial phases at all events, had been badly managed by the Russians. On the other hand the author whom I had to review was on the whole optimistic. Also I had to consider Bunny's character as a witness. He had a real and abiding hatred of the Soviet regime, a hatred that was made not less but more intense by his love for the Russian people and for their culture. He had been brought up in an atmosphere of enthusiasm not only for Russia but for the coming Revolution; his family home was close to that part of Surrey which Bunny's father had named 'Dostoevsky Corner', so large was the Russian minority there; he had rejoiced at the success of the Revolution in its early stages. One of the legends of Charleston, the date of which I cannot easily place, was a grand row between Bunny and Maynard at breakfast. According to Bunny – and I only have his version – Maynard in one of those fits of political euphoria to which he was subject, had declared that the Bolsheviks were doomed. The White Armies, supported by the allies, were ready to invade from all sides – the Revolutionaries would be crushed.

'They will not,' exclaimed Bunny. 'All that will happen is that more people will be killed; there will be more famine and misery.' With these words he knocked over a chair and went out of the room slamming the door with such violence that it was never the same again.

At some point Bunny's enthusiasm for the Bolsheviks waned and love was turned to hatred; according to Clive, Bunny felt for Russia what a man sometimes feels for an unfaithful mistress: he, but only he, might speak ill of her. In 1941 he was even more painfully torn; he was deeply patriotic, but he did not insist that we win our war single-handed. The Americans were very welcome, although their ideas about political warfare raised problems. But he wanted no help from Russia. He was not alone in this; there were, I have been told, some people in positions of power who, in 1939, hoped to land an army in Northern Finland, march through Russia (presumably receiving the surrender of that country) in order eventually to invade Germany by way of Poland. This idea was dropped rather abruptly in the spring of 1940.

There were many saner and more realistic people who were to

view the enormous popular enthusiasm for Russia and all things Russian with the utmost distaste, and who hoped that the two giants of the East would eventually wound and exhaust each other with fatal results for themselves. These however never asked for or hoped for a German victory over the Russians. Nor did Bunny in so many words, but his feelings led him very near to doing so.

Under the circumstances my review was less pessimistic than might have been expected. It is now preserved in the files of the *New Statesman* and if some scholar were interested he might read what I then wrote. My assessment was that the Russians would suffer some severe defeats but would very likely be able to turn the tables.

I have said that Bunny was much liked and valued by his colleagues in the Political Warfare Executive. The chief task of that organization was to provide directives for the foreign services of the BBC, for the 'black' propaganda which was supposed to come from occupied Europe, for the men who dropped leaflets or spread rumours etc. The BBC Foreign Services were admirable; their honesty really *was* the best policy, and I am glad that, despite the efforts of mean-minded politicians, they have survived. But there were moments when they could be silly. Thus in the spring of 1942 one of our broadcasters was sufficiently foolish to announce to the world that decisive battles would soon be fought on the Russian front. He was called to an interview at Political Warfare and was reminded that our information was that the Russians would probably sustain some heavy defeats. Now we could be quoted as saying that these would be 'decisive'. The wretched man could only say that he had merely intended to suggest that there would be some very big battles. 'A man' said Bunny, 'with no edge to his mind.'

I do not know whether the Germans did actually exploit this mistake; they had so much good news during the summer of 1942 that they hardly needed to. The Russians were driven back to the Caucasus, the British to the frontiers of Egypt, and in the Pacific the Japanese were victorious everywhere. It was not until the autumn that the tide began to turn. At the end of October the battle of El Alamein began; in November the Allies landed in North Africa.

I was at that time sharing the top storeys of No.41 Gordon Square with Bunny and Angelica. One day I came down rather late for breakfast and found that Bunny had already heard the news on the radio.

'The Russians are carrying all before them.' You might have thought from his tone of voice that the butter ration had been halved. I tried to get a little more information but he clearly found it so unpleasant to discuss the matter that I desisted. I had to wait until I got to the office before I could get a more detailed account of what became known as the Battle of Stalingrad. I am afraid that he must have suffered a good deal during the final years of the war (I had retired from Political Warfare and saw much less of him for a time). But the peace and the hostilities which followed it brought consolations of a kind.

By the end of the war Bunny and Angelica were not merely married but had become parents of a bevy of daughters. This resulted in a reconciliation with Vanessa. Bunny paid fairly frequent visits to Charleston, I think, though I can only remember one of them; it is fixed in my mind by two incidents which in a way were typical. It was in the late summer of 1944; France was being liberated but the enemy was still able to send infernal machines flying across the Channel. These sputtered through the air, became silent, and then fell to explode where they landed. A party of us was strolling on the gravel path in front of the house when one of these monsters flew overhead on its way northwards to London. One of our fighters gave chase; it was a dangerous manoeuvre, for if the pilot came too close and shot the thing it might easily explode in his face. We therefore watched with anxious excitement. We saw the 'plane approach, we saw its quarry burst suddenly into a ball of fire, heard a loud explosion and saw the fighter fly away unharmed.

We, who had been arguing amongst ourselves on I know not what topic, had fallen silent and remained silent as the aeroplane flew away on other business until Bunny remarked:

'And then the gentle little lamb

To talking put an end.'

A quotation I think from Ann and Jane Taylor which made us laugh.

Was it on the same weekend that I argued with Bunny about Jane Austen? Bunny had a great admiration for the novels, but he had strong reservations on the subject of *Emma*. Emma he maintained was a very unpleasant character, a desperate snob, callous, conceited and vain. There was nothing to be said for her. I replied that although she had her faults she did suffer from an unbearably silly father and that she bore his silliness with angelic patience.

For a moment Bunny was at a loss, but he was not a man who could easily be put down, and he responded, almost seriously: 'Well, we've only got Jane Austen's word for it.' Which is, I suppose, the highest praise that one can give a novelist.

The war brought restrictions and diversions which made it difficult to paint; one envied the old who, without incurring the slightest blame either from public opinion or private conscience, could go on painting whenever there was sufficient daylight. I was particularly fortunate in this regard. My sister was worse off; she got a load of troubles all in the same package: the inevitable hardships and annoyances of war were combined with the problems that arise when one has four daughters, all of them gifted, handsome, difficult and seemingly indefatigable. Hilton, Bunny's house, is a romantic and noble old building with spacious rooms, the windows of which look out upon a pleasant garden. If you go into the drawing room and, peering into the handsome fireplace, look up, you seem as it were to be gazing straight into the heavens. The upward draught is so strong that all the heat from any fire, howsoever large, is carried straight up and lost in the atmosphere. Or else the wind blows down the chimney and into the drawing room, passing rapidly from room to room until it ends up in the kitchen. In short, the house is as lovely as virtue and as cold as chastity. The hospitality was warm, but it needed to be white hot to make the sensitive visitor feel comfortable. (I am describing the house as it was forty years ago.)

I had the impression that Angelica found Hilton chilly and uncomfortable, a place where the echoing tumult of unbiddable children was hard to bear, a place where the neighbours all seemed to be Bunny's least interesting friends. It was not surprising that when from time to time she was able to escape, she should have done so in the company of her parents, and that they should have gone together to the shores of the Mediterranean.

Bunny it seemed to me had assumed the role of *père-de-famille* with all the energy and passion in this, his second marriage, that he had brought to his first. A new and important element in the situation was that he now saw himself as the prize bull in a herd of cows. He was usually in love with at least one of his daughters, and this did nothing to simplify or sweeten existence at Hilton. His very real and affectionate regard for his sons was an altogether calmer and more manageable emotion.

My own visits to Hilton began to change character, or rather, I myself changed character. I ceased to be the solitary bachelor who comes with an uncritical eye to talk, to paint perhaps, and play with the children. I became part of a ménage of my own: a husband and father, looking to see how things are managed in a family, how children are controlled, how meals are provided and produced. I came to observe and learn. From 1952 to 1959 I was employed at Newcastle-upon-Tyne; travelling between Sussex and Northumberland in an old car and on old roads with a growing family took two days and Hilton made a pleasant half-way house. The little Garnett girls liked petting and playing with their new baby cousins. We all of us looked forward to our fairly frequent visits, though on one occasion my wife Olivier and I found ourselves invited for a fortnight, not to stay with but to replace Bunny and Angelica and look after their children. It was a full-time job, and not my idea of a holiday.

However one year we all had a holiday together at Asolo, a lovely little hill town with a fine view over the Venetian plain. We took a handsome house called La Mura, built on the town wall. Although spacious, this had only three double bedrooms so we had rented two further rooms at the far end of the town. There were eleven of us – a pair of Garnetts, a pair of Bells, four Garnett girls, two Bell infants, and Bunny's younger son William, aged thirty-two. There was a meeting to decide who should sleep where.

Bunny, who saw himself as the monarch of this particular glen, asserted himself, insisting vehemently that his family should be united under one roof; they should all sleep at La Mura and the Bells should stay in the distant lodgings – an obvious and logical arrangement in his eyes. Olivier ventured that the Bells had hoped for a joint family holiday; if they were to be exiled their day would end when their children were put to bed, they being too small to be left by themselves; thus in the evenings the Bells would get neither dinner nor company. Furthermore, if William were to have a room of his own – as Bunny insisted that he should – the other two bedrooms at La Mura would be uncomfortably overcrowded. In the end her reasoning proved unanswerable. The two adolescent girls were delighted to saunter through the town after dinner, escorted by their brother, to their independent rooms, free from parental control. Bunny felt that he, the patriarch of the herd, had been hornswoggled, and though he yielded, he sulked.

Unfortunately he suffered other discontents, and for this I was responsible. Here I must explain that I drove to Asolo in our car, but the prospect of driving my family across Europe – it was hard enough to get them from Newcastle to Hilton – appalled me. The children and their mother therefore flew to Italy and I was thus able to offer a lift to a colleague. Eric Dobson was one of our most valued friends in Newcastle; he was intelligent, strikingly handsome and a gifted painter; he made a perfect travelling companion. I had assumed that when once he had reached Asolo he would want to adventure further – as a naval rating during the war he had fallen in love with Italy (insofar as Naples represented Italy) – but he seemed perfectly happy to remain in Asolo. He found rooms for himself in the town but spent most of his time at La Mura. He joined in our expeditions, he was invited to meals, he played poker and charades with us and in the mornings you might find him in the gardens, sometimes making a sketch but usually playing ping-pong with my nieces. The girls all loved him; everybody loved him – except Bunny, who was, simply, jealous. The trouble about being the monarch of the glen is that it is so difficult to endure competition.

Fate made some amends: it sent a very elegant young woman studying English at, I think, Milan University. She admired Bunny and considered that *Lady into Fox* showed a real understanding of 'the beastly world'. Sadly, she was the only person in Asolo whose attitude to Bunny could be described as reverential, and Bunny had come to need an occasional dose of reverence; I fancy that these occasions were becoming rather more frequent.

I wonder what the literary world thought of his novels? Is Bunny required reading in our universities as he is, I believe, in Japan? And ought one to think better of him if he is? I don't know; literary criticism is to my mind a strange and quite incomprehensible business. My own feeling is that his later novels – those which he wrote after 1945 – were not as good as *Lady into Fox* or *Pocahontas*, but what reason is there for thinking that my judgement is of importance to anyone else? None whatever as far as I can see.

What did Bunny think of himself? I don't know, but I suspect that there were moments when he liked to imagine that there were certain phrases which fell from the lips of professors talking to

English Literature students: 'Then of course there are masters of English prose such as Defoe, Borrow, Jeffries, David Garnett . . .' What he needed was some kind of public recognition. He accepted a CBE; I don't think that he displayed it, but then I'm not sure how one does display such a thing. A time was to come, however, when he was to seek a decoration which he could display.

This came at the end of his life, after he and Angelica had separated and the children were grown up. Bunny himself had settled in France. Like so many English people he was attracted by the material comforts and charms of that beautiful country, but, although a sociable character, he was content with the company of his fellow exiles and not fluent in French; this seemed a pity in a country where the shopkeeper and the peasant, not to speak of the *instituteur* and the priest, are frequently highly entertaining companions. But it was rather late to master a foreign language and Bunny's complaint, as it reached me through a third party, was not that he was starved of good conversation, but that he had to queue for service in shops. I cannot recall – and perhaps never knew – the full details of his grievances but they were in his view sufficiently severe to make him long for some badge of distinction that would put him at the head of the queue.

It seemed to me that Bunny needed a red ribbon. If he could be enlisted in the Légion d'honneur the village shop, at all events, would be impressed. I set about trying to obtain a decoration for him. I am not good at that sort of thing. I didn't know the right people, worse still I could not think of anything that could be urged in Bunny's favour, and that would qualify him as a friend of France. I wrote to the only person whom I thought might help me. Ritchie Calder was an old friend; he had become a peer. He had worked with Bunny in PWE, surely he would know of some great service rendered at a time of interallied fury (and there had been plenty of such times), some great blow struck for France. Ritchie was kind and sympathetic; he would obviously have liked to be helpful but he could think of nothing. I am sorry to say that in the end I could see no case for giving Bunny the Légion d'honneur save that he would have liked very much to have it.

He never knew of my activities – and in truth I was not very active. In the end he died undecorated. He left his body to science.

6

Maynard Keynes

I WAS FIVE years old and we were sitting in a boat, the ferry which took passengers across the Chichester Canal. Maynard was on my left; to my right were the salt waters of the estuary. With us were Clive, Vanessa, Duncan and my brother Julian. We had been at Eleanor, the Hutchinson's house near West Wittering, and we were now returning to our lodgings in Bosham. It was a hot day and we were refreshed by our cool, easy passage across the water. Maynard had taken off his straw hat and placed it upon the seat between us. It struck me that the hat might float. I took it and shied it out upon the water. It floated beautifully, bobbing up and down upon the little waves.

The ferry had to be diverted from its course, the boater recovered, and I to be reproved by my parents; Maynard couldn't have been nicer about it. It is my first memory of him, a very happy occasion.

About a year later the Bell 'family' settled at Charleston. Often of a Friday evening if one passed through the kitchen and into the lobby by the cellar door where the lamps and candles were kept, one would find a copy of the current *Evening Standard* – always a slightly astonishing thing for it looked so urban and remote in that primitive and countrified place – and when one saw it one knew that Maynard had come from his mysterious activities in London to spend the weekend with us.

At that time efforts were being made to decorate Charleston, which had once been a farmhouse and then a boarding-house and then a deserted house with a nice orchard but hardly any proper garden, and which was decorated only with wallpaper. Maynard did his bit – I use an expression which was then much employed –

addressing himself to the task of weeding the gravel path in front of the house; there was a lot of it and there were a lot of weeds. A labourer might do the job in an afternoon using a hoe, pulling up the weeds in a bank of little pebbles, mangling and bashing them so that they perished and could be extracted dead and withered by a man with a rake. A few deep-rooted weeds might survive to sprout again; this Maynard would not allow. He approached the gravel path with a 'prayer mat' – a rectangle of condemned carpet – fell on his knees, and with an old kitchen knife and the greatest care would extract every last vestige of vegetable matter from the ground. The patches thus cleared looked wonderfully tidy but they were not very large; they were the product of hours of devoted industry and one feared – seeing that the labourer could only devote himself to weeding on reasonably fine weekends throughout the summer – that by the time he had reached the end of his task a new growth of weeds would have sprung up at his rear. It was the least characteristic of his activities. When I saw Maynard devote himself to other tasks he was swift and usually efficient; only, in talking, he had a tiny stutter. It was as if the ideas came racing into his mind so fast and in such abundance that his tongue could not keep up with his thoughts.

As children, we at first believed the gossip of the kitchen and the farm where he was thought to be a spy because he carried a large black Treasury bag. Then we began slowly to regard him as a kind of oracle. There was a war in progress which seemed hardly to engage the attention of the grown-ups; but we had a governess and she had a cousin who was something or other on someone's staff. For a time this cousin provided us with inside information concerning the progress of the war, information of the most optimistic kind. Maynard, as we began to understand, was even more *au fait* with the progress of the war and, as always, supremely optimistic. Also there was something immensely exciting about his involvement in the conflict. There were occasions when he abandoned the gravel path in order to spend a few days in Paris. He met and talked with Mr Asquith and Mr Lloyd George; for us it was but a minor incident when he was dropped by Austen Chamberlain at the bottom of our drive with a Cézanne which he concealed in the hedge.* Maynard

---

* See *A Cézanne in the Hedge and Other Memories of Charleston and Bloomsbury*, ed. Hugh Lee, with a foreword by Michael Holroyd, 1992.

was our link with the great world of war and politics; he was amiable, communicative and amusing – the perfect friend for two inquisitive, politically-minded children.

When the war was over Maynard seemed to be more involved than ever in politics – that is, in the making of a peace treaty. At the same time I found the political problems which resulted from the armistice more comprehensible than the military problems had been.

One afternoon I found him sitting in his usual hidden corner of the orchard and the following exchange took place.

'Maynard, are you going back to France?'

'Yes.'

'Why?'

He explained that he was going to the Peace Conference in order to tell it how much Germany should pay in reparations, and on being questioned further, he said: 'I shall tell them that the Germans can't pay us more money than they have.'

It seemed, indeed it was, unanswerable. And yet I knew that he wanted the Germans to be, as one might say, 'let off lightly'. I knew also that the Allies wouldn't take Maynard's advice. This sounds a preposterous claim, but from what I had heard from servants, working men, daily newspapers, everyone except my own family, the vast majority of the people wanted the Germans to be treated as brutally as possible. If they couldn't find the money, they could at least be made thoroughly miserable. We wanted not justice but revenge, and Maynard would be called, as we had all been called, pro-German.

What with one thing and another I had come to believe in the existence of a vast intolerant majority, powerful, violent, and filled with hatred for the kind of things my parents (I use the term very loosely) valued. Certain pictures, certain political ideas, certain beliefs or, more exactly, disbeliefs, were valued by 'us' and hated by 'them'. 'They' would burn the works of Cézanne, vote for Lloyd George, fear God, honour the King and 'squeeze Germany till the pips squeaked'. It was an inexact but not extravagantly incorrect view of the world. My trouble was that the popular view was the view of people whom I liked, something therefore to which I was not totally opposed. I was at all events not so entirely in agreement with Maynard's attitude on reparations that I could not sympathize with the great Christian-chauvinist majority.

I have wandered far from Maynard, but as will be seen, for a purpose. In 1919 Maynard returned from Versailles in a state of some indignation, and spent the next month or two mainly at Charleston writing *The Economic Consequences of the Peace*, a splendid book.

For the next three or four years Maynard was a part of the family. He was in truth very much attached both to Duncan and to Vanessa. There was a general agreement – whether it was in any way formalized I do not know – that although we lived in separate establishments in various parts of 46 and 50 Gordon Square for most of the year, in August and September everyone should be at Charleston. This included Clive, although he and Maynard got on each other's nerves. When Vanessa and Duncan went to Italy, Maynard went with them.

Maynard twice ventured to bring his boyfriends to Charleston. The first occasion was a disaster; the disaster was called Gabriel Atkins. I do not remember him at Charleston, which perhaps is not surprising for the legend is that when Gabriel arrived all the regular inmates fled, leaving Maynard to deal with the situation that he had created; nor did they return until Mr Atkins had left. I came to know him well – rather too well – in later years when he was the companion of Mary Butts, by which time he had I suppose lost those charms which made him the toast of the British Sodom. Even so, I am astonished that he should have been Maynard's guest and catamite.

Maynard's second importation was a brilliant young man from Cambridge called Sebastian Sprott. Sebastian was not simply a guest, he was to be the tutor of us boys. I don't think he taught us much; perhaps he was too busy teaching himself German (when he left us he went to the Ruhr which had just been occupied by French troops). He was the first of several teachers who failed to teach me Latin. But we liked him very much. I wish that in the years that followed I had kept up that friendship, for something very remarkable happened to Sebastian: he vanished. At a fairly early age he went to teach at Nottingham University and clearly he liked the place, for he stayed there for years and years. When newly appointed he must have been an exquisite young person, slim, pale, long-haired, romantic. He wore a ring so exuberantly designed and so massively wrought that one feared that in attempting to lift his hand he might do himself an injury. When I next met him, about thirty years later, he was Professor of Philosophy – and of Psychology I think – at Nottingham. But Sebastian had vanished; Jack Sprott had taken his place, a sensible, bluff, breezy fellow who in some mysterious way had managed, while dropping all Sebastian's pretty absurdities, to keep all his sweet temper and fundamental good sense. Seeing him with his colleagues one understood more perfectly why he was so happy in Nottingham: they obviously loved him; he was, as it were, the licenced pederast of the university and must have attained that privileged situation long before his vice had been legalized.

Sebastian was the last of Maynard's catamites; in fact for a time he must have run concurrently with Lydia. They were neither of them involved in an adventure in which, for the first time, I saw Maynard openly and exuberantly intoxicated; it took place sometime between 1919 and 1923.

Boris Anrep had completed a mosaic in a chapel at the Military Academy, Sandhurst, and this was the object of our pilgrimage. Julian and I were allowed seats in a charabanc which also contained Augustus John, Mary Hutchinson, Lesley Jowett, Maynard, Duncan, Clive, Vanessa and Boris himself. There were lots of other people. We set off fairly early and went to see the decorated chapel. We then proceeded into the open country, stopping at a very beautiful place where there was open downland together with a noble forest. Here the grown-ups gathered in a circle around a bonfire, ate lunch and washed it down with champagne. Then they played kiss-in-the-ring – I remember Duncan catching and kissing Lesley Jowett. Finally they played another game: they set up a dozen or so empty bottles and bombarded them with others (also presumably empty). Vanessa excelled at this sport. Soon the ground beneath the trees was littered with a carpet of smashed glass. Julian and I, having helped ourselves to victuals, wandered away on our own, but not so far that we could not see the grown-ups at play. We were deeply shocked and distressed. We had always been told that places of outstanding natural beauty were to be respected. Only the worst kind of hooligan – or tripper – would leave broken glass behind him. This in our scale of morality was a crime; we were not in the least offended by what followed on the journey home.

On that journey I was seated between Vanessa and Maynard. There was some trouble at the beginning of it. John had made drawings of everyone on paper plates provided for the picnic (two of these are still at Charleston); the man sitting next to Vanessa stole a drawing belonging to the man in front of him and refused to give it back. Vanessa, in her best Hyde Park Gate manner, said she wanted to look at the drawing, got it, and at once handed it back to its rightful owner. The thief exploded in fury, but they didn't come to blows so I lost interest and began to pay attention to Maynard.

He was happy. He was happier still when he managed to buy an evening paper and found that something had risen – or perhaps fallen – on the stock market. He told me that he had made I don't know what enormous sum, and he gave me half a crown which, for me, *was* an enormous sum. He began to observe the pedestrians, respectable looking people returning I suppose from work in the City. They seemed to him unhappy and he decided to cheer them up. As the charabanc slowed down at a road junction he leant out over the side of the vehicle (it had no roof) and, raising his hat, serious, concerned, he addressed a prosperous looking citizen: 'Excuse me, Sir, excuse me, but I am afraid that you've lost your sense of personal identity.'

During the early years of the decade my life changed in such a manner that I found myself for a time more closely involved with Maynard than ever before. Julian left home and went to boarding school. I for a time was taught by Miss Rose Paul; then I went to a school in Gordon Square which educated girls and boys. Finally I spent some time at a school in Swiss Cottage. The Gordon Square school was convenient in that I had only to cross the square's garden for my lunch. I got it in the kitchen and there met the 'Click'. The Click was the servants' Bloomsbury, and here you might meet Annie the cook whom I didn't like and Blanche the parlourmaid, a more interesting character. Blanche – I never knew her by any other name – was a handsome girl from Dublin. Maynard had a high opinion of her; I gather that during the war, when life at 46 Gordon Square was crowded and complicated, Blanche was a tower of strength. She had to deal with a community which included not only Maynard but Sheppard (later Provost of Kings, Cambridge), Clive (which often meant Mary Hutchinson as well), Norton the mathematician, and a great many other people. When Sir Henry Wilson was assassinated by the IRA in 1922 she surprised me by saying that it was an excellent thing; that Sir Henry was 'a scourge of humanity' and better off dead; the troubles of Ireland were the fault of the Orange Men. I had never heard that side of the case and was a little shocked, but a few conversations with the grown-ups made me understand that a good many people agreed with her.

Blanche had a lover called Bam (I suppose he had some other name but I never heard it), and Bam was the leading figure in the Click when I knew it. Bam kept us – that is to say Annie the cook, Blanche, Mabel from the Stephens' part of No. 50, Grace Germany, a maid from our part of the same house, and perhaps some others – entertained with his accounts of South Africa and the First World War. It seemed that the main objective of the entire German navy had been to sink Bam. Indeed he was frequently torpedoed and often saved the lives of female passengers. I agreed with Grace who did not much like Bam and did not quite believe his stories. I am not sure what Maynard thought of Bam; they had an important interview at one time, although whether this was before Maynard found distressing evidence that Bam had performed an illegal operation on Blanche in Duncan's little back bedroom which lay behind No. 46, I do not know.

Grace, who became a great friend, succeeded poor Mad Mary, the delightful maid who in the end had to be incarcerated in a lunatic asylum. Grace herself, though nervous – if surprised she would leap into the air as though shot – was in fact a very sensible, sweet-natured girl, the daughter of a Norfolk farmer. She was destined to become the guardian angel of Charleston where she spent the greater part of her life.

Owing to the change in my educational arrangements I began to have lunch at school and lost sight of the Click, so I don't know what eventually happened to Bam and to Blanche, only that they left. I know that Maynard was very sorry to lose Blanche. At the same time I came to know Grace very well, and we were joined in the kitchen by a new and fascinating character, Lydia Lopokova.

I think that my first sight of Lydia was at a lunch party in which for some reason – or accident – I was included. Clive and Maynard were there, also Lydia, who was not the only member of the Ballet present. At that time it was taken for granted that the Ballet, being Russian, talked French. Clive was not the man to insult them by using any other language, and indeed the whole party spoke French

– all that is except Maynard and me. We had to listen mute and, in Maynard's case, furious, to a fast and enthusiastic chatter in which we could not join and, more particularly, to what was obviously a shameless flirtation between Clive and Lydia. When at last the party was over Maynard wondered how sensible people could amuse themselves by jabbering away in such a fashion. 'I don't believe' he declared, 'that they understand it themselves.'

It was thoughtless of Lydia for, although at that time she might have had more French than English, she was perfectly well able to communicate with Vanessa, who always spoke to her in English and with whom she usually had tea, wandering up from the rooms she rented in 50 Gordon Square and, later, in the kitchen where Grace and I understood English and nothing else.

'I write today to Barocchi to ask if he still think himself married to me.' In saying this to Vanessa, Lydia gave me a little shock; I had not imagined that she was a married woman. I think Vanessa also was a little disturbed: she did not care to hear Lydia making – as she foresaw – preparations for a second union. Then Lydia told us a very odd story. During the war she and Barocchi, together with the rest of the Ballet, had sailed from Europe to South America. Returning, their ship had been arrested by a vessel of the Royal Navy which made a search – presumably for contraband. Barocchi had taken fright and concealed their marriage lines in a place so secure that later on he was unable to recover them. What amazed and still amazes me is the idea that His Majesty's Fleet was supposed to feel an interest in the marriage of an Italian impresario and his Russian wife. Is it conceivable that he was in fact carrying a document of criminal or military importance? To Lydia, her husband's fears seemed quite reasonable.

These visits to Vanessa seemed to Lydia the pleasantest and most natural thing in the world; she took to making them at all times of day and enjoyed the opportunities for endless talk. Vanessa liked Lydia, but she liked her in reasonably small doses, and when these visits began to interfere with her painting, she protested to Maynard, who had the ungrateful task of telling Lydia that she was sometimes *de trop*. Lydia, not unnaturally, felt humiliated. It was the beginning of a painful schism which ended what had been a very happy relationship. Vanessa and Duncan had really formed a deeper friendship with Maynard than they could with Clive. It must have been quite soon after the war that Maynard, Duncan and Vanessa, at that time a seemingly unbreakable triangle, went to Italy on a spending spree. Maynard had made an immense amount of money by speculating on foreign currency. They went to Rome to spend it and had a lovely time buying pottery, furniture, and other things. Then they went to Florence and stayed at I Tatti with the Berensons, and it was there, when they went to visit the Berenson's neighbours, the Loesers, that Duncan was mistaken for Maynard and vice versa. Maynard described the appalling moment, after he had been looking at Loeser's pictures with Miss Loeser, when he came into the drawing room and found Duncan talking happily with the Governor of the Bank of Italy and other notables and telling them what they should do about the devaluation of the lira. He thought it more prudent to withdraw. Duncan did not realize what was happening until when leaving he was introduced to another guest as 'Economista Keynes'. The mistake was discovered when it was too late. Berenson was furious and became very rude to Duncan and Vanessa. Skidelsky in his life of Maynard Keynes calls this 'a prank', but it is quite clear both from Maynard's account and Duncan's that it was simply a mistake.*

It was not the only débâcle. When Maynard got home he found that the mark or the dollar had behaved in an unexpected way. Soon he had to write to Vanessa and Duncan and inform them that all was lost. Vanessa, who had entrusted him with all her money, realized that she would have to tell Clive that she was now penniless.

Maynard met them on their return and was able to reveal that the wreck was not quite as complete as they had feared. According to Vanessa it was she and Duncan who persuaded Maynard to go to Sir Ernest Cassel who in fact refloated him, and in the end Maynard was able to repay every penny that they had lost.

It is significant that they decided that Clive should know nothing of this business – I am sure that he did not know for if he had we should never have heard the last of it. The affair remained a secret between Maynard and the artists, who must at that time have formed a fairly solid entente. This, in its turn, may help us to understand the reactions of Maynard's friends to his marriage.

---

* That comedy (or tragedy) of errors has been described by Duncan himself, see *Charleston Magazine*, Issue 10, Autumn/Winter 1994

Here I must return to the story of Lydia. Expelled from Vanessa's painting room she sought company elsewhere and found it in the kitchen, much to the delight of Grace who worked there and of myself who loitered.

Lydia seemed perfectly happy in the kitchen. We adored her, she was so entertaining. Vanessa might not care for stories about Old Russia, stories of the steppes, of droshkies and moujiks, boyars and bombs, the samovar and the Nevski Prospekt. Grace and I were enchanted. Nor was this all that Lydia had to offer: one day we received two tickets for the Variety Show at the Coliseum. The ballet item was a treat; there was something magical about the transformation of our kitchen companion – a nice woman with an odd nose but not a raving beauty – into the almost supernaturally lovely creature who seemed blown towards us across the stage like a scrap of thistledown. That was the climax of the afternoon, but much had first to be enjoyed. We arrived early and saw everything. Beside the stage a little panel of light bulbs told us what number was being enacted. The ballet came on about No.10 following a little incursion of balletomanes; they had missed the Dolly Sisters and the man who sang patriotic songs, but they had also missed Harry Tate, the man with a squint and a miraculous moustache. They had not seen poor Harry constructing a wireless receiver, putting buckets on chairs, fastening wires to broom handles, bullying the mute, unsmiling youth whose look of silent, contemptuous despair remained unchanged while Harry, with the solemnity of a cathedral builder, raised his tottering contraption higher and higher to the amazement of the audience, many of whom were by now helplessly weeping with laughter. We waited breathless for the inevitable. It arrived. The whole affair came crashing to the stage while its creator surveyed the wreckage with eyes which went round and round in his head, each eye revolving in an opposing direction while his neatly waxed moustache followed suit. Meanwhile the silent boy remained silent. The ballet dancers were not the only artists on the stage of the Coliseum that afternoon.

Just as I was going to bed one evening, Maynard burst into the room and told me to get dressed, I was to come with him to a box at Covent Garden. The Opera House, which had fallen on evil days, was that night to see the first performance of a revue called *You'd Be Surprised* starring George Robey; also the ballet – or at least a bit of it, including Massine and Lydia; these were to appear in the second half of the revue. In the first we were shown, amongst other things, a remarkable *tableau-vivant*. The curtain rose to display a view of rocky mountains against a setting sun; in the foreground were more rocks which formed the shores of a pond, contrived upon the floor by means of a carpet of silver paper. Seated upon the rocks was a tribe of Red Indians, but they were none of them red and all of them young ladies. They wore very little and remained motionless, like models in a life class. They were quite silent and so was the audience until Lydia, who was sitting beside me in the Royal Box, exclaimed: 'Oh, it is to make you to *womit!*' The whole audience turned toward us, or rather to me, for Lydia had vanished. Nevertheless, I enjoyed George Robey. The next day the papers told the public: 'Covent Garden Revue Falls Flat', and in fact it was soon withdrawn.

Maynard offered me entertainments of another kind. Every Saturday afternoon he hired a Daimler and a chauffeur and took us – me and Lydia – to see the sights of London: the Tower, Westminster Abbey, Hampton Court, St Paul's, and on one occasion the Hogarth Press at Richmond. He felt that I should be educated. Certainly I was entertained, but I think that he had another motive; he wanted, without appearing to do so, to educate Lydia. They were soon to be married and he wanted his wife to know as much as possible about England; how better could he do this than by educating me? I remember a scrap of conversation which is perhaps worth recording. It took place in Westminster Abbey.

Lydia: 'Quentin, do you believe in God?'

Q. (after a moment's indecision): 'No Lydia, I don't.'

Lydia: 'Neither do I, but it would be nice to believe.'

Maynard: 'It would be comforting.'

I was in some ways precocious, but on the whole young for my age. I was at times, I suspect, tactless, difficult and conceited. But I cannot remember ever having a sharp word from Maynard or from Lydia. They were very kind to me and to each other; only once did I see them fall out. That was at lunch when there was a dispute about a picture of Lydia by Duncan. Lydia was wearing a tunic with a very short skirt, and Duncan had been rather over-enthusiastic in his drawing of her legs. 'Instead of saying what a lovely dancer, they will say what a large naked Lydia.' Maynard was jocular, and indeed was trying to pass the whole thing off as a jest. But it misfired. Lydia turned red as a turkey cock. 'Oh Maynarr,' she wailed, and almost burst into tears; it was embarrassing, all the more so because neither I, nor I think Maynard, was perfectly sure of the nature of his offence.

I suppose I was dreadfully spoilt by them. I had such fun, such treats, such glimpses of two romantic worlds – that of public affairs and that of the ballet. It could not last. I knew well enough that a grim world of public school awaited me, a world where there would be no fun, no treats and, though I did not then know it, far less education. But there was a stay of execution. I spent one term in Paris and this gave me a different view of Maynard and Lydia. They arrived quite unexpectedly at 96 Boulevard Port Royale bearing tickets for the ballet *La Boutique Fantasque* at La Cigale. Now Lydia took the lead, chattering fluently with Madame Pinault. I attempted, in vain, to get Monsieur Pinault and Maynard to converse; I knew that they were in agreement about French foreign policy, but it was no use. And again, *chez* Picasso, Lydia was left in command, to speak in French to the painter and in her own tongue to the then Madame Picasso.

Maynard's marriage, like so many of his undertakings, was a vast success. Lydia was a devoted wife, and in his last years her devotion was heroic. From the first she realized that there was a great part of his life which to her was more or less incomprehensible. He for his part made allowances for her need to maintain old friendships, some of which he found boring. He delighted in her oddities, in her constant battle with the English language; he supported her in her theatrical excursions. But he may have regretted the fun and freedom of the days when he, Vanessa and Duncan formed a triumvirate. *They* surely did; for them life was permanently impoverished.

For a time we almost lost sight of the Keyneses, although the newspapers were full of their marriage. Presently they returned and became our neighbours at Tilton. It was then that Vanessa put a large notice by the gate at which travellers turned right if they were bound for Charleston, left if they were going to Tilton. The notice bore one word: OUT. This had nothing to do with the fact that the Keyneses were now so close to us – ostensibly at all events. It was originally painted and displayed because Freddie Mayor – a nice little picture dealer – having drunk far too much while lunching with two other dealers in Brighton, drove with them to Charleston, arriving unannounced and unwanted.

It is true, however, that Vanessa and Duncan also suffered from a few uninvited visits made by Lydia and Maynard and friends from the world of fashion, culture, and the ballet; they, and particularly Vanessa, having lost a precious morning's work, became so anxious as to be quite neurotic about these invasions. Once, when I came home with something urgent to discuss, I could not find them until I got to the top spare room (now 'Vanessa's Studio').

Vanessa was over-sensitive in her fear of being interrupted at Charleston by the arrival of unwanted visitors. But it must be remembered that she had suffered greatly. Lydia was never as serious a menace as Barbara Bagenal. But when I wanted to see her I had to go to Tilton, and I myself found a small but sensible change in our relationship.

But there were always meetings, birthday parties and other jollifications, not to speak of those big evening parties at Gordon Square which were enriched with dramatic performances; but to these I was not invited until my school days were over.

The most outspoken critic of Maynard at Charleston was Clive; he had never enjoyed that close companionship which had assumed an apparently indissoluble form when during 1914–18 Maynard was living largely at Charleston. He and Clive disagreed about almost everything. Now that the war was over, Clive could gravitate naturally to a francophile position all the more easily because the French had become the reactionaries of Europe; while Maynard's sympathies were German.

Clive objected strongly to Maynard's table manners. It was true that he was an acquisitive eater and would gather toast, marmalade, butter, sugar and condiments into a small area around his plate, helping himself as the occasion demanded. But a far more serious grievance was Maynard's claim to omniscience. Of course there were a great many subjects concerning which he was better informed than anyone at Charleston, but there were a few which he would have done better to have left alone. When, after a brief tour of the Quantocks, Maynard described a method of stag hunting which involved not only horses and hounds but men armed with rifles, Clive was contemptuous and never tired of repeating the story.

When he married, Maynard became more socially ambitious and more reactionary in his politics. But if Leonard Woolf is to be believed – and I have always found him the most believable of men –

long before Maynard had become a landed gentleman he might have become a peer.

According to Leonard the Labour Party – presumably during Ramsay MacDonald's first administration – decided to offer Maynard a peerage. Leonard was asked to sound him out. He found Maynard in his bath at 46 Gordon Square and made the offer which Maynard (who probably did not want to be identified with Labour, or perhaps any other party) refused. Whether he would have taken a peerage from Baldwin one cannot tell.

When he married, Maynard took Tilton on a long lease and, when the farmer left it, he was ready to farm it himself. It was a dairy farm with a little arable land and some woodland, enough to justify the maintenance of a gamekeeper. Maynard was in fact establishing himself as a country gentleman, producing tuberculin-tested milk, a covey of partridges and a few brace of pheasant. And this involved him in just the kind of activity that Clive might criticize.

But Maynard was in love with the idea of being on his own land, or at least of being a highly respected tenant holding a 99-year lease. He had discovered that, by the happiest coincidence, he had settled upon a property acquired at the time of the Conquest by a Norman proto-Keynes. Years later, when he was ennobled, he asked me to emblazon his arms which, if I remember rightly, were azure a bend wavuly argent. The wavuly bend he told me commemorated the winding stream which flowed through the Norman home of his race. I made some ineffectual sceptical noises; I had thought that since no one in the eleventh century was armigerous, this seemed improbable. But he didn't listen to me.

If Maynard cultivated a feudal system of his own, it has also to be said that he felt not only the right to impose duties on others, but also the duty to aid and protect his vassals. I saw this principle working, and working wonderfully, in the case of Edgar Weller.

Edgar Weller was a handsome young man from the neighbouring parish who at one time courted Grace; he then married Ruby, a nice woman who served the Keyneses, and he became the Keyneses chauffeur. Edgar was fond of a drink and having drunk became argumentative. One evening he drank too much and argued much too much with the police in the village of Ringmer. He was locked up in a building which he attempted, not without some success, to demolish. He was charged with a number of offences and summoned to appear before the magistrates in Lewes.

Maynard said that he would do what he could for the poor fellow; amongst other things he offered to give evidence. Together with Vanessa and Duncan I went with him to the trial. That Edgar would be found guilty could hardly be doubted; we hoped that there might be mitigating circumstances. But there was something else: a bold, brutal barrister from London who fell upon the police evidence like a savage dog upon a rat. Then came the police surgeon, a more convincing figure than the over-confident constable who had preceded him; his evidence seemed conclusive. The defence tore it to pieces and the poor man crept out of the court in a battered condition.

Then Maynard gave evidence, and the nature of the proceedings changed. He and the Chairman of the Bench conversed like old friends – which indeed they were. Maynard explained that Edgar had been a soldier. 'In France?' Well, he was a little young for that, but had an excellent record, having served in Jamaica. There he had contracted a form of malaria which when it recurred made the patient behave wildly, as though violently drunk. But in truth he was a steady and reliable man.

'You'd say that in general he was a perfectly good sort of chap?'

'Yes indeed.'

'Case dismissed.'

Maynard gave us lunch afterwards. He was justifiably pleased with himself. Edgar did suffer from some further bouts of 'malaria' and on one occasion shot the keeper's dog. But he never had to face another court of law. Rather surprisingly he told me later that standing in the dock he felt the most awful idiot. He didn't look it.

Maynard did not shoot, but having acquired some woods and arable land together with a keeper and a keeper's cottage, he felt it proper to rear some birds and to invite Clive and a few local farmers for a few days' sport. He himself would walk out with the guns and, as Lydia thought, overtire himself. He had been very ill.

'Maynarr, you must come home soon.'

'I'll come home to lunch.'

'Then you must lie down after lunch.'

'Yes yes, I will lie, I'm lying now.'

This was in the latter days of peace when Lydia was battling hard to keep him from overworking. Maynard was an extremely bad patient and there was something heroic about Lydia's persistent care for him in his last years.

The keeper, Mr Churchill, fascinated Maynard. He was a man who lived for his birds; as Maynard remarked, he was not really very much interested in the sportsmen; they were merely an instrument for culling the bird population – and there were some fine pheasants – Lydia called them the 'firebirds' – which were not to be shot at. In 1939 he complained that the war would put an end to all serious shooting. The rides through the wood were always kept perfectly trim and clear, he slaughtered vermin – a category which included dogs, foxes, cats, and endangered species of birds. Even in wartime a cartload of what was deemed to be spoilt corn found its way into his woods.

When Lydia was cold she wore an enormous amount of clothes: she looked like a pillar-box that has been draped in half-mourning; but when she was hot she took them all off – all of them.

'But Maynard, what would Mr Churchill say if he found Lydia naked among the raspberries – as she often is?'

'It's alright; he wouldn't believe his eyes.'

And yet there must have been times when she was recklessly exposed. Sir Roger Stevens who was in Washington during the Second World War once went to Maynard's hotel to see him on urgent business. It was during a heat wave. He found the door of the Keyneses apartment open; he ventured in; he went from room to empty room and finally came to a kitchen containing a large refrigerator. The door was open. Lydia was crouched within, stark naked. She at one time used to walk over the downs reciting the poetry of T.S. Eliot; in doing this she would strip bare to the waist. The late Lord Gage once met her and she, modestly seeking to cover her breasts, pulled up her skirts to her chin. Unfortunately she wore nothing beneath her skirt.

Lydia and I never lost that early friendship which always united us. I enjoyed her company when we were tête-à-tête. When she gossiped or talked about old days with the ballet she was delightful, but when she attempted to discuss politics she ceased to charm; and when one met her with Maynard one longed, like the French poet, to say '*Sois charmante et tais toi.*'

In the spring of 1940, when the Germans invaded Norway, the Keyneses came over to Charleston and were very much welcomed by Clive and by me; we both felt that things might be going very wrong (as indeed they were) and we hoped that Maynard might enlighten us.

Unluckily Clive started on the wrong note; he said that he thought that the Germans were winning. Before he could finish his sentence Lydia interrupted him – 'Oh Clive, you *must* not say that; you must *not* say that you want the Germans to win.'

'My dear Lydia, I was saying nothing of the kind. I was saying –'

'No! You must *not* say that –'

'But Lydia –'

That was the entire substance of their conversation. Clive was never able to make Lydia understand what he had said; she would listen only to herself. My own attempts to break this absurd and infuriating deadlock were in vain. Duncan went to sleep; Vanessa was not interested; but Maynard, I knew, could at any moment have called Lydia to order, instead of which he lay back, smiling, with his eyes – by far his best feature – half closed, apparently enjoying Lydia's absurdity and Clive's discomfiture. It was an infuriating evening. I suppose that Clive brought out the worst in Lydia, and because in Clive's presence Maynard allowed Lydia her head, there was no remedy.

I return to the last months of the peace. Being alone at Charleston at that time, I spent a good deal of time at Tilton. The Keyneses were kind and hospitable. Lydia gave me lessons in Russian, Maynard in economics. I made no progress in either study but I enjoyed their company and in spite of political differences I still found them sympathetic. Maynard no doubt thought me silly and wrong-minded, I thought him a deplorable reactionary, but I had known him too long and liked him too well for political differences to separate us. We both loved Lydia and as a politician he did not need to take me seriously (I discuss our differences in Appendix II). We disagreed most strongly in 1937 and 1938; but the war made us forget this. It had the effect of bringing me into a closer relationship with Maynard. I needed a job in which I could at once do something useful; I found it on the second day of the war driving a tractor on Maynard's farm.

Maynard had brought one of the men employed by King's College to manage their estates and put him in charge of Tilton. Logan Thomson was a common-sensical Yorkshireman, a good organizer with an ability, which I much admired, to make correct estimates of what the weather would do, what his men would do, and what his land would yield. His men often differed from him, making their own guesses, based of course on longer experience of the local weather and the nature of the soil, guesses which he, Logan, always treated with respect but would on occasion overrule. So far as I know, he only had one disaster at Tilton – that was when he left a tractor undrained and was caught by a sharp frost (he met the damage out of his own pocket). He got good work from his men; some of them were very old – one old boy had been a private at Spion Kop. A younger soldier was the ploughman (he enjoyed himself enormously in the Home Guard), and a one-handed man was the most thoughtful and ingenious of the labourers. It is an extraordinary thing, a farm, a little world of friendships and enmities; we were about fifteen people, including three landgirls.

Logan was a bachelor and, so Lydia said, his heart had been broken by a handsome Scandinavian girl; she and Logan used to drive around the farm together and seemed, all through the summer of 1938, to be inseparable. I suspect that old Mrs Thomson who, with Thomson *pére*, lived in the farmhouse at Tilton, was responsible for ending the affair. If it had not been ended Logan's story would have been very different.

To outward appearances there was only one thing about Logan that was peculiar. He slept until about 9 o'clock in the morning – an extraordinary thing in a farmer. Only once, in my experience, did he rise early. His appearance created panic: quite a lot of his men had followed Logan's example – in part at all events – and this one day's early rising restored discipline wonderfully. As one got to know him better one discovered that he was late in rising because he had been reading late into the night, and in fact he was fairly well read not only in agricultural science but in modern literature. He often borrowed novels from the Keyneses. But one discovered this slowly. He certainly did not parade his intellectual accomplishments.

Logan had a great admiration for Maynard and loved to tell stories of his employer's triumphs amongst the local farmers. There was a long tale about a neighbour's fence – or was it Maynard's own? At all events, the neighbour paid for it to be repaired. Maynard had convinced him not only that it was his legal duty to undertake this but that it was in truth an expenditure by which he, the neighbour, would profit. Logan got immense pleasure from describing the fellow's bewilderment, his inability to see a flaw in Maynard's argument, and his fear that he had in some way been outwitted.

Logan got on extremely well with Maynard and was I think rather proud to be employed by so distinguished a man, and certainly Maynard considered himself well served. One day, when I was rolling a pasture, Maynard came round to tell me, as he told everyone else on the farm, that Tilton was to be made a partnership between him, Lydia and Logan. Every eventuality he told me, had been taken care of, and they would know just what to do if any one of the triumvirate were to die or go dotty.

'Supposing' I said, 'you all go dotty at the same time?'

'The one thing the lawyers overlooked,' he replied.

In the end something not wholly unlike this did happen.

Logan's pride in being employed by a distinguished man was to some extent shared by his workforce. But this was compounded with another feeling. In the second year of the war Logan announced that the allowance of milk – one of the labourers' perks on a dairy farm – was to be increased; simultaneously it was announced that the milk had to be collected in appropriate cans, i.e. those which would contain exactly the permitted ration. Until then it had been taken away in large containers which, if over-generously filled, could hold very much more than this. In fine, Maynard's benevolent act was calculated to reduce the amount of milk consumed on the farm. The beauty of it was that no one could possibly complain.

There were of course other forms of generosity – presents brought back after American visits, and entertainments of various kinds. The strangest of these was a recital by Lydia, disguised I think in a mackintosh together with a rather bewildered chorus of local children, of *The Forsaken Merman.* 'Children dear, was it yesterday?'

About a year before the war Maynard came over from Tilton and asked me to make a mask for a guy; he was giving a Bonfire Night party, and they needed a guy to burn. I was happy to oblige, made a mask, and joined the party. In Lewes and the surrounding villages November 5th was in the past a great opportunity for drinking beer, letting off fireworks and denouncing Popery (Lewes had martyrs in the Marian persecution). There were bonfires and fireworks in many villages so this was very much a part of local tradition, although I do not think that Tilton had had its own bonfire within living memory.

It was quite a jolly affair, though I think it was a mistake to lay the bonfire, as this one was laid, in an open field. But the guy burned well, there was some beer, the bonfire prayer was recited. I thought no more about it until I had been a farm labourer for some months and my friend Becket Standen, the brightest of the farm workers, said to me: 'What did you think of that bonfire party? *We* thought it a proper waste of money.'

'But surely it's the tradition round here to celebrate Guy Fawkes Day? Lord Gage has a bonfire at Firle.'

'Lord Gage is a lord and knows how the thing should be done. This was just a pretence.'

'But Mr Keynes thought that everyone would enjoy it.'

Becket shook his head. 'It wasn't real.'

The path of the traditionalist is indeed a hard one.

I had already ceased to be a farm worker and was in fact in hospital when I heard that Maynard was dead. The news had been expected for some time but was not the less depressing for that. A few years later there was a change in my own life which took me away from Charleston. When, however, Olivier and I came south for a vacation there was always an invitation from Lydia. Logan would usually be there. In fact it seemed that a ménage of a kind had been established – of what kind it was hard to say. Indeed the whole management of the place was, to me, mysterious. For a long time Lydia and Logan seemed never to eat at home; they would go to Lewes and eat there.

The hall at Tilton was still full of things that had been purchased in America during the war in order to survive something like a state of siege: tins of powdered milk filled shelves, and to complete the oddity of the scene the police had done their best to safeguard the contents of the house. On one of the outer walls was an enormous alarm; a gigantic object shaped liked some Brobdingnagian bicycle bell was attached to the brickwork. Inside, the pictures of Maynard's collection – Cézanne, Matisse, Seurat, Delacroix – were hung just below the ceiling in order, so I was told, to make it more difficult for burglars to snatch and carry them off. Thieves were also discouraged by the simple expedient of leaving the road between Tilton and the A27 in a state of disrepair; here indeed was an obstacle that might discourage the most resolute marauder.

By the time we returned to Sussex for good in 1967 a drastic change had occurred. Tilton was abandoned; the pictures had gone to Cambridge, Lydia was in a Seaford nursing home, Logan in another. Of the two, Logan was the most to be pitied. He seemed in reasonable health but was hopelessly bored. He told me that nobody came to see him, which was not quite accurate for I did meet a farmer who had been his neighbour and there may have been others. He refused books, saying that he could not read them, and when supplied with a 'talking book' could not use it. Once or twice in conversation he told me that he was able at times to see Lydia – which was in fact not possible. The only thing that I could do for him was to bring him oranges. In the end he told me that he was dying and wanted to die. I have never seen anyone so completely deprived of curiosity or the capacity for enjoyment.

The last time I saw Lydia I found her in bed in quite a pleasant room in what was, I suppose, a superior nursing home. She surprised me greatly by greeting me in French. She seemed unwilling to converse in any other language and I was thankful that she hadn't reverted to Russian. I think she did most of the talking; she seemed in very good spirits, chatting away about her early days in London, about the ballet and the fun we had had together. She never spoke about Maynard or Logan; nor did I. She died a few weeks later.

7

Roger Fry

'I HEARD FALSEHOOD taught, and was compelled to deny it. Nothing else was possible to me, I knew not how much or how little might come of the business, or whether I was fit for it.'* Those are Ruskin's words. He says better than I could what I felt when, like him, I began to reply to people who, so it seemed to me, were grossly unfair to a great man.

There the resemblance ends; Ruskin went on to defend Turner in five large volumes. I defended Roger Fry in a number of articles, reviews and letters to the press all of which have, I imagine, been forgotten. Actually I have written more about Ruskin than about Roger; also I owe more to him. Roger enlarged my understanding of an art in which I had been instructed by other people; Ruskin taught me an important lesson concerning an art which I had regarded as a mere convenience but which was, for him, a passionate affair with the muse. Moreover he had two voices; one is that of *Modern Painters*, ornate, majestic and didactic, the other is that of *Praeterita*, plain, passionate and subtly magical. In both Ruskin could be sublime; Roger could be sublime only in a few wonderful moments in his lectures such as that which Virginia, his first biographer, has described. One can learn from Ruskin – not to draw but to write – and he is a good teacher; at all events *Modern Painters* is today still inimitable, by which I mean that the student is not tempted to write a pastiche.

Ruskin clearly had considerable charm but not if one had views of

---

* Preface to *Modern Painters*, Vol. V

one's own about art and wanted to express them. Ruskin wanted to talk, Roger wanted to listen. I am content to know and to learn from Ruskin through the medium of the printed page.

To know Roger in person was a treat. When I was born he had already fallen in love with Vanessa and one of the things that brought them together was the fact that he, as the father of two children, was able to sympathize with her at a time when I, a nameless and ailing brat, seemed ready to leave the world which I had so recently entered.

His presence and indeed his charm are amongst my earliest memories. Julian recalled that evening when Roger, having filled two clay pipes with coal dust, placed them on the fire, there to emit lovely jets of blue flame.* I, too, clearly remember that beautiful demonstration although it must have been made before I was six years old. I cannot have been very much older when, playing that game in which one likens one's friends to animals, I compared Roger to an elephant. I do not think that my childish comparison was wholly inapt: vast but gentle, formidable but friendly, provided with a trunk that could perform wonderful ingenuities. It was certainly thus that I saw him at the time nor I think did my image become wholly unrecognizable in later years.

He was the best of teachers for one longed to be taught by him. I remember a happy morning in his garden at Dalmeny Avenue in London when I was twelve or thirteen trying, first on my own and later with his assistance, to fashion a toy which, because it had both a heavy and a buoyant element, would neither sink nor float in his pond.

I suppose it was at about the same time that he took me to the National Gallery, where I hoped that he would tell me what I should or should not admire. He surprised me greatly by insisting that I should tell *him* what to like. It came as rather a shock and I must confess that I found it much more congenial when we discussed science. As a scientist he could usually provide useful information, more than when I asked about art. He had at that time a picture by Kokoschka on his walls which I admired because it was almost or wholly abstract; I was somewhat at a loss when he asked me what else I found to admire in it.

---

* *Julian Bell*, ed. Quentin Bell, Hogarth Press, 1938, p. 10

We children loved him and indeed respected him greatly. And yet from quite an early age we began to laugh at him. This didn't seem to us odd; it was more or less what we felt about Duncan, Clive and Vanessa, but in the case of Roger the laughter was perhaps louder because of the strange mixture of wisdom and folly with which he entertained us. Roger's credulity was what most amused us, it was in fact the negative side of his scientific ability. I don't think it applied to works of art where usually his sensibility acted promptly and his judgements were swift and final. One glance and he would dismiss a thing as a fake or a fraud or, alternatively, produce that long sigh of delight which would be followed by an exclamation: 'My word, that's swell.'

But patent medicines were another matter, and that was not all; he insisted that any new idea should be given a fair trial, that nothing should be dismissed out of hand. Desmond MacCarthy complained that Roger would never listen to 'the still small voice that whispers *fiddlesticks*', but *that*, Roger would reply, was what was said when astronomers suggested that the earth moved round the sun. True enough, but it must be allowed that Roger had a positive affection for the marvellous. Those improbable explanations to which most of us turn only when all the prosaic explanations of ordinary life have been dismissed were for him the starting point of an enquiry which usually ended in something sufficiently banal, but which began with earth-shaking suppositions. I do not use that adverb in a purely figurative sense. Consider the story of the tides.

Julian Fry, yachting on the Solent, found that the tide turned twenty minutes later than he had expected. Little knowing what trouble this would cause he mentioned the fact in a letter to his father. You or I receiving this information would, if we thought anything of the matter, have concluded that the boy's watch needed an overhaul, or that he was misinformed about the time of the tides or that the Solent, because it diverges into two channels, might well be perplexing in its tidal motions. Roger had a more apocalyptic explanation which he offered to Vanessa and T.S. Eliot when they came to dine with him at Dalmeny Avenue. 'The tides', he said,' are governed by the moon. If the moon goes astray so will the tides. Why then should the moon misbehave? Clearly because something is happening in the solar system and the solar system could only be disturbed by some foreign body, some 'dark star' flying into our part of the heavens. This alien asteroid which has shaken the moon in its orbit must inevitably be drawn to the superior mass of our own planet. It will strike the earth and that will be the end of us.'

To describe, in plain prose, the convincing, sensible, sweetly reasonable quality of Roger's manner when uttering this ludicrous absurdity is beyond me. It must suffice to say that even Vanessa, who had been listening with affectionate amusement to Roger's tales of mystery and imagination for years, was made uneasy. As for the unhappy author of *Prufrock*, he was in despair. He returned with Vanessa and a bundle of poems in the tram which in those days took one from Dalmeny Avenue to the Tottenham Court Road. From thence the painter and the poet made their way eastwards in gloomy silence towards Bloomsbury. Suddenly Eliot raised despairing hands towards the errant moon; he had left his poems on the tram.

Clearly Roger could, for a time at all events, believe in the fantasies of his own imagination; the astonishing thing was that for a time he could convince others. Eliot to be sure was a sitting duck; in later life he could believe in any star so long as it was not too dark to shine on Bethlehem. But take the case of Leonard, not only the most sceptical of men, but the most obstinate in his opinions. Did you or anyone else ever hear Leonard say 'I was mistaken', asked William Plomer. Certainly no one was less likely to say anything of the kind, or to need to say it; nevertheless I once heard Leonard admit that when Roger maintained that this planet would in future be governed by birds, he listened patiently, fascinated by Roger's ingenuity and, for a spell, convinced.

Clive, who provided Virginia with most of the accounts of Roger's credulity for her biography, hedged a little. 'Of course one day Roger will back a winner and we shall all look stupid.' 'Might there not be, it was suggested, a scientific method for testing the value of works of art? The suggestion was acted upon. Next week he was found, according to gossip, swinging a weight attached to a bit of string above a canvas by Cézanne or himself and attempting to measure by eye the extent of the oscillation.'*

This was, admittedly, gossip and I think untrue, but it is certainly true that Roger was an ardent believer in the miracles of Monsieur

* Virginia Woolf, *Roger Fry*, 1940, Chapter 11

Coué, the apostle of auto-suggestion, in the black box that could provide instant diagnoses, and in a great many other wonderful inventions. I recall a scrap of conversation:

Vanessa: 'But Roger, do you really think that if I lost a leg I could learn to grow another simply by thinking about it?'
Roger: 'If a lobster can grow a new leg why shouldn't you do likewise?'

It must be allowed that Roger could be credulous even in an area where he usually knew better. A young woman – almost any young woman, but it helped if she were attractive – might show him a watercolour in which he would discover the evidence of considerable talent (in this he resembled Ruskin). Not surprisingly Vanessa found his optimism tiresome. Indeed he was inclined to discover taste and talent in everyone. His Quaker ancestors had found God in everyman. Roger did not believe in God but he found aesthetic sensibility everywhere. We have to remember that he belonged to a generation which was looking with new eyes at the art of Africa, Polynesia and other hitherto unlikely places. Also he was amongst the first to offer encouragement to that great teacher Marion Richardson and her pupils. He made some mistakes but he also made some important discoveries.

Roger knew that we laughed at his credulity and in later years he could join in the laughter. Meeting him in Paris shortly before his death I found that he wore an amulet around his neck. It contained iodine. 'It is supposed' he said with a smile, 'to be good for my rheumatism. Perhaps it is.' On the same occasion, which shows his realism, he remarked, 'Ever since the war [World War I] the French have been unreasonable about Germany; now that they are becoming more reasonable the Germans are themselves becoming unreasonable. It will end in war.'

*

I suppose I knew that Roger was a considerable figure in the world of art and art expertise, a person sufficiently public to be the object of widespread admiration, affection and hatred. But I should have been puzzled to say just why he was loved, hated and respected. I was never told to respect him or indeed to love him, he was simply, unaffectedly and beautifully 'there'.

It came therefore as a considerable surprise to me, a youth of seventeen living in Munich, to find when 'Herr Professor Fry' passed through Bavaria on his way to Vienna, Dresden and Berlin that I could claim to be on intimate terms with a great man. He was, I now perceived, a person for whom doors were opened, curtains drawn, cupboards unlocked, a man of power who with a single brief exclamation of pleasure or contempt could justify or prohibit the use of a name, which when emphatically given could be translated into hard cash.

I remember the agonies of one dealer who hoped that one of his belongings – a panel picture – might be attributed to Masaccio and came as near as he dared to offering a bribe, an offer which Roger, I think quite genuinely, failed even to understand. Or again the agitated lady in Dresden, 'Oh Herr Fry, you *do* think it's a Cézanne?'

'Oh my God yes!'

But the most memorable of these interviews was with a gentleman who it was said owned all the sugar-beet in Hungary. He was an amateur painter and he had some fine things. At the front door of his home we encountered a dog; when we entered it did likewise and seemed perfectly at home. The sugar-beet magnate spoke (I think) Magyar – he had only a little German; I had to interpret although I had even less, not enough at any rate to ask him why the dog was allowed the freedom of the house. Finally we came to an enormous canvas filled with horses, soldiers and emblematic females. 'Did Herr Fry think it might be by Vasari?' Herr Fry thought it quite possible. And what did he think of it as a picture? I had some difficulty in achieving an adequate translation; Roger did not often use strong language. After this we made our way to the door, accompanied by our host and two amiable servants. As we prepared to leave we were asked whether we were taking our dog with us.

According to Helen the dog had 'misbehaved' on a priceless eighteenth-century sofa – which reminds me that I should have introduced Helen Anrep, sometime wife of Boris Anrep the mosaicist; she was Roger's last mistress (in effect his second wife). Helen, who had her own views of Vasari not to speak of Raphael ('I could have told that young man a thing or two'), and indeed of most subjects, was in many ways the perfect companion for Roger, argumentative, teasing, difficult but essentially warm-hearted and devoted; she was sometimes but not always a strong enough character to resist his impetuosity.

Clive has described how the Bell family and its guests were coerced by Roger and obliged to emulate his insatiable lust for continuous strenuous activity.* Helen provided a much-needed brake when she came with him on his travels. Not that it always worked. I remember one occasion when Roger got up at, I think five in the morning, in order to catch a steamer which would take him across a lake to a railway station, from which he could travel further for an hour or so to catch a bus which would take him to a place where he would be near a church which might or might not have been decorated by Tiepolo. Helen refused to accompany him.

Such excursions on our tour through Germany and Austria were, however, exceptional. Our usual programme in Vienna or Dresden started with a visit to the galleries; we would arrive when the doors opened; by about 12.30 Helen would begin to complain of hunger or fatigue. 'But Helen we've only just arrived.' With luck the gallery would close at 2 o'clock; then we would find 'that little place' which Roger had noticed as having a Magyar name and perhaps Hungarian goulash. After lunch Helen might persuade him to take a rest, but there were still churches to be visited and then perhaps a concert and finally the opera.

Roger had a passion for Monteverdi – a passion which Eddy Sackville-West, then considered an authority on music, considered highly absurd. The real disadvantage of such an admiration during our tour was that there was little chance to hear seventeenth-century opera in the great opera houses of Munich, Vienna and Dresden. I myself had just learnt to admire Giuseppe Verdi and Roger, who would give anything a trial, did come and listen to *Otello* in Vienna and was considerably impressed.

I think that Roger enjoyed his journey through Germany and Austria, there were a good many things in German *Kunstforschung* that he found admirable. But if he found Central Europe impressive his greatest enthusiasm lay elsewhere. England, Bird's Custard Island as he used to call it, he considered philistine and indeed barbarous; there were a great many of his compatriots whom he liked and it was here that he usually made his home, but he was never

---

* See Clive Bell, *Old Friends*, Chatto & Windus, 1956, p. 85

enthusiastic about the English as he was about France and the French. It is not easy to be enthusiastic about an entire nation, and even Roger had to admit that there were quite a lot of people in France who had to be considered exceptions. But fate brought him in touch with a couple who were exactly what he hoped and sometimes believed all the French to be, although not French in a Parisian sense. Marie Mauron *née* Roumanille only, so far as I could discover, spoke Provençal to her parents. When Roger came into their lives, Marie was a school teacher at Les Baux; she must at that time have been a very attractive young woman with a tremendous gift for conversation. I remember an occasion many years later when, entertaining us in a restaurant, she not only reduced us to happy tears but made the waiter so helpless with laughter that he could not do his job properly. It is hardly surprising that having met Roger and seen how delightful and how funny he was she at once became his friend for life. Her husband was a still greater acquisition although he, at the time of his first meeting with Roger, could hardly have been cheerful company. Charles Mauron, like Marie, was a Provençal; he was a man of formidable intellect; amongst many other things he was a chemist and it was natural that he should have found employment in a soap factory in Marseilles. An explosion in the factory injured his face and very nearly blinded him. When Roger found him he was recovering from this accident but it was still doubtful whether he would ever again have the use of his eyes. Understandably he was sunk in deep depression; he could do nothing but sit still and worry. Roger himself was recovering from a love affair which had ended in tragedy and left him deeply depressed.

Roger saw that Charles must have an occupation. He knew English and with Roger's help he could at once become a translator. It so happened that Roger was reading a book that deserved to be translated; it was called *A Passage to India*. He pulled it out of his pocket for them to begin at once to translate it.

'And so' said Charles, 'he led me straight into the Marabar Caves.'

It was the beginning of a new life for Charles. He made English friends of an older generation; of these Morgan Forster was the most devoted; a younger generation, my brother and his friends, made the Maurons, who moved presently to St Rémy, a further link between England and Provence.

Charles did in the end become totally blind but not for many years, indeed there was a time when he used to ride down from the Mas d'Angirany into the centre of St Rémy on a motor bicycle, and so far as I know never had an accident. It was interesting with this in mind to hear him – with a real concern although not without laughter – deplore Roger's method of travelling through France.

Here I must retrace my steps. The machine age did not really arrive in force (so far as my family was concerned) until 1927 when the Woolfs bought a Singer and we bought a Renault. Meanwhile Bunny bought an aeroplane; in this machine he flew from Huntingdon to Firle landing on the 'back field' behind Charleston, but not without damage. The damage was suffered by Roger's motor car which was just coming up Charleston drive when Roger caught sight of Bunny preparing to land. He was deeply interested in the sight, so interested in fact that he ran slap into a gate post.

Roger's car did not differ from most inexpensive vehicles; in this it was unlike his celebrated bicycle which indeed differed totally from nearly all other bicycles. It had been made by a 'little man' (Roger could always discover a 'little man') and on some principle (could it have been cantilevers?) which rendered it unique. It was so striking an object that in every French village in which the thing was parked a little knot of excited villagers – such as might collect around a notice proclaiming a change in government – would gather to comment and to wonder; but although less unconventional than his bicycle, his motor car was also a centre of attention.

'The French' Roger said to Charles, 'are a happy people; wherever I go I hear laughter.' Charles did not doubt that this was the case, having seen Roger driving on the wrong side of the road, behind him a mass of easels, canvases, paint boxes, books, bottles and packages of all shapes and sizes surmounted by a tall *diable*. This, it should be said, was not a fiend but a tall portable chimney with a kind of hat or conical roof.

When Roger collided with a lorry no damage was done except to the feelings of the lorry driver who was incensed when Roger explained that it was customary in England to drive on the left and it was surprising on the whole that such accidents didn't occur more frequently. 'You don't expect me to congratulate you?' said the lorry driver.

I have in my time met a good many people who could be classed as intellectuals. People who when they have been offered an idea will set upon it joyously and pursue it with unflagging enthusiasm, but none who had such an appetite and stamina for the chase as Charles Mauron. He talked endlessly, brilliantly and continuously with an erudition which he took for granted. He was sometimes comic, often profound and never boring. Many years later, visiting Charles and his second wife, Alice, I found that fountain of ideas and discussion still flowing freely. More than once, coming down to breakfast he would greet me with 'Now, where were we?' and we would resume the discussion just where he had left it about midnight on the previous evening.

Unfortunately I never witnessed a serious discussion between Charles and Roger but I imagine that it would have been much the same, although Roger no doubt would have given him a better run for his money. In the days when my brother and his Cambridge friends filled the Mas d'Angirany with laughter and flirtation, the conversation would have been more general and Marie would have played an important role.

It was at a meeting of that kind, or so I gather, that Charles devastated the company with a supremely tactless remark. Much later I asked Marie whether her husband was often guilty of such gaffes. No, she said, it was exceptional; she and Charles were then living a double life, they had a house full of guests to entertain, and though they tried not to show it, they were living in a nightmare.

'But why?'

'We had just heard that Roger was dead.'

8

Leonard Woolf

'BUT WHAT', IT may be asked, 'about Virginia? Is she not the best of the bunch, the brightest star in this galaxy? How on earth could you exclude her?'

Some older readers may anticipate my reply. About twenty years ago I wrote a life of Virginia; it is still in print. To her I devoted far more space than to any of those whom I have discussed in these pages. I still have things that I want to say about her, here and in other chapters; also I devote Appendix I to a discussion of *Three Guineas*. Meanwhile there is Leonard.

I must have been aware of him before I was of an age to remember him. I was two years old when he married Virginia and by the time he became distinct as a person it was still as part of a solid entity – the Woolfs. At that time the Woolfs inhabited Asham, a lovely house which lay in a valley of the South Downs about six miles from Charleston. We, the Bells, came to Charleston in the autumn of 1916. I recall his presence in the summers of 1917 and 1918 when picnic parties met on the lower slopes of the hills above Firle. I recall also an invasion of Asham by us children which earned a stern rebuke from the Woolfs. It had been preceded by a similar explosion for which Bunny Garnett and two young women were responsible. The incident is of importance here only because it made me aware that, whereas our parents and many of their friends spoiled us outrageously, Leonard was an altogether tougher proposition. My sister, Angelica, describes in *Deceived with Kindness* how she made a similar discovery.

In 1918 Leonard again found it necessary to impose discipline, but on this occasion we got a rather better notion of why he had to do so. My brother and I were sent to the Woolfs following the birth of Angelica. Leonard and Virginia gave us a lovely time at Asham and we then removed to Hogarth House, Richmond. Leonard finally expelled us, sending us to 46 Gordon Square, for a reason which he explained to us. Virginia had had a tooth extracted – a thing which usually made her ill – and the presence of two noisy boys gave her a headache. Virginia's headaches were a just cause for alarm. Leonard said enough to make us understand this and we ourselves, who by this time knew and liked him, accepted the situation without difficulty. I suppose this was my first intimation of Virginia's nervous fragility and of Leonard's continuous task of preserving her. It was not for many years that I understood how much he had to do and how well he did it.

Presently he began to entertain us. 'Now old Woolf will tell you his traveller's tales,' Virginia would say, which was unfair for Leonard was a very truthful man. We were somehow aware of this, and, because one felt that he was not romancing, his stories of the gorgeous east and above all of the fauna of Ceylon, of apes and peacocks, of his tame panther and his adventures amongst the pearl fishers were accepted without reserve; they were a constant source of delight.

I wish that I could remember more of the Ceylonese stories, or for that matter of his stories of early days in Kensington and Putney. I have a picture, not I think too inexact, of a close centripetal Jewish home, the widowed Mrs Woolf and her large family living in genteel poverty whilst maintaining a brave front.

Once staying with him I came down to breakfast which had been laid for two (Virginia broke her fast in bed). Leonard was in the kitchen, but a book, which obviously provided his early morning reading before the post came, lay by his plate. I could read just enough to discover that it was the *Lysistrata*. Like many of us, Leonard had been subjected to an intensive saturation of the classics when at school, but unlike most of us he had retained and used what he learnt.

After Putney and St Paul's, Trinity College, Cambridge must have been a wonderful and exhilarating experience. For Leonard, unlike his friends Lytton Strachey and Thoby Stephen, this translation to a society where one was free to think and to speak, must have been glorious but almost intimidating. His friends came from homes which, unlike Putney, were in a sense preparations for Cambridge. For him it must have been very unfamiliar territory. The fact that he was liked, accepted, elected to the Apostles and became a central figure amongst the intellectuals of his generation is to the credit of all parties. I would add here that it enables us to assess and to put in its proper perspective the assertion that the set in which he now found himself was anti-semitic. Here Leonard, who was to meet so many of the great and powerful men of his age, met G.E. Moore, the only one according to him who really was great. Leonard was a part of the nucleus that was to become Bloomsbury. He met those two beautiful women the Miss Stephens, Vanessa and Virginia. And then suddenly it was all over. One may envy him the education that he gained through talking to his Cambridge friends, but it was not the kind of education that would impress the Civil Service examiners. He had very little money and no powerful relations. He had to be content with employment far from home, to collect a fox terrier and the entire works of Voltaire and to set sail for Ceylon.

He spent seven years in that island, returning in 1911 to find his old Cambridge friends together with some additions and changes. Bloomsbury was in full bloom. G.E. Moore was still its prophet, but it also worshipped Cézanne. Clive Bell, a semi-detached member of the intellectual group at Trinity, was now at the centre of things and, after Thoby Stephen's death in 1906, had married Vanessa Stephen. Virginia, still unmarried, was flirting desperately with Clive. Leonard, who had long meditated the possibility of marrying her, now fell deeply in love. He determined to marry her. It would appear to be the one moment in his life in which he lost his calm, but he was finally successful. Clive was not pleased and, from this time on, although there was never I think an open quarrel between the two men, there was a lasting antipathy.

To Clive it seemed that Leonard was too austere, too political, too critical of that which he considered frivolous or wordly. He missed all the jolly and decorative side of life; this made him censorious and puritanical and limited his appreciation of the arts. In short he was a 'kill-joy'. Clive never quite forgave Leonard for having been an Apostle while he, Clive, was not. Leonard thought Clive an intellectual lightweight whose views on politics and life in general were those of a timid, spoilt and selfish man; as a critic he was superficial, as a man fussy, snobbish and frequently ridiculous.

The difference between the two men was exacerbated by the fact that Leonard had always to preserve Virginia from social pleasures which, if taken in excess, were bad for her health. He knew too well that if Virginia stayed too long at a party she might have one of her headaches on the following day. Virginia herself also knew this very well, but then she did love parties. Thus about ten o'clock, when Virginia was enjoying herself enormously and the company was enjoying her, Leonard would suddenly announce that the time had come for them to return to Richmond and Virginia would depart with him reluctantly. Clive always suspected that Leonard was, as we say in the nursery, 'doing it on purpose'. He half believed that the precaution was unnecessary; he may sometimes have been right, but Leonard had to be over-cautious.

Both of them, if pressed, would admit that the other had some good qualities. Clive was a kind man, Leonard was virtuous. But these were concessions which could only be extracted with some labour.

Leonard was very critical of *Art*. He considered that Clive was too much of a formalist and was, in consequence, very unsound in his judgement of Rembrandt. Here he was in the right, but I think that, in conversation at all events, Leonard went too far in the opposite direction, espousing a theory which took no account of our valuation of those works of art the literary content of which is invisible.

I have discussed Clive's work on civilization and Leonard's opposing view in my chapter on Clive, and here it need only be said that they differed very profoundly, the one seeing the civilized man as the member of a social élite, the other seeing him as an impartial rationalist – and here I found myself in disagreement with both parties.

Again I must recall another dispute. It took place when the Woolfs were staying at Charleston at Christmas 1927 and Vita Sackville-West came to lunch. Clive and Virginia were enthusiastic about the visitor, praising her beauty and speaking with admiration of her ancient aristocratic lineage. 'What snobs they are,' said Leonard who, it should be mentioned, became and remained a friend of Vita. It was to Julian that he addressed his remark and I am sure that Julian agreed.

I think that it is true to say that in this period, say 1926–33, Julian and I were divided by the fact that I was greatly attracted to Clive and Clive's views while Julian was in general agreement with Leonard. I was charmed by Clive's wordly panache, his urbanity and his sense of fun, while Julian, serious, sometimes ruthlessly serious, a member of the Labour Party, an Apostle, unworldly, interested in poetry and at times displaying a kind of intellectual puritanism, was probably at that time Leonard's favourite nephew. Perhaps it should also be said that Clive's influence on me did me no service with either Mr or Mrs Woolf; at one time I was regarded by them both as a very precious, affected young man. Even when I began to take an interest in socialist politics my brand of socialism deviated from Leonard's and Julian's; they were both deeply distrustful of the communists and, while critical of the Labour Party leadership, essentially and firmly social democrats. While I was always wanting to see a united front with the extreme left, they kept to a straight and fairly narrow path.

All this needs in various ways to be qualified, partly because Julian's relation with his aunt was more complex than that which united him with his uncle. Julian loved to tease Virginia, producing parodies of her style while she – and this was also true of Leonard – could be severely critical of Julian's writings. I, on the other hand, joined with Virginia in a series of lampoons (which no one took very seriously), and wanted to be a painter which meant that I was not a competitor.

Also I should remember how much I owe to Leonard who, during the 'thirties, certainly put a number of commissions in my way; for whom I decorated walls and tables and who also gave me my first political task, writing for the Fabian Society an account of the Sino-Japanese conflict of 1931–2, which was also my first literary undertaking.

It is not an easy thing to write about people one knows well; behind every statement concerning friends and relations there is a great mass of unstated information which colours one's opinions but which cannot easily be conveyed to the reader. When I say that there was a considerable rivalry between Charleston and Monks House (to where Leonard and Virginia moved in 1919) I do not mean that the Bells and the Woolfs lived on the same terms as the Capulets and the Montagues. Perhaps one might come rather nearer the mark by comparing the differences between the two households with those which separated the Musgraves at the Great House from those at Uppercross Cottage.

There was a certain amount of gentle teasing. Leonard thought and thought rightly that the garden at Monks House was much finer and better tended than that at Charleston. When in summer he visited Charleston, he proceeded, after reducing his dogs to obedient silence, to go round the garden with Vanessa giving and taking advice in the friendliest manner. I doubt whether he thought much of our odd habit of cultivating globe artichokes mainly for their flowers. Nor, I think, when the Bells visited Monks House did we comment upon the Woolfs' treatment of the tiles in the living room upstairs. Here indeed there must have been faults on both sides. There had been a miscalculation, there were two tiles too many. The Woolfs set the tiles around the fireplace and laid the two supernumerary tiles flat upon the hearth, thus creating the oddest effect. I could never look at that absurd arrangement without wondering how my aunt and uncle could face it daily.

Their house itself was to us Charlestonians odd and uncomfortable; it seemed to consist of two cottages knocked together. There was a big room downstairs made by the amalgamation of several pokey little rooms; here the Rodmell Labour Party used to meet; it was increasingly used for storing apples. Some convenient rooms were created up above. There was a kitchen which at one time featured an almost constant stream across the floor; this was supposed to be one of the main tributaries of the River Ouse. Two more rooms were added on at the northern end of the house; one had to go out of doors in order to reach Virginia's bedroom. Behind the house sat a bust of Virginia's grandfather Sir James Stephen, the Colonial Secretary, on whose head last thing at night Leonard would go out and pee.

In 1923, when Charleston was not available and the Woolfs were in Spain, Julian, Vanessa and I spent three weeks in Monks House.

Did you think Rodmell very inferior to Charleston? I suppose so: but then what a pleasure that was! How the Wolves can live here: how stuffy; how ridiculous their decorations are etc. etc. That was what Dolphin said to Duncan when they settled in at night.

VW to VB, 1 April 1923

Monks House was full of books. It seemed full to bursting although I do not think that at that time there were books on the stairs as there were later. The place was then fairly primitive, but then so was Charleston. The great drawback of Monks House, according to Vanessa, was that it was in a village so that one could hardly avoid seeing a great deal of one's neighbours.

In the 1920s the land lying to the north of the house was offered for sale; speculative builders were interested. Leonard stepped in and acquired it; it was a strip of grassland as long as the house and garden though not very wide. Leonard had a use for it: he had played bowls at Cambridge and decided to make his newly acquired land into a bowling green. The reader probably thinks of a bowling green as a piece of grass as smooth as an ice rink; the bowling green at Monks House *was* fairly smooth in places although sometimes an apparently level area might conceal an invisible declivity, but apart from these irregularities there were flower beds and rough grass on one side, and on the other an abrupt slope which, if a bowl were thrown too hard, would carry it with great rapidity down into a hedge; finally there was a pond surrounded by a gently sloping concrete embankment which seemed to invite a carelessly thrown bowl into its depths.

Leonard and Virginia played on that green whenever they could and Leonard usually won. They played so frequently that they came to know every capricious oddity of the terrain. We visitors usually lost, but when one played a foursome Leonard might find himself with a companion who could lose the game for him. This was a trouble which he could prevent. Leonard not only played a very good game of bowls, he could teach others to do likewise. I have seen him with a complete novice, a person who seemed to have no aptitude for games of any kind, teaching her, with a few words of friendly but authoritative advice, to get into the right position to aim and to bowl with such an increase of skill that the partner who had begun as a liability ended by becoming an asset.

The reader will have noticed the pronoun in the foregoing paragraph. Yes, Leonard played mainly with female partners. I think that this was always his tendency but it became particularly true in later years. He was largely introduced to politics by women and some of his first works of political journalism were concerned with women. I do not think that he ever spoke or wrote about the men of the co-operative movement with anything like the enthusiasm which he felt for the Women's Guild. He was always sympathetic, sometimes more sympathetic than Virginia, in his attitude to the women who worked in his house and in his office.

The same cannot be said for his relationship with young men in the Hogarth Press. He employed a series of bright young men: Ralph Partridge, George (Dadie) Rylands, Angus Davidson and John Lehmann. George Rylands remained on good terms with Leonard but was glad to leave, Angus Davidson lasted longer but suffered more, Ralph Partridge parted on bad terms. The only one, however, of whom I can speak with any authority was John Lehmann. At a lunch party in 50 Gordon Square John's sister Rosamond told the company that he was considering applying for a job in the Hogarth Press; what advice should she give him?

'Do you *like* your brother?' asked Ralph Partridge.

John in fact was aware of the fate of his predecessors but with the confidence of youth he believed that he could succeed where others had failed. At first it seemed that he was right; he managed to get on fairly well with Leonard. Virginia described him with enthusiasm; she always found these young men sympathetic and hoped that they would prevent Leonard from overworking. 'Lehmann may do: a tight aquiline boy, pink, with the adorable curls of youth; yes, but persistent, sharp.' (VW, 10 January 1931)

A year and a half later the situation had changed; John had his grievances. '. . . Nessa put his case for him and against the irascible Leonard and the hard work and the underpay . . . I'm not specially sympathetic.' (VW, 19 May 1932)

Vanessa was not unprejudiced; John was Julian's friend and for a short time not only my friend but my lover, but she would not have been his advocate if she had not believed that he had a pretty good case. There were faults on both sides – that is a bromide, but I believe true. It was, I guess, a case of Greek meeting Greek; John had considerable abilities as a publisher, believed in himself and was impatient of the menial tasks which Leonard thought good training for a beginner. He could be as ruthless as Leonard and showed it when, without a word of warning, he left.

That, one believed was the end of the matter. The amazing thing is that it was only the beginning. In January 1938 Leonard offered John a partnership and the management of the Hogarth Press and

John accepted, buying out Virginia's share in the business. At the time he told his friends that although he had to serve with Leah he would win his Rachel (see Genesis XXIX.20); to me it appeared that Proverbs 11 would have been more to the point – 'as a dog returneth to its vomit, so a fool returneth to his folly.'

It seemed as though I had been rather too hasty. In 1938 and 1939 there was no serious trouble. As Leonard put it: 'John I think always wanted to get control of the press.' Leonard almost but not quite wanted to let it go. In 1938 he was tired and ill and had reached the limits of even his capacity for hard work. He and Virginia discussed the possibility of putting the press into the hands of a co-operative of what Virginia called 'the young brainies', Isherwood, Auden, Spender and of course John. The co-operative idea faded out but John remained and he had the money to buy himself in. There had already been a reconciliation; I suppose it seemed the obvious thing to do, but Leonard's first intention seems to have been to relax control altogether and this was something that he could not bring himself to do. The firm became a dyarchy and thus continued until just after the war when John attempted to buy Leonard out, was outmanoeuvred and found that his Rachel was ravished from him.

Leonard's account of his dealings with John is not ungenerous. He admits that he was probably responsible for the breakdown of John's apprenticeship; it may have been this that persuaded him to give John a further trial. John is a good deal less fair-minded. Although I heard a great many criticisms of Leonard at the time and since, I have always found it hard to imagine him completely losing his temper. I never knew him do anything of the kind even though I was of the wrong sex and on certain topics held what he considered the wrong opinions. In one respect he did think me decidedly lacking in decent feelings: he considered me unsympathetic to the brute creation. I thought him silly in his enthusiasm for livestock.

Monks House was densely populated with our dumb friends. I had nothing against the shoals of goldfish which inhabited Leonard's ponds. I could tolerate his large colony of miniature tortoises, his cats were inoffensive, his dogs, though tiresome, were tolerable; but I drew the line, and so I think did many others, at Mitz the marmoset.

Those who are wise enough not to keep a marmoset may need to be informed that marmosets are very small monkeys which I believe inhabit trees; in aspect they bear a certain resemblance to the late Dr Goebbels and when Leonard was so imprudent as to take Mitz by motor car through Nazi Germany I feared the authorities might perceive the resemblance and take offence. Like Dr Goebbels Mitz was talkative; it seemed to be in a perpetual state of vicious fury; ugly at all times, it became hideous when it vented its spite at the world. It was deeply in love with Leonard and would spit out its jealousy upon the rest of humanity. Perhaps it was showing its affection when it crouched upon his arm and defecated upon him; this was so much its favourite occupation that Leonard had to have waterproofing upon the sleeves of his jacket.

Leonard would visit the zoo and talk marmosets with the keepers; they were distressed by the fact that these exiles from the tropics tended to die during an English winter. One always hoped for a severe frost that would finish Mitz, but Leonard took infinite pains to keep it well wrapped up in a cosy place. On one occasion Mitz nearly escaped by climbing to the topmost bough of a tree; it refused to come down, despite the offer of its favourite delicacies. Then, with his usual acumen, Leonard summoned Virginia and took her in his arms. Mitz was down in a trice chattering in jealous fury.

This story reminds me of another in which Mitz played no part. I had it from Dr Rutherford, Leonard's physician. Leonard rang him one morning saying that he felt rather unwell; the medical orders were that he should stay in bed, the doctor had a lot of work to do but would call early in the afternoon. It so happened that he had less work than he expected; he arrived at Monks House in the middle of the morning to find that his patient was working hard in the top of a tree, high up, if not so high as Mitz; his task being done he descended to find himself confronted by his physician. It was the only time, said Rutherford, that I ever saw him out of countenance. Leonard kept Mitz alive for what seemed like many years; in the end I think it died of old age.

The period 1930–42 was a bad one for Leonard. The great task of his life from 1912 to 1941 was to keep Virginia alive and sane. The completion of any novel was marked by a time of great danger and *The Years* was almost too much for her sanity. Julian's death and Vanessa's subsequent ill health added to her depression but worse almost than anything was the appalling international situation.

I was at Monks House on 3 September 1939 when Chamberlain

declared war on Germany and we still did not know whether the French would join us. A lot of time was spent listening to the radio, the BBC seemed to be in a state of disarray that afternoon, many people were expecting an air raid, and in fact there was a warning which turned out to be a false alarm. But we did have time for a game of bowls and for once I won.

The public history of the following months, the fall of Poland, the 'phony' war, the German victories in the west, the isolation and defence of Britain need not be described by me, nor do I need to do more than touch on the fact that Leonard and Virginia had their store of poison ready in case we should be invaded. It was after a period of comparative peace and quiet, or at all events of dangers less imminent than those through which we had passed in 1940, that the final blow fell and Virginia killed herself on 28 March 1941. I did not see Leonard for some days after that event. When he did come to Charleston I was horrified at the spectacle of his despair, stoic though he was: it was dreadful and I cannot feel much charity for those imbeciles who have since maintained that he did not love Virginia.

It is not easy to write about what was for us a domestic tragedy, nor is it easy – although the difficulties here are of a very different nature – to describe the happy and fortunate events that were to follow.

The person who saved Leonard from the depths of despair was Mrs Ian Parsons (Trekkie Ritchie). She lives not far from us. We know her well and if I were to tell the world what we think of her she would probably blush and almost certainly tell me not to be absurd. He certainly was fortunate; old age is not a cheerful condition and Leonard certainly was not cheerful when he met her, but I'm not sure that with her to help him he did not enjoy an autumn more splendid than his spring.

One point on which I happen to be well informed should be made. It could be surmised that Leonard's sister-in-law and her family at Charleston might be a little put out by discovering that a charming woman quite unconnected with Bloomsbury should have been Leonard's rescuer from depression and should have earned his grateful affection. The fact is that Charleston liked Trekkie and was immensely grateful to her.

And so he lived happily ever after – it would be pleasant indeed if any truthful biographer could use these words. Certainly the last thirty odd years of Leonard's life were not without their miseries: the memory of his ultimate failure to save Virginia, his own maladies (he was a remarkably healthy man but still he could be unwell), the death of friends, of dogs and cats, of plants even, were a vexation, and the state of the world something much more than a vexation. And yet his may justly be called a happy old age, largely I think because Trekkie was by his side, also because he was able to rest a little. He lightened the enormous load of political work which he had carried for about thirty years, which meant that he had the leisure to write the things that he wanted to write. He had the pleasure of defeating John Lehmann's scheme for obtaining the Hogarth Press and the more important pleasure of seeing that enterprise established in what he considered a good home, that is to say with his friends Chatto and Windus, friends with whom he never quarrelled. This allowed him to keep some control over his darling firm and at the same time to relinquish all the more tiresome chores involved in publishing. In fact it proved the right and proper solution to the problem that had for so many years afflicted him.

The new arrangement of his life gave him time not only to write but to travel. He went to Greece and, with a serendipity not unlike that of Roger Fry, exhibited a rare gift for meeting and conversing with people whom he found intelligent and sympathetic. On the Acropolis he fell into conversation with a 'tout selling post cards' – 'the intelligence, knowledge, humanity of this man were extraordinary'. I expect that the postcard merchant would have said the same of him.

Although he had never been a Zionist, and had foreseen the disasters that would arise when a Jewish state was created in what had been an Arab country, he fell in love with Palestine and its inhabitants and he met a taxi driver who, I gather, agreed with Leonard and Lucretius in thinking that religion is a great trouble maker (as it surely is).

Finally he went back to Ceylon and here met everyone: the peasants and the village workers whom he had known when he was a young man and also the elected rulers of Ceylon. Here I shall reproduce some words that I wrote about Leonard in order to contradict him. At the end of a lifetime of thankless work on committees he declared that 'it had all been time wasted'. To this I replied: 'It cannot often happen that when a period of Imperial rule is over and a people has won its liberty, a returning civil servant, and a severe one too, is kindly received.' Leonard had something like a hero's welcome. The long hours in committee rooms had, after all, borne some fruit. And to this I would add that Leonard himself had not been expecting so cordial a reception. 'What a life he has led,' said E.M. Forster, 'and how well he has led it.'

9

The MacCarthys

I KNEW DESMOND and have tried to describe him in my biography of Virginia Woolf. I could make it worse but not better, therefore I repeat the following words:

Desmond, in the imagination of his friends, was going to be the successor of Henry James. Hearing him talk you could believe that. Even when he had sunk beneath repeated failures to float magazines, to produce copy on time, to meet the demands of bailiffs, to cope with life at all, still he had only to speak in order to command, not so much attention as affection, to fill one with delight, and, when he was in the vein, to convince one that he was the master of some prodigious treasury. He had only to put his hand into his pocket and draw out whatever you might wish – subtlety, brilliance or deep imaginative richness. It was 'ask and have,' for he was the most carelessly generous, the most intellectually spendthrift of men. How few plays have ever enchanted one half so much as Desmond's small talk.

Conversation was his art, and for him the tragedy was that he should have chosen so ephemeral a medium. For Virginia there was an inconvenience of another kind; he would turn up at Richmond for dinner, uninvited very probably, and probably committed to a dinner elsewhere, charm his way out of his social crimes on the telephone, talk enchantingly until the small hours, insist that he be called early so that he might attend to urgent business on the morrow, wake up a trifle late, dawdle somewhat over breakfast, find a passage in *The Times* to excite his ridicule, enter into a lively discussion of Ibsen, declare he must be off, pick up a book which reminded him of something which, in short, would keep him talking until about 12.45, when he would have to ring up and charm the person who had been waiting in an office for him since 10, and at the same time deal with the complications arising from the fact that he had engaged himself to two different hostesses for lunch, and that it was now 1 o'clock, and it would take forty minutes to get from Richmond to the West End. In all this Desmond had been practising his art – the art of conversation.

In a better world he would have been paid for talking, he could then have earned a fortune with his tongue, but he could not even envisage that as a possibility. He planned to write a great novel, if ever he could find the time and the energy. What he did was write journalism – very good journalism sometimes, but nothing to be compared with the Jamesian or Tolstoyan opus of which, in his youth, he had dreamed.

Now the great talker, like the great actor has (or had) no chance of survival; people may talk of him as they talk of Mrs Siddons or Paganini, or as I am talking now, but they can do no more than try to conjure a shadow from the past. The work of art itself has gone.

And of course there are other difficulties. Hugh and Mirabel Cecil have written an excellent biography of Desmond and of Molly his wife.* I knew Desmond only for a relatively short time and Molly I hardly knew at all. And yet I want to say a few things about the MacCarthys and their children.

Let me start with the children. I knew them before I knew their parents. In the summer of 1917 Molly brought them, Michael, Rachel and Dermod, to Charleston. Dermod seemed too young for our attention, but Michael and Julian, Rachel and I were almost coevals. We invited them for a sail on Charleston pond in the punt; it sank, we declared that we had all been very brave about it, we became friends. But almost at once, so it seemed, Rachel and I disagreed.

'Do you believe in fairies?' asked she.

'No,' said I.

'I do,' said Rachel.

'No one believes in fairies,' I replied.

'Irish people do,' she said, adding 'and I'm Irish', at which point Michael interrupted: 'No you're not, we conquered the Irish but we are not Irish', and the conversation took a different turn. When and whether Rachel stopped believing in fairies I do not know; she was a natural believer.

---

* *Clever Hearts*, Gollancz, 1990

About ten years elapsed. Then I was invited by Ray Strachey to spend a 'free week' in a house near Haslemere called 'The Mud Hut'. It deserved its name. Ray had invited a party of adolescents to come and fend for themselves; the girls cooked, the boys washed up. There was a bathing pool into which everyone was thrown, there were tents and ragging, there was noise, confusion and squalor. In the middle of it all, like patience on a monument, sat poor Rachel. I was about fifteen or sixteen so she was perhaps seventeen, but in fact very much older than I. Neat, pretty, modestly well dressed, in short a young lady and very like her mother. She was thoroughly bored and unhappy. What seemed to console her, and delighted me, was that she found me, under the circumstances, congenial. I was very immature, I was neither handsome nor well dressed, but I came from a world that she knew. We had friends in common, we had read the same books, we knew the same people, we neither of us much cared for the amenities of The Mud Hut, and before we parted she told me that I had been a comfort – which it is a comfortable thing to be. When the 'free week' ended we parted on good terms.

When we met again I considered myself grown up. As for Rachel, at The Mud Hut she had planned to become a publisher's reader, but now it was her ambition to go on the stage. In fact when I met her in the drawing room of 46 Gordon Square she was rehearsing. Wearing a free translation of early Victorian dress she danced and laid a bouquet before a cenotaph while a gramophone played Chopin's preludes. She was to perform it at one of the Keyneses' theatrical parties. She looked enchanting.

I was now able to take her to dine in Soho and to the theatre. The flirtation was a mild affair but it excited Molly's vehement disapproval. It was her habit to intercept and question her daughter when she returned from such outings and I daresay that Rachel, a truthful girl, admitted that when I brought her home to Wellington Square, I kissed her goodbye. One would hardly describe this as 'loose living' but this, according to Hugh and Mirabel Cecil, was the charge against her.

When Ralph and Frances Partridge invited me to join them on a Spanish holiday to which Rachel was also bidden Molly wrote a fierce letter to say that if I was of the party Rachel would not join them. I was therefore disinvited and felt somewhat aggrieved.

A study of the Cecils' biography explains Molly's wrath. Molly, by Bloomsbury standards, was both chaste and respectable, but she had enjoyed a lively flirtation with Clive. Clive was a lot more skilful and enterprising than I at the age of eighteen, or indeed at any age, and brought Molly to the very edge of adultery. The affair went far enough to give Desmond an excuse for his own infidelities.

Thus, when she saw her own ewe lamb in danger, as she saw it, of being hurt by a chip off the old block she was frightened and enraged. I felt hardly used. Molly, I thought, should have realized that I was a sheep in wolf's clothing.

But in retrospect I see that I was rather thoughtless. I am sure that I did not in fact injure Rachel in any way, but I did not measure the possible consequences of what seemed to me a harmless flirtation and if I had in any way deterred Rachel from making the good and charming marriage that eventually she did make it would have been a disaster.

Actually I remember being pleased when I heard of her engagement to David Cecil. I already knew and liked him very much. I remember discussing religion with him and hearing him say that he was not interested in the question: 'Does God exist?', but rather, 'What sort of God is he?'. This seemed to me a really terrible subject for discussion and one that might easily lead to blasphemy, but David seemed quite happy about it and I did not try to press the point.

Seeing David and Rachel together I felt that there was a kind of lovely innocence about them. They lived in a private world so fair that they mistrusted any phenomenon which lay outside it. Walking once from Charleston to Firle we came across a bull and some cows and although I assured them that a bull in female company was harmless they insisted on going through another field. That was understandable, but their subsequent alarm at the spectacle of a flock of sheep was so grotesque that for a moment I thought they must be teasing me. But no, it was quite genuine anxiety.

We had different friends and different interests. I rarely met them but it was pleasant when I did. I heard news of them from Ralph and Frances Partridge and never doubted that they were both happy and respectable. Imagine then my horror and astonishment when the newspapers announced that Rachel was in prison. I knew that Rachel couldn't be a criminal so what on earth had happened?

It transpired that she had committed some microscopic offence, parked her car in the wrong place, something of that kind, and she received a summons. I imagine that she more or less chose to forget it. So they sent another summons, and then another and another, until in the end the only thing that the authorities could do was to arrest her. After bailing her out David wrote a short letter to the magistrate in which, so he said, the words 'nursing mother' appeared five times. Everything ended happily. It seems to me that there is something very MacCarthyesque about this story: the obstinate refusal to confront a tiresome situation and then the increasing reluctance to face ineluctable facts was typical of both Rachel's father and her mother.

I saw Rachel for the last time when she accompanied David who was opening some tedious meeting in Brighton; the circumstances prevented us from conversing. She still looked amazingly young. My last encounter with David resulted from a book that he wrote about Jane Austen. I reviewed it and there was much to praise, but I did think that the darker side of the Austen family history should have been mentioned. This review brought me two letters: in one the correspondent agreed with me, the other was from David himself and contained nothing save gratitude.

I hardly knew Michael, the MacCarthy's eldest son, but he once spent a night at Charleston when I was living there by myself. He did most of the talking and indeed he had much to say. He had ridden on horseback from Buenos Aires to the Straits of Magellan across a land that grew colder and more desolate as he approached the South Pole, feeding on mutton which he killed *en route*, conscientiously hanging up the pelts for the owners to find. I am told that his story has been written and I hope it may be published.

Michael struck me as being unlike either of his parents both in person and character; he seemed to me a very practical man. Dermod, whom I knew much better, looked remarkably like his father and had much of Desmond's charm; in his choice of a profession he realized one of Desmond's unfulfilled ambitions – an ambition which perhaps was better unfulfilled. It is true that Dermod once told me that he could be as vague and as forgetful as any man, but he was too modest. He was to become a celebrated paediatrician; I would trust a diagnosis by him but not by his father. To be sure Desmond's bedside manner would have been worth a shelf full of pills and one can imagine him keeping some aged hypochondriac alive forever simply by sympathy. But, to return to his younger son, having myself suffered from a multitude of ailments and been in and out of hospital for years, and having also been attended and my life saved by some distinguished physicians, I still very much regret that I was never Dermod's patient.

We didn't pay much attention to him when he was a little boy, but as he grew older he developed wonderfully and I fully sympathized with his father's agonies when he was stationed in the Far East on board an aircraft carrier. Then he came home, and before you could say entente cordiale, he was married to a very beautiful young Frenchwoman. This indeed was my impression but in fact it seems that there were difficulties with Molly. I gather that she complained loudly. Marie France, she allowed, had every charm, but it seemed that she didn't have much else. In saying this Molly continually interrupted herself saying, 'I suppose you'll think me very worldly'. I suppose she was, but Molly had led a pretty hard life.

The physician is the priest of modern society. He is feared and loved, he regulates life and death, and seeing that most of us expect only one life we pay him the attention which we once accorded to those who imposed punishments and rewards in the afterlife. Thus, when a priest goes astray we smile but when a physician errs we are shocked. When Dermod told me a story concerning the errors of a medical man I was a little shocked.

It was like this: Dermod and another doctor were discussing a case. A child had been examined and the other doctor had arranged an operation. The operation was successful and the patient made a good recovery. But Dermod had been privy to the examination and had been quite sure that there had been no need for surgery. In fact the operation had been completely unnecessary. Dermod felt, rightly I suppose, that his colleague ought to know what he had done. He told him; it can't have been an easy thing to say, or to hear. The feelings of Dermod's colleague were so strong that he replied with his fist. For a moment it seemed that the two physicians would come to blows. The worst did not happen, Dermod's assailant calmed down (perhaps the Hippocratic oath forbids fisticuffs) and peace on I know not what terms was restored. Dermod, though surprised was also amused, and told his sad story with art and with humour. I never saw him 'put out' in anything.

One side of his activities was for years unknown to me: he sailed a small boat and seemed positively to enjoy perils and discomforts that many people would have given much to avoid. He wrote a book about his adventures in small boats. I read it and enjoyed it enormously. I wanted to tell him how good it was but he unexpectedly died before I could do so.

I return to Desmond himself. My first clear memory of him must date from about 1923. He came to lunch with Vanessa and I was there. I asked for something from Vanessa, he intervened and I got it. 'Were *you* spoiled as a child?' she asked. 'I was ruined; I remember my mother saying: "You *can't* spoil that child."'

Then he asked what I was reading. I was reading Sherlock Holmes. He adopted the voice of some elderly pedant who bids young people never to lay their Virgil aside. 'My boy,' he said, 'keep up your Holmes, don't neglect your Holmes as you grow older, so many young men do.'

I liked him very much but I didn't see much more of him for several years; sometimes when Rachel brought me to their house in Wellington Square I would find him. Once he astonished me by giving me half a crown so that I could get home, and once, commenting on Shaw's *Philanderer* which Rachel and I were to see that evening, he quoted those lines in which a character, on being told that an old friend is now a dramatic critic, replies: 'How jolly it must be to go to the theatre for nothing'. The bitterest lines, said Desmond, that were ever written for the stage.

I got to know him really well when in about 1938 I was admitted to the Memoir Club. I heard him read an account of his old and awful friend G.A. Paley, and I remember how, when Desmond mentioned that the MacCarthys might make a home next door to Paley, a despairing cry was heard. 'Oh no!' said Molly, and one knew just how much she had suffered. Molly was the founder and for many years the secretary of the Club. She was in a way a problem because fate, with hideous cruelty, had made her incurably deaf. She had to be placed at dinner and at the subsequent meeting in a position in which she might hear something even when, as usually happened, her hearing aid had broken down.

I remember one lovely evening, after the meeting was over, Desmond suggesting that we walk together. We passed some grand house and he pointed to it saying: 'That was my hide-out'. He told me then how he had played a rather cruel joke on Michael. They had come to that house. 'I must leave you here,' he said, pulled a key from his pocket, opened the door and vanished, leaving his son bewildered – and perhaps indignant – on the pavement.

'But Desmond, how did you manage it?'

Christabel Aberconway, a lady of great wealth but of diminutive intellect had written a novel; even she perceived that she was illiterate. She therefore turned for help to Clive and Desmond. According to Clive he did no more than delete the word 'and' which occurred about forty times on each page. Desmond's aim was more ambitious. He had, in effect to rewrite the book.

The Divine Gift by Christabel Aberconway was a literary curiosity. The story (which I have read) was silly beyond words but it was very well written. 'Surely', one of the reviewers exclaimed, 'Lady Aberconway should not be wasting her very considerable literary talent on rubbish of this kind'. Desmond must have been amused. He needed a private place for what was then a secret task. Lady Aberconway, in whose house there were many mansions, lent him a room and gave him the key.

You must imagine this story told in a leisurely way with some interruptions by me so that it took us very pleasantly to Pall Mall; here I made my way to the Reform Club while Desmond went next door to the Travellers'. At the doors of the Reform I halted. Desmond seemed to be in trouble; he was having some kind of difficulty with those rails which, we are told, were installed for the convenience of the aged Talleyrand. I went to look and found that Desmond was having an affectionate conversation with a cat.

What did he look like? I should know for, at the end of the war or just after it, he was frequently at Charleston, a guest much appreciated by the artists for he was always willing to sit for his portrait. He was placed upon a model's throne and from thence read to us, usually from Henry James. My own painting was not good, but I modelled his head in clay. Aesthetically the thing was not a great success, but it was a speaking likeness of Desmond as an old man. He was getting very bald and I was able to describe the extraordinary shape of his skull, but there is no point in further trying to put into words that which I have recorded in dimensions.*

Of his general appearance I speak with hesitation. Molly always

---

* This piece of sculpture now stands in the Library at Charleston

declared that her husband looked dreadfully shabby and I suppose that in the smart world which – rather to the sorrow of his unfashionable friends – he often frequented, he must have appeared untidy and perhaps ragged. Even Virginia found fault with his clothes, but that a man who looked like a scarecrow could have charmed the birds from the trees seems unlikely. I must admit that I am not an arbiter elegantiarum and I suppose that Molly was; she, to be sure, always looked and behaved like a perfect lady. I remember her lady-like consideration for the susceptibilities of the waiters at the Soho restaurant where the Memoir Club met. Discussing the size of a tip she spared their feelings by conversing in French. The fact that the waiters *were* French somewhat defeated her purpose, but the intention was admirable.

She and Desmond seemed in some ways ill-matched; she came from a refined home, she took the privileges and the duties of her class for granted and although she may not have believed in fairies she resembled her daughter in capacity for belief. She welcomed the discipline and the romantic authority of a church which, in this country, has a great appeal for the upper classes.

It was she who invented the term Bloomsbury and she is generally thought of as a member of that group. And yet she was at best a semi-detached member. A letter has recently come to light in which Vanessa and others implored her not to become wholly detached. In this her friends were successful. But it is also true that when she found herself in the promiscuous and libertarian society of Vanessa, Duncan, Maynard and Clive at Asham both she and they were disconcerted.

Desmond, who never lost the scepticism of Cambridge and was at ease in a libertarian society, seemed to belong altogether to Bloomsbury. Also, unlike Molly, he had political sympathies. As a boy he had a passion for Gladstone and had been moved by party political feelings when he rejoiced to see his leader ascend as he entered his home two steps at a time. He, or more probably a friend, had also witnessed the grand old man's rage and agony when hot soup acted cruelly upon his damaged eye. 'I had thought that *I, I* might have been spared the purgation of pain.' All of which made me suppose Desmond, with his Irish sympathies, a Gladstonian liberal. But in fact, although his political feelings were strong he seemed to have little interest in political action.

One evening at Charleston he described the fighting at the Four Courts, which he had witnessed and which had horrified him, as well it might; but what surprised us was his astonishment that such a thing could happen. Clive and I both felt that it was almost to be expected that those who fought for liberty should in the end fight one another. There were plenty of historical precedents, but Desmond seemed uninterested in history.

Clive, who delighted in Desmond's company, had one favourite story which he loved to repeat. Desmond had been invited by Wilfrid Scawen Blunt to shoot duck at Ampton. Desmond was a very poor shot and Blunt, knowing this, placed him in a station where large quantities of some very precious and peculiar breed would 'come over'. Now, as I know well, even a very bad shot sometimes has one of those days when he simply cannot miss. Desmond's performance was miraculous, his bag enormous and Blunt, who had only himself to blame, found it hard to be polite. This story pleased Clive even more than that of Desmond at Chatsworth rising late and meeting his hostess together with various other ladies, in a passage. It was Sunday morning and they were dressed for church. Desmond tried to slip past in his pyjamas, a brimming chamber-pot in his hand. Tolstoy it seemed, had said that emptying this was a service which no man should leave to someone else.

In writing about Desmond it is hard not to become over anecdotal; nevertheless I offer two more specimens because they also give a notion of Desmond's friend Max Beerbohm.

The first concerns a visit to Brighton by Max and Desmond. They shared a room in a hotel near the front. It was a fine morning and getting late when Max got up and looked out of the window. He called on Desmond to join him, but Desmond preferred to stay in bed. Max went on looking at the world outside and began to describe it. The sea that morning was calm, the parade almost deserted, out in the middle distance with her sails languidly flapping was a fishing boat, but the beauty of the scene was completed by the luminosity of the sea beneath a pure sky. Desmond could stand it no more, he leapt out of bed, joined Max at the window, looked out – and saw a blank brick wall.

The other incident took place at Rapallo. Here Max was the host and Desmond a visitor. When he arrived Max had to confess that there would be no room for Desmond, but one in an adjoining house was available. It was inhabited by a White Russian family and they could spare a room; they were very pleasant people with children and they would not disturb him at all; he could come and go as he pleased only would he please be careful not to make a noise when he went through the house at night?

Desmond meanwhile was getting more and more depressed. Why on earth couldn't Max have found a room for him at a hotel? Max interrupted his thoughts by saying: 'Dear Desmond, you have wonderful manners'.

It may well be that the reader does not find these stories as amusing as I did when Desmond told them. My transcription no doubt loses a great deal, but what you really miss is Desmond's voice; it is that which the world has lost.

10

Meetings with Morgan

THE GROWN-UPS had gone out and I was alone at Charleston. To be precise I was on the lawn in front of the house. From thence I could see anyone who came up the drive. Visitors, in those days, were rare but there were usually a few trippers who passed by on their way to Firle. We mistrusted trippers, therefore I looked with disapproval at a traveller whom I should probably have described as 'uninteresting' or 'unremarkable'. He approached slowly, stopped, opened the gate and asked whether he was at Charleston and, if so, were my parents at home.

I observed that he carried a bag and I think that he told me his name was Forster but it would have meant nothing to me. I was a schoolboy, not very well read, and socially unaccomplished. For all I knew he might have come to mend the 'independent' boiler which, as usual, was out of order. The last time a stranger had arrived at Charleston Roger Fry had taken him straight up to the WC and told him how to mend it. He turned out to be not the plumber but Lord Gage.

The visitor suggested that we go into the walled garden and there he began to talk. It soon became clear that he was not a plumber and, although I was still unable to place him, I had no difficulty in deciding that he was an extremely nice person. I record a fraction of our conversation.

He told me of a philosopher who was obsessed by one particular problem but was unable to find time in which to examine it thoroughly. When the war came he was sent to guard a warehouse. It was an easy but monotonous task. At last he had time in which to deal with the matter that obsessed him; he arrived at a conclusion, discovered that his life's work was done, and died.

We both laughed, although it was in a way a tragic story, but Morgan told it in his own way, a way calculated to amuse an adolescent. It was a rather 'grown-up' story, hence flattering and already I enjoyed flattery.

Afterwards, when the grown-ups had returned and the visit was over Clive told me that Morgan was our greatest living novelist. He appealed to Virginia to confirm his judgement and Virginia, after a moment's hesitation, agreed. I was also told that he had been considerably impressed by my ability to entertain an unexpected guest. I did not question the truth of this statement which made me even more self-satisfied than before.

Thereafter I saw him from time to time but always in company. When we did meet again tête-à-tête I was more or less grown up. We were travelling together from Lewes to London having met by chance on Lewes station platform. He had been staying with the Woolfs at Monks House and had much to say about Leonard. Leonard was an old friend; they had both been Apostles, Leonard had taught him to ride a horse – this was long ago, just before Morgan's first visit to India. Now he was enthusiastic about Leonard as a gardener. His gifts were, Morgan said, magical; he had a mysterious power over plants and animals. Under his care they prospered in an astonishing way, they multiplied, sprouted and flourished in abundance.

He said less, but interested me more, when he told me of what he intended to do when he got to London; there, it seemed, he enjoyed the company of the proletariat. I wanted to hear more about his life in a very unfashionable part of town but felt that it might be indiscreet to ask many questions.

When I did see him in London he was living in a perfectly respectable district, No. 26 Brunswick Square, and the talk was not of the proletariat but of T.E. Lawrence. His walls were covered at that time with pastel studies of the leaders of the Arab revolt by Eric Kennington. These I did not admire. At first sight the affinity between Morgan, a gentle and pacific character, and that great military leader seemed strange to me, but they were both attracted to persons of their own sex and both found that they needed sometimes to escape from eminent and public positions into a condition of sympathetic obscurity.

I found that Morgan did not want to discuss his own refuge which I think was somewhere south of the Thames. But presently he did give me a notion of the company that he kept, and I was considerably impressed.

In those days there was an Opera House in Charlotte Street called La Scala; it did indeed house opera but on the occasion to which I refer it was offering Chekhov. There was a place where one could promenade during intervals and here I met Morgan who introduced me to a friend, a handsome young man with natural good manners. Morgan left us and we talked about the play. Then, for some reason, I asked him what he did.

'I am a policeman,' he answered.

He was not very like my notion of a policeman and he seemed even less like one when he said, not without a certain modest pride, that he had never made an arrest.

'But if people misbehave, what do you do?'

'I reason with them, it always works.'

In those days our policemen really *were* wonderful.

We, by which I mean English-speaking people, usually explode in fits of laughter when we discover that *Howards End* is known to the French as *Le Legs de Mrs Wilcox*, but this is the least of the difficulties of the translator, after all the number of English people who read Morgan in French is small. In the 1930s Morgan was concerned with the French translation of T.E. Lawrence's *Seven Pillars of Wisdom*; an attempt had already been made in which the translator had rendered the warning cry of 'Snake! Snake!', with which irresponsible Arabs alarmed their comrades in the desert, as *'le cri du serpent'*. This, together with many other blunders, led Morgan to propose another translator. It was Roger Fry who suggested that Charles Mauron should translate *A Passage to India*, thus Morgan became his close friend. Charles found the *Seven Pillars of Wisdom* a long and difficult job but his work was, I am told, well thought of. (Charles, and Marguerite Yourcenar, are still considered Morgan's best French translators.)

Morgan came to know Charles well and was perhaps, after Roger, the most welcome guest at St Rémy. For a time I tried to assist in the translation of *The Longest Journey*; this must have been around 1950 and by that time Charles was completely blind. It was an instructive occupation. It taught me something about Morgan as a writer and something also about French usage. *The Longest Journey* is a chaste work, nevertheless Charles found certain passages which, if literally translated, could appear vulgar and obscene. We were also faced by certain phrases which presented very great difficulties. Take, for instance, ' "I like our new lettering," he said thoughtfully. The words "Stewart Ansell" were repeated again and again along the High Street – curly gold letters that seemed to float in tanks of glazed chocolate.'

It was the final phrase which puzzled Charles; I am not sure that it may not puzzle some of my readers. Can one still find those glossy fascia boards which used to be common enough on English shop fronts and which Morgan has indeed very beautifully described? Charles had not seen them; he was perplexed by the 'tanks of glazed chocolate' and I found them hard to explain in words. A drawing might have been useful, but not to a blind man.

How we ultimately conveyed this phrase I do not remember. I never knew what Morgan himself thought of that translation or indeed whether he indulged in the instructive pastime of reading one's own words in a foreign tongue.

I don't think that I saw much of him during the years leading up to the Second World War. I heard a good deal about his political activities at that time but they did not touch my own and it was not until the war had begun that Morgan once more visited Charleston.

In that very cold winter of 1939/40 Morgan came to stay at Monks House. The Woolfs were, very properly, economizing on fuel. Morgan felt that they were really too economical. His bedroom was served by a thing called a 'Cozy stove', adequate at most times but in that bitter season not cosy enough. Poor Morgan crouched over it, but found it inadequate even when, in his efforts to keep warm, he set his trousers on fire.

When he came on to Charleston he was rather less enthusiastic than usual about Monks House. With his left trouser leg carbonized he cut a rather pathetic figure. In addition to the usual Charlestonians he found there Raymond Mortimer. Now Raymond, perhaps the most intimate of Clive's men friends and a constant visitor to Charleston, was a stylish figure. If *he* had burnt his trousers there would have been plenty of alternative pairs, all beautifully pressed and smartly angular, in his well-stocked suitcase.

Naturally Morgan's misadventure was discussed; then, for the first time in my experience at Charleston, there was a general discussion of men's clothes. It was not a very friendly discussion. Raymond did not hide his opinion of Morgan's taste in dress (it was certainly unadventurous). Morgan did hide his opinion of Raymond's smart wardrobe, but one got the impression that he was holding his fire. Instead he let Vanessa speak up for him. She declared that Morgan's clothes had the merit of simplicity while Raymond – she didn't quite say it – was vulgar. Clive spoke up for Raymond; altogether dinner was not a great success.

After dinner I went upstairs, as I usually did, to write. Was it then that I began to plan my first published work *On Human Finery*? Possibly, but whatever it was, it was interrupted by Vanessa calling out: 'The house is on fire! This time it's serious.' It was serious.

Somewhere behind the boiler at the far end of the hall where there is now a head by Marcel Gimond, there was a crevice through which one could look into a large hollow space; this lay between the hall and the kitchen. Here there was a fearful and formidable blaze. The space was contained by glowing walls of red-hot timber and lively flames. The crevice, which we tried in vain to enlarge, provided the only access to the fire and it was through this that we attempted to throw or spurt water. While some of us did this others used the telephone, recently installed, to call the fire brigade. By the time they arrived we had just succeeded in extinguishing the flames which gave way to a great volume of smoke and steam. I should mention that our two guests brought pails of water from the kitchen.

The firemen finished the job, demolishing a great deal of the brickwork and turning their hose upon the dying fire. Meanwhile the disagreement between Morgan and Raymond was forgotten. Our rescuers – I think there were six of them – all fine young men and very amiable, were invited to rest and to refresh themselves. Beer was produced in generous quantities; Morgan and Raymond joined them. I don't know how the evening ended for the rest of us went to bed, but clearly our guests were going to enjoy themselves.

*

Q. 'It seems to me, Morgan, that you were near but not exactly *in* Bloomsbury.'

M. 'What makes you think that?'

Q. 'Well, you preferred Beethoven to Mozart.'

M. (smiling) 'Ah, but I was young then.'

That is the only scrap of information that I can retrieve from a meeting with Morgan in 1970, and it was irrelevant. I had come to talk to him about Virginia, whose biography I was trying to write. He was living with old friends, the policeman whom I had met before and the policeman's wife who, like her husband, was an interesting character. I was told by others that she was the most popular woman in Coventry since Lady Godiva. She had, it seems, distinguished herself by her courage, intelligence and enterprise during the terrible bombardment of Coventry in 1941. They were both obviously devoted to Morgan and it was pleasant to find him in a refuge at once comfortable and sympathetic; it was there that he died.

It was pleasing that he was happy amongst friends, for he was now getting very old, but in terms of research my visit was a failure. At first Morgan did not want to talk about Virginia and when he did talk of her he said nothing that was not already pretty well known.

I saw him again on his eightieth birthday, but I don't think he saw me. It was at King's; Noel Annan was our host and made an admirable speech. There was a large and distinguished company including, as was proper, a strong delegation from India.

A Passage to India is not my favourite amongst Morgan's novels, but it did make me think in a new way about the British Raj. From an early age I had a vast admiration for the works of Rudyard Kipling, an admiration which I once discussed with Morgan and which he shared, although with some reservations. I suppose that I also had some misgivings about Kipling's politics, but at all events I was convinced that the British had – despite some lapses – done a great deal of useful work in India – an opinion which was reinforced by what I knew of the work of Stracheys, Stephens etc. in the subcontinent. The British had brought the blessing of good government and naturally the governed would be grateful. It was in making this assumption that I erred.

Morgan would not have denied the practical virtues of the British. He gives his hard-working civilian the virtues of sincerity and industry but not much else; we cannot be surprised that his efforts to be just do not earn him the affection of the people. But far more interesting and crucial to his argument, Mr Fielding, the friend of the Indians and their advocate and champion, finds eve· hen he befriends and genuinely likes an Indian that there is an invisible barrier.

' "We shall drive every blasted Englishman into the sea, and then ..." he concluded, half kissing him, "you and I shall be friends." '

It is a simple and, as it seemed to me, a convincing argument. With the best will in the world one cannot love an alien ruler and the fact (if it be a fact) that the ruler is wise, enlightened and liberal-minded does not endear the ruler to the ruled; indeed it may be an additional cause of irritation.

This Morgan made clear to me and to thousands of others; slowly but surely he changed public opinion, so that while Churchill talked of collecting the women and children and if necessary fighting our way to the sea, India was liberated and we parted as friends. It was one of the greatest achievements of the Attlee government. That wise abdication was I believe made possible by Morgan.

I I

The Stracheys

'I HAVE DONE with the French, I will have no more of them.' The speaker was Miss Dorothy Strachey; the time was September 1899. Captain Dreyfus had again been condemned.

When she recalled these words Dorothy had for about thirty years been the wife of the French painter Simon Bussy. She was the friend and the translator of André Gide, also an important intermediary between French and British literary culture.

It had, as she admitted, been a rash statement but it was not, as I had supposed, the outburst of an inexperienced girl. Dorothy was born in 1866, the third child of that fertile pair, Sir Richard and Lady Strachey. In 1899 the momentous educational experience at Les Ruches, an adventure which Dorothy was later to use in her long short story *Olivia*, was a thing of the past; she was living at home, nearing middle age, caring for her many juniors and in particular for young Lytton. Also, as it now appears, she was tragically involved with a platonic lover of whom she never spoke, except in a letter to Gide, who had left her broken-hearted. It was, I imagine, on the rebound from that hidden passion that she fell into the arms of Simon Bussy.

When she first saw him he was invisible. This may sound a little Irish, but in fact he was muffled in bandages; when these were removed she would have found a pugnacious looking little man with very bright, intelligent eyes. He had nearly lost his sight – and that would have indeed been a tragedy – while he was cooking a meal upon a petroleum stove and it exploded.

In hospital, surrounded by incomprehensible foreigners and

distressed by incomprehensible regulations, his condition, already miserable, grew desperate. Somehow his despair became known to the Strachey family. It was decided – probably by Lady Strachey – that a young cousin (it was Duncan Grant) should go to John Singer Sargent, at that time the most celebrated painter in London, and tell him that a young and promising French artist was alone and very unhappy in a London hospital. Could Mr Sargent do anything for him?

He certainly could: brushing matrons and nurses aside he made his way to the bed where the young artist lay, heard his story, met, crushed, charmed and impressed the people in authority so that henceforward M. Bussy was treated like royalty. He soon recovered and was able to accept an invitation from the Stracheys at Lancaster Gate.

Simon Bussy was the son of a cobbler in Dôle, where he received his first training in drawing; in 1890, when he was twenty, he was admitted to the Ecole des Beaux Arts. Here, in the studio of Gustave Moreau, his companions were, amongst others, Matisse and, I think, Rouault.* Matisse was to remain his friend and to receive his advice for the rest of his life.

Simon was one of those painters who command the respect of other painters and of a few art critics, but who remain unnoticed by dealers and patrons. And yet he did not lack power. Looking at his earlier work it is clear that he had studied Degas and perhaps Cézanne to some purpose. He had gifts which might not only have pleased but excited the world. His early portraits are complex, highly and successfully organized. But although he had qualities which would have placed him among the *fauves* he preferred to cultivate his '*petite sensation*', and this led him to the minute study of isolated objects – a fish, a lizard, a bird. These he described very carefully with a perfect understanding of their shapes and with an uncompromising use of pure local colour, exactly as anyone might see them, anyone that is who could examine them with endless patience and affection. To the careless observer he seemed as dull as virtue, so perfectly honest that it hurt.

In 1903 all this lay in the future but already he was considered a

---

*I had this from Simon himself, but the friendship is not mentioned in the catalogue: *Exposition Simon Bussy et ses amis*, Besançon, 1970

bad match for Dorothy. There were nine other Strachey children, four of them girls and very little money for anyone. Nevertheless the Bussys found a home which was exactly what they wanted in a most expensive part of France, that is to say at Roquebrune between Monte Carlo and Mentone. Here the Bussys spent the winter months; in the summer they came to London and about 1921 when I first began to know them they were our neighbours at 51 Gordon Square.

The Bussys had married in 1903 and their only child Jane-Simone, called Janie after her grandmother Lady Strachey, was born in 1906. In 1918 Dorothy fell deeply in love with André Gide. He was forty-nine, she was fifty-two. The story of their one-sided love affair is recorded in a remarkable correspondence.

*

One day, when I was about six years old, an entirely new figure appeared upon the lawn of Wissett Lodge. It was a large, sprawling figure wearing a yellow waistcoat; in my imagination I likened it to some amphibious creature, a frog or a newt, but on a heroic scale, a creature with long limbs who blinked at the world through black-rimmed spectacles and when questioned uttered a faint croak. It was called Lytton. I found him very amiable.

I saw him again three years later at Charleston. We boys had been promoted, allowed that is to join the grown-ups for dinner. By this time I knew something about him. Our cousins, Michael and Peggy Bell, had mentioned his name; he had it appeared been denounced as a scoundrel by one of their grown-up friends, for he, Lytton, had written a book called *Eminent Victorians* 'which blackened the reputation of decent and distinguished people'. This sounded fun; we looked forward to his appearance with pleasure and here he was drinking soup at our table. How, I wondered, would he deal with it? It was thick white soup. How would it get past his beard? He seemed unaware of the difficulty and then, sure enough, he had a thick snowy growth on his upper lip. Did he realize how absurd he looked? Perhaps he did for with one deft wipe with his napkin he removed it, whereupon Vanessa said to him: 'Lytton, how do you like being famous?' He considered this briefly and then, with what sounded like an expiring croak he replied: 'Vaguely pleasant'.

In the early 1920s the Strachey family arrived to join Maynard

Keynes and the Bells in Gordon Square. Lady Strachey, with a contingent of daughters, came to No. 51, the two top floors of the house being reserved for the Bussy family. Lytton also found a room in the Square, as did James, his younger brother, and James's wife Alix; these two analysed patients at No. 41 while another couple Adrian and Karin Stephen (my uncle and aunt) did likewise at No. 50 where we also lived. Raymond Mortimer was at the end of the Square and presently the Woolfs established themselves together with the Hogarth Press nearby in Tavistock Square. Bloomsbury then gained a geographical reality which it lacked hitherto.

As children we sometimes played the annoying but not too mischievous game of 'parcel post'. Neat little packages were thrown on Sunday mornings from the top windows of No. 50 to lie, conspicuous and tempting, on the pavement below. Passers-by, often immaculately dressed Irvingites on their way to worship in the Catholic Apostolic church on the other side of the Square, would sometimes stop and gaze at these innocent looking parcels; usually they would kick them into the gutter before picking them up and examining them more closely, then, at last, yielding to curiosity, they would break the seals, violate the tissue paper wrapping and find a saucy message and/or a handful of rubbish. The whole thing would be thrown back angrily into the gutter. We always hoped we would catch someone we knew, a Keynes, a Bell or a Strachey, an aunt or uncle, but they did not seem to be abroad on Sunday morning.

To us at No. 50 it seemed that the culture of the 1920s was all around us, but it was different at No. 51. In place of the Cézannesque still-lifes, white walls, Grant and Bell decorations, clean abstracts and other modernities, one found a dark hall with a notice board which told one which Stracheys were in and which were out; somewhere in the gloom one perceived a signed photograph of Joseph Joachim complete with violin, on the first landing hung Robert Browning with an appropriate quotation, beyond him the armorial achievements of the Strachey family with another appropriate quotation (in Latin). It was not until you reached the top of the house that you were reminded of the twentieth century by a big fauve portrait of Janie Bussy by her father, a very fine picture.

But if the nineteenth century predominated upon the lower storeys of No. 51 it was a particularly poetical, musical and eccentric aspect of that century. It was said that at meal times the Strachey children devoured literature; each Strachey had a book and guests were left virtually tête-à-tête with Lady Strachey. I gather that when the conversation was not literary it was musical. Mrs Bartle Grant (Duncan's mother) recollected a scrap of conversation overheard when two Stracheys were leaving a concert hall: 'My dear, *did* you hear that F sharp?'

In *Howards End* Morgan Forster has left a notion of the Stracheys at home, but what one remembers is their way of speaking; one needs some form of musical notation faithfully to reproduce the peculiar character of the Strachey voice. A tiny echo thereof may still sometimes be heard when Frances Partridge speaks but otherwise, so far as I know, it is now mute.

About this time, that is to say in the early 1920s, I was walking every morning in the company of the girl next door, who was Janie Bussy, to an address in Mecklenburg Square. Here Miss Rose Paul educated us. She was in some way connected with the Stracheys. She was a Hellenist who had taught boys at Owen's School, Islington, until there were no boys left who attempted to learn Greek. She remained connected with the school through its headmaster Mr Cholmeley; the connection had I gather been romantic but was now so ancient as to be respectable. What Janie learnt from her I do not know. Dorothy had wanted her to be taught to write a précis and complained that Miss Paul had failed her. When she left, Miss Paul congratulated Janie upon her mathematical ability which was indeed considerable. Me she taught a little French and the history of Athens from the time of Marathon to the end of the Peloponnesian war.

I am afraid that poor Janie found me a great trial, not when we were with Miss Paul, but during the walks to and from Mecklenburg Square. It was not a long walk; we went through the rather squalid areas around Marchmont Street and then into St George's Gardens, which had once been a cemetery; there we would stop to look at the tomb of Anna Cromwell, the Protector's daughter. It was not a spectacular monument, but we both liked it and would pause to admire it on our way. Thus for a moment it brought us together, but there was not much else to do so; we were a strangely assorted pair.

Clive called Janie a '*jolie laide*'; certainly she was never in any regular sense a beauty, but she always looked distinguished. She had her father's little black button eyes and yet they could become beautiful when she spoke or smiled. She had her mother's hump, but also a delicacy of articulation, a sinuous grace which reminded one of the odalisques of Ingres. She carried herself and she dressed with wonderful simplicity; she stepped over the London pavements like a fastidious cat.

I was about ten years old and very fat, my hair was red and so was my face. My clothes were stretched almost to bursting point by the nearly impossible task of keeping abreast with my rotundity. My socks were in a state of semi-permanent collapse. As for my boots they were at once decrepit and volatile, as Vanessa once found when she approached our front door and one of them came sailing through the air to land at her feet. The condition of the boot went some way to explain its eccentric behaviour. The boot laces, often broken and mended with string or wire, had become deeply involved, entangled, and finally absorbed by the boot proper, while this had become so deformed that the thing had to be put on as though it had been a slipper. It was taken off in the same way, but sometimes as in the present instance, with an impatient kick which sent it flying through the window (which luckily was open) to fall into the street below.

It will be understood that I was hardly a proper companion for any respectable person, let alone a rather shy, very carefully adorned young lady. And so we gazed at Anna Cromwell's tomb in silence and found very little to say to each other on the way back to Gordon Square. And presently Janie went back to France and I went to school and several years passed during which I saw nothing or very little of the Bussy family.

But there were other Stracheys. I was once taken into a half-darkened room and introduced to a lady all in black whom I knew to be Lady Strachey; but far more important was my introduction to the youngest of her daughters, Marjorie. Marjorie was asked to teach me to play the piano. Perceiving at once that I should never learn to play she also observed that when I struck a wrong note, as I usually did, I found the effect so painful that I would give up in despair. From this she argued that I might not be entirely devoid of natural taste. She made me understand a little of what *Fidelio* was about, she made me listen to Leonora No. 3, she took me to concerts, she made Schumann's *Kinderzehnen* moving and exciting.

Sadly, she couldn't take me very far for I was soon taken away from London, but she gave me a greater appetite for music and did something to satisfy it. She also gave me an example of really efficient teaching.

She gave me another about thirty years later. At this time I was myself teaching art at a girls' school in Lewes; here my 'studio' was separated from a music room by a partition so thin that I could hear everything next door. In this way I was able to hear singing lessons taking place which did not arouse my enthusiasm. But one day when I was making preparations for an art class (this in my opinion is the one essential thing in art teaching), I heard Marjorie give a lesson on the Risorgimento. It was not a very scholarly performance. But Marjorie was enthusiastic: she had no use for the Austrians and the Ultramontanes and at first I, who do not share the Victorian belief in nationalism, listened unsympathetically to her expressions of contempt for 'that beast Napoleon III', and also to her enthusiasm for Garibaldi. But Marjorie's enthusiasm was infectious: she made the whole struggle seem real, she echoed the sentiments of the Brownings and of the English zealots for the Italian cause with such force and so persuasively that I was seduced; yes, Napoleon III *was* a treacherous beast. And although I complained later that she ought to give the other side of the picture (as I believe she did) I was deeply impressed by her ability to bring history to life.

Marjorie was indeed a wonderfully effective teacher, this despite the fact that her very 'Strachey' voice could put people off. But it wasn't her voice, it was her face that was her misfortune. The Stracheys were not a beautiful family, but one can believe that, when young, Dorothy had a certain charm. Marjorie when young was, to judge by photographs, a fright. There was something cruel about the manner in which fate had treated her: her talents were all for teaching and persuading, just a little outward charm would have helped her so much. And yet she had the courage to hold and even to enrapture an audience by exploiting her very ugliness. That she could sing, dance and recite proves her courage, but there was something almost inconceivably brave about her resolve to make herself look really atrocious. I once saw her rehearse a performance clad in black tights into which she had forced a bright scarlet cushion suggestive of some indecent deformity. Thus clad she danced across the floor and sang nursery rhymes, or what had been nursery rhymes, until Marjorie converted them by her manner and her innuendoes into something unspeakably sinister and macabre. When, in the middle of this outrageous performance, a corner of the scarlet cushion began to slip down between her black silk-stockinged legs the effect was overwhelming.

That particular performance was delivered to the wrong audience. Cultivated ladies from Hampstead and Kensington who had come to be entertained by Miss Strachey were bewildered, shocked and horrified. Finally most of them left the room. But younger and more hardened spectators were delighted. If one could take it, it was well worth taking.

Vanessa once said of Marjorie that she was the best, the most moral person whom she knew and I am inclined to agree with her; she always seemed to me to be entirely without malice or ill-temper although she could be moved to fury by any kind of cruelty or injustice. Her sister Dorothy resembled her in this – but I do not think she would have much cared for Marjorie's nursery rhymes; she, Dorothy, seemed to belong to an earlier generation.

I did not know Dorothy at all well until about 1935 but her daughter Janie was a fairly constant visitor at Charleston in the late 1920s. She was then Julian's friend rather than mine for not only was he nearer her age but they were more interested in and better read than I in both French and English literature. I could talk only about painting, nor did I know much about that. Janie then would talk with Julian about Pope or Heredia while giving some time to Clive with whom she cultivated a decorous flirtation. Our daily walks from Gordon Square to Mecklenburg Square and back hardly constituted a link. In fact it was not until after I had attempted to educate myself on the top of an alp that I got to know all the Bussy family well.

In the autumn of 1934 I was advised to spend the winter by the Mediterranean. It was welcome advice for I was attempting to write something about the principality of Monaco and the Bussy family were living within easy walking distance of that tiny state.

In preparing for my sojourn *chez* Bussy at Roquebrune I realized that I should be staying with people much better educated than I; it was a little terrifying but it might be salutary. In only one respect did I feel that I might be better informed than my hosts. At that time young people in England were discovering that they were political animals: they read the *Daily Worker*, they read John Strachey, they even read Marx. I considered myself quite as well read as my English friends. As for the highly cultivated, extremely well-read Bussys, they had always seemed to me to live in a rarified atmosphere, they were above politics and probably had never even heard of Karl Marx. I was completely wrong.

Dorothy was an intelligent, amusing, open-minded person, an ambassador of culture, as much at home with French as with English literature; exceptionally gifted, she seemed the type of the fair-minded English liberal. In fact she was a communist and a follower of Trotsky. She described him to André Gide as 'one of the greatest people the world has ever produced.'* I think that Dorothy had been swayed by her daughter, although Gide may have also influenced her; this was the time when he was flirting with and later rejecting Stalinism. Who influenced whom I do not know. Janie herself once described her sudden passion for the great heretic Trotsky: she saw his image on a cinema screen and, in a sense, fell in love with him rather in the manner of Paul on the road to Damascus. Janie herself would certainly have rejected this comparison and indeed I would not suggest it if I could at all rationalize her conversion. I can only say that she did in fact develop an interest in the creator of the Fourth International and devoted her very considerable intellect to the study of Marxist theory.

There were many enthusiasts who were content to read John Strachey and the Communist manifesto of 1848; those who like me could claim to have read *Das Kapital* from cover to cover tended to be rather smug about it, but Janie was familiar with *The Theses on Feuerbach*, Lenin's *Empirio Criticism* and much else which, because it was in German or Russian, was unknown to me. What was more, she thoroughly understood what she read. I remember one occasion when I giggled at a remark by Engels in *Anti-Dühring*. Engels had been accused of tampering with the virginity of the square root of minus one. She pointed out that Engels was in fact at fault and explained the matter so clearly that for a few moments I actually understood the maidenly qualities of that non-entity.

We argued incessantly, though amicably, but on a battlefield

---

*Dorothy Bussy to André Gide, 12 November 1936

which was new to me. In England I was accustomed to being denounced as a bourgeois social democrat by Yvonne Kapp who was also, in her way, a very convincing and formidable opponent, but at La Souco I faced a learned expert who condemned both me and my British adversaries. It was disconcerting but, in a way, exhilarating. For me the arguments were always coloured by my feeling that a comrade should be politically active. Yvonne was magnificently active; Janie, despite her intellectual brilliance, seemed no more than a parlour communist; that was an opinion which I was obliged later to revise.

Simon Bussy had been in left-wing politics long before the Russian Revolution, but although he continued to hold 'progressive' political opinions he said little about them. Indeed usually he seemed not to want to say much about anything. But he had an old friend in Nice who could make him loquacious. One Sunday morning, soon after my arrival at La Souco, Dorothy remarked that she would not be surprised if Matisse were to come over from Nice in time for tea.

For me it was rather as though she had said: 'I daresay Jesus Christ will drop in after lunch.' I had been vaguely aware that Simon knew Matisse, but somehow I had not supposed that he would come round for tea as though he were an ordinary human being. For me, indeed, he was no ordinary human being, but rather a very extraordinary superhuman being. I have compared him by implication with the second person of the Trinity; I will push the comparison no further than to say that in his painting there did seem to me a divine element, and if one may imagine a deity who worked in oils on canvas then he would have been something like Henri Matisse. It will therefore be easily imagined that when the noise of doors opening and voices informed me that I shared a roof with him, my emotions were formidable. Not that I could be at all precise in my anticipations; fate had placed me fairly close to ringside and I believed that I could recognize a champion on sight, but equally it had taught me that great men are great in many different ways. Matisse would clearly be gigantic, but he might also be a surprise.

He was.

When I opened the drawing-room door I concluded that there had been some silly mistake. The guest who was discussing the weather with the Bussy family was indeed a 'fine figure of a man', comfortably plump, fairly tall, his person assisted by an excellent tailor, and altogether very carefully trimmed. But of greatness I could see no trace. The chance visitor whom I had so absurdly supposed to be Matisse might well be eminent in the world of insurance or real estate, but he could not, surely, be the creator of *La Ronde*. Here a difficulty arose. I knew what Matisse looked like, there were photographs, there was a self-portrait – and these, absurdly but undeniably, referred to the amiable philistine to whom I was now being presented in terms which left no doubt that I was shaking the hand of the master himself.

The mind flies swiftly from one hypothesis to another. I realized that I was being crass. When Matisse explained that the average temperature of Nice was slightly higher (or it may have been slightly lower) than that of Mentone, there was some magic in his meteorology which I must have missed. If only I could rise to the height of his real meaning, that meaning which was too subtle for my apprehension, I should be enchanted. I tried to soar to his sublimities. It was hard work.

He soon forgot about the weather and turned to his usual topic, which was Matisse. I was not, and never became, a close friend; nevertheless, there were occasions when he did tell me something of his agonies. They were not the agonies of a creator; rather, they were the agonies of a dealer who held very valuable stock and felt that the market did not realize its full value. There were occasions when he alluded to the appalling fact that there were persons who had not understood that he was superior to other painters. He did actually shed tears over certain well-worn clippings, brought out from an inside pocket and re-read with indignation. These were tears not of self-pity but rather of pity for erring mankind which, with invincible ignorance, ventured to find fault with his art or – just as bad – bestowed too much praise upon Monsieur Picasso. He was a painter of undoubted talent but one whose pictures suffered from the irredeemable fault of not having been painted by Henri Matisse.

Vanity was too feeble a word with which to describe the feelings of Matisse for Matisse. There was something candid, innocent and sincere about his approach to himself which entirely disarmed criticism – and, after all, that immense talent was genuine. But although the great man's adoration of himself was justifiable and, in its innocence, forgivable, nothing could make it an entertaining topic of conversation. The Bussy family, which had offered no comment until after I had met the master, took the view that Matisse was the greatest living painter, the greatest living egoist, and the greatest living bore. Why then did they continue to receive him Sunday after Sunday? Partly I think because he was Simon's oldest friend, partly because sometimes one did get a glimpse of the real Matisse. The Matisse with whom one attempted to converse *chez* les Bussy seemed like Henry James's poet – an unreal phantom who discussed trivialities downstairs while the real man was sitting in the room above writing immortal verse. Indeed, in a painter, such a division of the personality seems less improbable, for the art of painting is even further from the art of conversation than is that of poetry. Listening to Matisse talking about art and life, genius and talent, age and youth, all with particular reference to himself, one could indeed imagine the man of genius was somewhere else talking to himself in a pictorial language of almost incomprehensible beauty.

Of those sublime communications I heard nothing. Others who were closer to him may have been able to hear something in his talk as great as the things that he could say in paint. For my part, I was content and more than content when the great man could, for a moment, forget his greatness and chat in human tones. This did occasionally happen, as when Matisse would reminisce with Simon on life and larks at the Ecole des Beaux-Arts. At that time, it seems, one was either a mystic or an anarchist. Simon had been an anarchist. 'And what were you, Monsieur Matisse?' asked Janie. Unfortunately, the remark reminded the master of what he had become. He cleared his throat, filled his chest, and gathered around him an invisible cloak of sententious genius, before answering that when he was a young man it had seemed to him that there were already too many people trying to put brakes upon the progress of humanity, whereas now . . . 'Now,' interjected Janie, 'it is you who slam on the brakes.' The remark left Matisse spluttering in angry confusion. One would hardly have imagined from Janie's modest but masterly memoir that she would have been so impertinent, and indeed such interjections were very rare.

On another occasion, irritated by the memoirs of Alice B. Toklas, Matisse remarked that Mademoiselle Gertrude Stein could speak with no authority concerning the avant-garde in France because she knew far too little French, and on this subject he refused to be drawn into further comments. These little diversions from his usual theme did offer the hope that he could be interesting if not brilliant. And indeed one Sunday afternoon, forgetting himself in the happiest manner, he remembered something he had heard and seen. Could it have been in the South Pacific? And was it perhaps connected with the culture of pearls? It is exasperating that this sudden excursion, a simple and humorous story expressed without the slightest pomposity, should have vanished from my mind. We all agreed that it was a memorable afternoon and that Matisse had been charming.

I have said enough, I hope, to suggest that, so far as my own observation goes, Matisse was happier in his dealings with the muses than with his fellow human beings; perhaps one may conclude with a note on Matisse and the machine. This is hearsay, for when I knew him the great man was conveyed hither and thither by a chauffeur as befitted a potentate. But there had been a time when the master himself was at the wheel. I gather that he never actually made the complete journey from Nice to Mentone (it was all of ten miles); his progress was impeded by the fact that whenever he was approached or overtaken by another vehicle he pulled up on the pavement, at the same time stalling the engine. Even in those days there was quite a lot of traffic along the Côte d'Azur, so his progress was slow indeed. This was tiresome, but the spectacle of Matisse turning round on a busy and sinuous road, flanked on one side by a rocky wall and on the other by a precipice, stopping dead sometimes upon the verge and sometimes in the middle of the highway, and then starting again, with sudden impetuosity either forwards or in reverse, was too much for the nerves of anyone who loved Matisse or painting, not to speak of those of his passengers. I was told that he had never had a serious accident. The Fates, no doubt, treated him with proper respect.

Janie wrote a more extensive and better informed account of Matisse which was published in the *Burlington Magazine* and described some of the dramas in the life of the great man. Here I would like to add some notes on her own. I don't think there is much that I can add concerning the years between 1935 and 1939. We met quite frequently when the Bussy family was in London, and the old debates continued in an atmosphere of growing political gloom, but always with some gaiety. In one of those years Janie exhibited her paintings in London. I have one of those paintings: a quiet, sensitive, intelligent work but not vigorous, not a work of genius.

In 1940 the Bussy family was in Nice. It was not a good place in which to spend the war years. She wrote letters to us at Charleston throughout the occupation, sometimes using a false signature for of course they had to be censored. One could not tell what she was doing although one might guess. Nor was she much more informative when she got back to England. She had much to say about the comedies and tragedies of life, but it was only through others that I learned that she was in charge of a clandestine press and was in constant danger. If either of us was an armchair politician at that time it was I.

In the post-war years the Bussy family became reorganized; formerly it had been Simon and Dorothy who looked after an invalid daughter, now it was Janie who cared for her parents. Simon died in 1954. Six years later, on a memorable day when I saw New York for the first time, I received a letter telling me that Janie was dead. She had been overcome by the fumes of a geyser while taking a hot bath. Dorothy died two days later.

12

Ottoline Morrell

THERE HAVE BEEN many portraits of Ottoline. Most of them are feeble and misleading, but there is one to which I must allude: it is by Simon Bussy and it hangs in the National Portrait Gallery. Unlike the photographs it gives one a vivid and decorative account of her face – the most remarkable face that I have ever seen. Alas, Simon gives us no more than that; if only he could have described her from the hem of her skirts to her topmost plumes what a masterpiece he might have produced! Also, he might have forestalled much that I now want to say, or perhaps to repeat, for I have already written a little about that remarkable woman.

One encountered Ottoline as one might encounter an abstract painting: one admired the colours, the *matière*, the disposition of forms, one was amazed by the brilliance and the audacity of the composition, it was all stupendous, gorgeous, a little overwhelming and highly dramatic. Her voice was in a sense musical, she roared like any sucking dove, rolling her words along her vast Hapsburg jaw in a thrilling manner as became so majestic a figure. But to me it seemed that her manner was more interesting than her chatter; when carefully considered one found that her remarks were not very profound. Some of her distinguished friends may have stimulated her to brilliance; I could not do likewise.

Miranda Seymour in a long and sympathetic biographical study leaves us with a picture which, despite some bad draughtsmanship, seems to me convincing.* She makes Ottoline appear a well-

---

*Miranda Seymour, *Ottoline Morrell: Life on the Grand Scale*, Hodder & Stoughton, 1992.

disposed and certainly not a wicked woman, deeply religious, rather stupid and decidedly dull. It was perhaps a certain incongruity between her outward appearance – which suggested stupendous dramatic possibilities – and her banal pronouncements which led to confusion. One judged her, perhaps unfairly, as a fraud. Clearly she had an appetite for distinguished society and although her husband could hardly have satisfied this need she did attract some extremely remarkable men; perhaps in their company she could reflect a brilliance which the rest of us were unable to elicit.

> We have just got to know a wonderful Lady Ottoline Morrell, who has the head of a Medusa; but she is very simple and innocent in spite of it, and worships the arts.*

This was the beginning of Bloomsbury's connection with Ottoline. Miranda Seymour is, as might be expected, very severe on Bloomsbury which, so she tells us, was guilty of assassinating Ottoline's character. But when she talks of Bloomsbury what does she mean? When faced by that elusive entity she, like so many others, fails to inspire confidence.

> The two main families of the Bloomsbury Group were the Stracheys and the Stephens. The strongest influence in the formation of the group in its earliest days were the Apostles, male members of the elite and secretive Cambridge discussion group to which Vanessa and Virginia Stephen had been introduced by their brother, Thoby, before his early death in 1906 [sic].†

In fairness it must be said that Ms Seymour does not usually write like this or stray so far from the facts. She believes that Bloomsbury disapproved of Ottoline because she was religious; she forgets that atheists have a much better reputation for tolerance than Christians and that those who could accept the piety of T.S. Eliot would hardly object to that of Ottoline.

But we never do discover who belonged to this band of assassins, or rather who did not. I doubt whether Ottoline knew Saxon Sydney-Turner, E.M. Forster or Marjorie Strachey well enough to

*Virginia Woolf to Madge Vaughan, May 1909.
† Seymour, p. 76.

find in them friends or they a victim. Her great champion in Bloomsbury was Maynard Keynes, also perhaps Desmond MacCarthy. But it is Duncan Grant who, according to Ms Seymour, was Ottoline's main supporter and 'defended her from mockery whenever an opportunity to do so arose'. Duncan certainly had opportunities to defend Ottoline from mockery; whether he can be said actually to have taken them is another matter. I heard him tell several stories about Ottoline; of these I publish one for it does show the lovely innocence of her mind. In telling it Duncan imitated, as he very beautifully could, the unique quality of Ottoline's voice. She had told him how, when coming home to Garsington after a long absence, the Morrells found a bird in the drawing room, 'and what do you think it was?' asked Ottoline. 'It was a cuckoo' – one must imagine that last word ending on a long drawn-out vowel – 'now wasn't that a strange thing to bring into the house? A cuckoo...'

It was indeed a strange thing to happen and a stranger story to tell. I had this from Duncan long after Ottoline's death, and this I think was the case with all the stories and jokes about Ottoline that I heard; they took the form of gossip, they were recorded in letters and diaries; no one wished to hurt Ottoline's feelings, no one in Bloomsbury that is. This is also true of Virginia for although she took 'people like Ottoline' as a point of departure for Mrs Dalloway, the portrait which she eventually drew is not, and was not intended to be, recognizable.

Aldous Huxley, Gilbert Cannan and D.H. Lawrence were not so polite, indeed they seem to have set out deliberately to wound the poor woman. It is a fact which critics of Bloomsbury would do well to ponder.

I first met Ottoline when I was about six. She came as a visitor to Wissett Lodge. Here, it was said by Vanessa, I used to follow her about the house making obscene gestures. I have no recollection of this but I do have a vivid memory of Ottoline's departure. I took one look at her sitting high above me in the trap that was to bear her away and burst into floods of tears by saying: 'What's all that for?' The grown-ups explained that I was overcome by grief when I realized that she was to leave. In fact I was moved by a more complicated emotion.

Let me try to explain. During her sojourn in Wissett Ottoline had dressed – for her – quietly. Wissett was a place where the inhabitants lived simple and on the whole industrious lives; splendour was out of place. But when Ottoline was travelling she was clad in full regimentals, or at least she was that morning. She was wearing odd clothes, gorgeous but dilapidated, priceless brocades which, having become semi-detached, were fastened perilously with magnificent jewels and safety pins; the eye travelling upwards was dazzled by a glittering multitude of pearls and, still ascending, one found Ottoline's face. In itself magnificently improbable, it was now painted with a reckless abandon such as J.M.W. Turner gives us when describing a sunset; then came a shock of golden hair and more pearls until at last she exploded heavenwards in a soaring confusion of nodding ostrich feathers.

With all this overwhelmingly splendid finery perched high above me upon the frail structure of the trap I felt – although I could not then find words for it (I still find it hard) – that the laws of nature had been annulled, that I was as they say 'seeing things'. I howled as I would have howled if an earthquake had hit the house – in a sense it had.

Ottoline as a guest was difficult. When she had gone Vanessa burst out, saying that her visit had nearly destroyed us. 'I've decided that woman isn't for me. I hope I shall never spend more than a few hours in her presence again – or at the most one weekend a year. This is final. Not,' she added characteristically, 'that I dislike her'. Miranda Seymour overlooks this qualification but it was important; Vanessa was an exacting hostess and there were many people of whom she disapproved as guests but whom she would accept easily in other situations. Thus it was that a few months later Julian and I found ourselves at Garsington.

Julian – Ottoline's daughter – must at some point have been put more or less in charge of us. We were enlisted in a game in which she pretended to be the corpse of a princess, a walking corpse attended by the rest of the party who were employed as priests, mourners etc. I myself was supposed to march with downcast head behind the imaginary catafalque. It seemed to me a damned silly game. But I was vaguely aware that the garden was lovely, even in winter, less extensive but more beautiful than Seend. Of the house and its inhabitants I can remember nothing. I do recollect the story of a peacock which died a natural death and then appeared roast at table. I feel reasonably sure that this was pure myth.

Miranda Seymour continues: 'Vanessa's children were encouraged to perform parodies of her [Ottoline] before audiences which consisted principally of Ottoline's friends.'* I have no recollection of these performances nor do I think that I or my brother had the kind of histrionic talent which would have made such things possible. The origins of this fantasy may be found in Virginia's diaries dated 20 September 1927, eleven years after the events that we have been considering, when my sister (aged nine) 'rigged up in a long black shawl, acted Lady Cornflax & Lady Ottoline at Charleston'. Her performance was charming but had not much to do with either of these ladies. I am sure Ottoline would not have been in the least distressed if she had been present. Angelica gave us an idea of how a great lady looked and behaved in company as a nine year old might have imagined her; it was in no sense a parody.

For me Ottoline was at that time a memory. I had not seen her, or I do not remember seeing her, during the fifteen years which had elapsed since that apocalyptic vision of 1916. It was not until the summer of 1931 that I was able to refresh my memory. At that time I inhabited a studio in Rome, in the via Margutta which skirts the Pincian. At times when I had money in my pockets I made my way to the Piazza di Spagna, turned into the via della Croce and turning right came to an excellent restaurant where the pasta was good and the bills tolerable and one ate under the shade of trees in a pleasant garden. Here too was congenial company: Eddie, now Sir Edward Playfair, Jimmy Sheehan, then celebrated as a war reporter, Duncan, Alberto Moravia, Philip (Pipsy) and his wife Ottoline.

In that distinguished company I found myself, or at least considered myself, grown up. I had sense enough however to realize that I must be an observer rather than an important contributor to the conversation, and as such I devoted much of my attention to Ottoline. We were fifteen years older but I was now capable of seeing that even in her late maturity Ottoline had a certain erotic appeal; also, despite the fact that here, as in any company, she was the most remarkable component, as a conversationalist she could hardly be considered brilliant. She remained of course a memorable sight and whereas in London, or even at Garsington, she could hardly fail to appear exotic, here, in the eternal city, she was thoroughly at home.

---

* Seymour, p. 178.

Rome in fact seemed the proper habitation for Ottoline; it is an intrepid city, a city which may have been guilty of many things but never of timidity. What courage it must have taken to build the Coliseum, or Trajan's Column, St Peter's or indeed the Monumento Vittorio Emmanuele. Nor was it only in bricks and marble that the Romans were courageous: the exuberance of their architecture was echoed in their internal decoration. The ceilings of Fra Pozzo and Pietro da Cortona, for example, which rise from an imitation of the mouldings and ornaments of the church so cleverly counterfeited that the eye looks upwards to where holy personages, airborne amidst feigned architecture, fly through the heavens. We cannot tell where solid fact ends and illusion begins. Higher still a multitude of angels and putti soar to dizzy altitudes until at last in the highest heavens we observe the Holy Trinity. Very much, in fact what I observed at Wissett Lodge in the summer of 1916.

The atheistic tourist tends to regard the illusionism of the *seicento* with a limited enthusiasm; he sees in the vertiginous *trompe l'oeil* of the period no more than a technical *tour de force*. Compared to Poussin such pictorial conjuring tricks appear sufficiently trivial and considered as expressions of faith unconvincing, indeed like the liquefying blood of St Januarius it seems a mockery and a travesty of truly religious emotion.

But ecclesiastical art is, or was, the medium through which the churches explained religion to a poor and illiterate congregation. The people of Rome in the seventeenth century were certainly poor and in all probability illiterate. They took the baroque at face value; were they so very different in the year 1931? I doubt it.

It is said that when Lytton Strachey happened to arrive at Naples on Easter Sunday he caused a commotion. The 'better' class of people was shocked and turned away in disgust, but the *lazzaroni* greeted him joyously with a murmur of: 'Yea indeed he is risen'. May we venture to suppose that Ottoline unconsciously visited the inhabitants of the Trastevere in a rather similar manner?

Here, as far as I can remember them, are the facts. There were five of us: Ottoline, Duncan, Jimmy Sheehan, Pipsy and I. Ottoline and Duncan walked a few paces ahead. We in the rear moved slowly for Ottoline and Duncan had much to say to each other and sometimes came to a halt. We, the rearguard, kept our station, glad I daresay to pause for although it was late afternoon, the full heat of the Italian summer was beginning. Behind us was a group of urchins, waiting, it seemed, for the appropriate moment to beg for *soldi*.

Ottoline was dressed as though for a garden party. I cannot provide a full inventory of her finery, but there was an enormous hat crowned with plumage, a wealth of jewellery and, what struck one most forcibly, a train which raised a little cloud from the dust of the Trastevere. Presently I became aware that the children had been joined by a number of older people and then that these had been joined by a still larger throng. It was a perfectly civil crowd, but evidently excited. Why, one wondered, had it collected? It could not be anything to do with the perfectly ordinary and respectable people in the rear; it must be Ottoline. What did these people expect?

I did not think, despite the train, that Ottoline looked a figure of fun; there was something dignified, almost regal, about her appearance, nor did I hear any laughing from behind us. She was, simply, a magnificent spectacle and something astonishing. The Romans could have seen nothing like her since Queen Christina lay naked upon the roof of her Palazzo, or perhaps since the time of the Caesars. I felt that they were now expecting something – I knew not what, neither perhaps did they. I began to feel rather uneasy and so, manifestly, did Pipsy. Ottoline and Duncan on the other hand seemed perfectly unaware of an audience which was perhaps expecting a miracle. And how, if she did become aware of the popular emotion, would Ottoline react? I had heard stories of her unpredictable behaviour in crises, of how she slapped the face of a Conservative candidate when Pipsy lost a by-election. Would she do something dreadful – or perhaps something quite charming – if she became aware of her situation? I suspected that the crowd was moved by religious feelings and could be dreadfully disappointed; might we be lynched or torn to pieces? In fact I was scared.

And then, suddenly, simply, without the least fuss, the crisis was over. We came to the doors of the church – possibly Santa Maria in Trastevere – Duncan pulled back the leather curtain at the door; Ottoline went into the dark interior; we did likewise and the crowd did not follow us. I cannot remember what we did or said in the church. We remained for quite a long time and departed through another door into some kind of piazza where there was an aged *carozza*; the Morrells entered it and drove away. I think I went home by myself.

That momentary vision of Ottoline taking part in a scene in which her presence seemed entirely appropriate, but of which she was quite unconscious, was so splendid that later on I wondered whether it ever happened; and yet it did. It marked the high point of the story of Ottoline in Rome – that is to say the story as I saw it. What followed all seemed bathos.

In London I saw Ottoline from time to time; she asked me to Gower Street and there I sometimes had the pleasure of talking to Walter de la Mare, and various Irish men of letters. It was not very exciting; but there was Ottoline and she, as a spectacle, was always rewarding.

13

Ethel Smyth

VIRGINIA WOOLF DIED in 1941 and to many people it seemed that her reputation would die with her. The men and women who make opinions in universities, in the media, in editorial offices and upon other seats of judgement, condemned her. She was a snob, a rentier, she told malicious stories about her friends, she lived in Bloomsbury. It followed – for the moral purity of our censors is exquisite, their judgements rigorous – that Virginia Woolf was without talent and had better be forgotten. In the 'fifties and 'sixties it seemed that this advice had been heeded; like Bloomsbury itself, Mrs Woolf was dismissed. True, her publisher took a different view: he pointed out that her novels continued to sell very nicely thank you. But Leonard Woolf was clearly biased. Another voice, that of Desmond MacCarthy, was also raised, but so far as I know only in private. About a year after Virginia's death he prophesied that her reputation would slump. 'But', he added, 'there is a cyclical movement, and it will rise again.' He did not live to see how good a prophet he had been.

In the late 1960s I was engaged in writing Virginia's life. 'A pity', they said, 'that no one will be interested.' But presently it seemed that some people *were* interested and then it appeared that America, God bless her, was very much interested. This transatlantic rumour grew into a mighty roar which, crossing the oceans, has been picked up in this country and disseminated throughout the world. When therefore the *New Yorker* in March 1991 announced a revival of the kind of hostility towards Virginia and Bloomsbury with which I was so familiar 40 years ago, I suspected that Desmond's cycle was still turning. The same article also recorded that some sharp criticisms were coming from what might seem an unexpected source – the feminists. I found this interesting in that I had myself suggested that Virginia Woolf's feminism (she detested the word, but I can find no other) was not entirely suited to a modern feminist audience. Such an audience might rejoice in the argumentative power of *A Room of One's Own*, but the tone was too mild, too conciliatory. Virginia believed in tolerance, she believed in persuasion; in a word, she was unheroic. In 1938 she could say with proud assurance: 'scarcely a human being in the course of history has fallen to a woman's rifle'. Today that statement seems less unquestionably true, for today women in the United States and elsewhere have been armed and trained as soldiers. To what extent that development has been welcomed by American feminists I do not know, but certainly it would have been deplored by the author of *A Room of One's Own*. All of which leads me to wonder whether our transatlantic cousins might not now prefer a suffragette to a suffragist.

These terms require some words of explanation. The National Union of Women's Suffrage Societies, formed in 1897 under the leadership of Millicent Fawcett and usually referred to as 'suffragists', worked for the same reforms as the Women's Social and Political Union – the 'suffragettes' – created in 1903 and dominated by Emmeline Pankhurst and her daughter Christabel. The suffragists believed in the value of rational argument and were averse to violence of any kind, the suffragettes were not. Naturally it was the suffragettes who captured the attention of the public and who are remembered today. It was not simply that they marched to the sound of splintering glass and outraged feelings; they displayed military virtues of the highest order: superb tactical invention, good staff work, prudent audacity, heroic stoicism and unshakeable discipline; they excelled in all these things. And when, in 1914, their battle still unwon, they turned from civil to international strife, it was a thousand pities that the Pankhursts were not given command of the Allied armies and had to content themselves with urging their countrymen towards the killing-grounds commanded by their inept brothers.

When the war was over, Mrs Pankhurst and Christabel found their occupation gone: English women over the age of thirty had been given the vote, a gift which did not seem quite so precious as it had appeared when it was still being fought for. And when, ten

years later, complete equality was achieved (without fuss or violence of any kind), Mrs Pankhurst had but a month to live and the
suffragettes were history. But the struggle was by no means over,
for another suffragette appeared to carry on the battle in her own
way.

In October 1928 Virginia Woolf gave two lectures to the women's
colleges at Cambridge. These were rewritten and published a year
later as *A Room of One's Own*. There must have been many veterans
from the heroic past who read those persuasive arguments and devastating ironies with the delighted feeling that they had gained an
ally. There was one notable suffragette who, reading the book, fell in
love with its author and hurried round to 52 Tavistock Square. She
was Ethel Smyth.

> An old woman of seventy-one has fallen in love with me. It is at once
> hideous and horrid and melancholy-sad. It is like being caught by a
> giant crab.

Thus Virginia, writing to me in May 1930. I was living abroad and
had to take my aunt's complaints on trust, but even then I did not
believe that Dame Ethel was so hideous and horrid as Virginia suggested. Nor was she. She had been a militant, having given two years
to working for the cause; she had broken windows, been thrown
into prison, and for a time had been very much in love with Mrs
Pankhurst. Ethel Smyth was indeed one of nature's suffragettes,
tremendously brave and vigorous, riding straight to hounds and
demanding vociferously that her rights as a musician should be recognized; mocking, scolding, complaining. She was, like Mrs
Pankhurst, a staunch Conservative and, unlike the suffragette
leader, the daughter of a general, the companion of an Empress and a
friend of Kaiser Wilhelm II.

I cannot remember under what circumstances I first met her. It
was at Charleston. I think that she arrived by accident, for otherwise
I do not see why I should have carried her bags across the fields
down to the Swingates where she could catch a bus. At any rate she
was gracious and grateful for my services. I liked her and longed to
ask her to sit for her portrait. I hadn't the courage, and in truth a
Rembrandt was needed to deal properly with Ethel as an old
woman. That immensely strong face, surmounted by a wild disor-
der of hair, above which was an even more wildly improbable hat,

was almost too paintable to be painted. I have, nevertheless, attempted to make a sketch from a photograph (see plate 12).

What Ethel thought of me I am not sure. Virginia, always a mistress of romantic fiction, reported that 'she adores you . . . and would marry you, given a dog's chance'. Also she said that I was like a dog. True, she qualified this by saying 'a sheepdog'. That was not quite the impression that I, as a young man, was trying to create. Yet one could not but admire her courage and fortitude, her panache and her fun. Of her music I cannot speak, but certainly there is something tremendously engaging about her writing; she may sometimes be absurd, yet she is often very amusing, and she is always highly readable.

Why then did Virginia say that Ethel was like a giant crab? Well, I think that this *was* what she was like. Virginia enjoyed Ethel's good qualities but she did want to call her soul her own, and if you are attached to a giant crab, a crab which pinches and will not let go, a crab which demands love, makes scenes and is perpetually bombarding you with questions and assertions, you begin to feel that your soul is being taken over. And yet it was Ethel who felt that she was the aggrieved party. She was much more in love with Virginia than Virginia was with her, and she suffered. They parted company and then, because Virginia did indeed like her, they were reconciled – until the next quarrel.

I did not witness much of this painful business, but I remember one meeting which gave me a taste of it. It began at an exhibition at Agnew's, where I ran into the Woolfs with Ethel. Ethel was complaining loudly of the manner in which she had been treated by I know not what conductor. It was a long and involved tale, and clearly Leonard and Virginia had heard it already. I had really come to look at the pictures, but Leonard persuaded me to accompany them home in a taxi, and it was in the taxi that Leonard, trusting to poor Ethel's deafness, said to me: 'Can't you shut her up, Quentin?' Unfortunately he had not realized that the interior of a taxi may serve as a kind of sounding box in which even the deaf may hear. Ethel heard; and the situation which had been tedious became unpleasant. By the time we got to Tavistock Square, Ethel had changed tack. Seeking, I fear, to annoy Leonard, she had begun to abuse the socialists. She was very rude about them, and I, foolishly no doubt, produced arguments to which she hardly listened (and could perhaps hardly hear) but I fear that she heard enough to demote me from the status of sheepdog to that of mongrel.

Bernard Shaw had recently published a book called *The Intelligent Woman's Guide to Socialism and Capitalism*, and this excited Ethel's scorn and anger. Virginia, thoroughly bored by all this, tried to change the subject, but in vain. Ethel went on and on with really dreadful persistence until at last Leonard could no longer resist the obvious retort, 'Perhaps it was not addressed to you, Ethel.'

Stopped in mid-career, she asked Leonard what he had said. He had to repeat himself twice, speaking very loudly, before the remark could be understood.

When later I heard that Ethel was coming to Charleston, I was a little worried at the prospect of meeting her again. It was foolish of me. If she remembered my perversity, it was most certainly forgiven; it was probably forgotten.

But I must explain why Ethel was at Charleston. In truth, she had now fallen in love with Vanessa. It was a little inconsistent of her to do so, for Ethel detested Bloomsbury. She had made an exception when she fell in love with Virginia, and a further more dubious exception in the case of Leonard; but to proceed from that and conceive a passion for Virginia's sister was surely carrying inconsistency rather far. Nor was that all: she was extremely friendly with Duncan Grant. She was one of that fairly large set of people who detested Bloomsbury but did not carry their enmity to the point of actually disliking the company of members of the group whom they happened to meet. Nor can it be said that those whom Ethel liked made any enormous effort to please her. Vanessa, with her sister's example before her and being of a more cautious temperament – also, it should be said, being quite indifferent to the rights and wrongs of her sex – was in no hurry to respond to Ethel's advances. 'You are a little like your sainted sister', observed Ethel.

Nevertheless there she was at Charleston, having lunch with Vanessa, Duncan, my sister and myself. Ethel had at some time written the score of a ballet entitled *Fête Galante*. I do not know whether the music had received public performance, but the ballet had not been staged. Now I think someone influential had seen that the composition had merits. Also, Ethel had a hoard, a sum of money called 'Last Illness Fund'. She decided that she would rather have a ballet than a last illness and was ready to spend the fund – a typically spirited decision. Scenery and costumes would need to be designed, and this was where Vanessa came in. Ethel came to lunch to tell us all about it.

If I remember rightly, Ethel began on another topic, a new novel by Maurice Baring. She told us at some length about the plot and explained why in her opinion the book was a masterpiece. Fortunately, Virginia being absent, there was no one to contradict her. The painters were quite ready to take Maurice Baring on trust. Then, towards the end of the meal, she turned to the matter in hand. She described, and went on describing, the plot of *Fête Galante*, and then, noticing that she was sitting with her back to a piano, she turned and began to illustrate her meaning with her music. It was an extraordinary, a stupendous performance; I remember it very clearly. What I had forgotten until my sister reminded me was the deplorable fact that she and I disgraced ourselves.

I must try, although it will not be easy, to mitigate our offence. Ethel was in full fig. Despite that fact that it was a warm summer's day, she was lunching in a tremendously tailored tweed suit, crowned with one of her astonishing tricornes. She attacked the piano as though it had been a music critic, and the piano was obviously getting the worst of it; she sang out in what seemed to us an odd manner, only breaking off to exclaim in a voice as powerful as that of a huntsman who sees the fox breaking cover: 'A simple melody, a simple melody, as simple as Beethoven!' It was this, I think, which led me to exchange glances with Angelica – not, I hope, actually to giggle, but rather to lose that proper stance in which a member of the home team should listen to the music of a guest. Unfortunately we were observed, and felt in disgrace – not that Ethel stopped for a moment.

But she seemed still in a sunny mood when, after lunch, we went out into the walled garden in the hope that there might be a cooling breeze. Breeze or no breeze, Ethel went on talking, and talking, and talking . . . She was talking, I think, about herself, and she talked principally to Vanessa. Presently we found ourselves at that north-eastern corner of the walled garden which now bears some mosaics and a pool. At this point we, the disgraceful young, had fallen to the rear. Ethel was walking and talking with Vanessa and Duncan; they turned up the path that leads towards the house and after a step or two Duncan fell back and joined us. 'I think I am going to faint,' he said. 'I'm too bored to stand any more.' We found a seat for him, leaving Vanessa to carry on the battle alone. I like to think that I went to her assistance, but I am afraid that it is improbable. Also, it would be nice to be able to say that *Fête Galante* was in every way an enormous success; in fact I do not think it was ever danced.

Nobody comes badly out of this story, except of course my sister and myself, and Angelica was little more than a child. Vanessa and Duncan were indeed victims, but not the victims of ill-will. Ethel clearly had no notion of the pain she was inflicting on them – or on Virginia, for that matter; she simply felt the need to testify, to proclaim the excellence of her art, the rightness of her opinions, her immense and unswerving faith in herself. To do that she had only to pour out her soul, and she had so much soul to pour out that poor Duncan, on that occasion the weaker vessel, could not contain the awful weight of testimony.

Had Ethel been a suffragist, she might have been more careful in her manner, approaching her listeners upon common ground, seasoning her arguments with wit, sugaring the pill of faith with a tactful placebo. But Ethel was a suffragette; she disdained such artifices, she proclaimed the truth as she saw it, sword in hand, and was in consequence a dead bore. So perhaps was Joan of Arc. It is an occupational disease of heroes and heroines, and Ethel was certainly heroic; which is why, in a nation defended by a corps of Amazons, many may find her more to their taste than a suffragist like Virginia.

14

Claude Rogers and Lawrence Gowing

WHEN I WAS eighteen I went to Paris. I was fortunate in being able to do so and to spend a great part of my youth in that lovely city. Nevertheless, in one important respect Paris was a disappointment. It had been the theatre of war in the long conflict of modern painting – a campaign which might be considered to have been more or less permanent since the time of Ingres and Delacroix. I arrived therefore feeling that I might serve as a recruit in the battle of 'modern' art. It did not take me long to discover that the battle was over. The victory of the 'moderns' which, in London, was still disputed, had for years been conceded by the French; the supremacy of the conquerors, of whom Picasso and Matisse were the most eminent, was acknowledged by the public. It was impossible, however hard one might try – and I did try quite hard – to find in the Surrealists a new power which would renew the conflict which our predecessors had so brilliantly waged in the years before I was old enough to bear arms.

If one wanted to go on painting, the logical solution of one's problem seemed to be to find something in nature which seemed interesting and to describe it as accurately as one could. That now seems obvious, but it took me a very long time to reach this conclusion and, when I did, it appeared that a group of young painters were already thinking upon the same lines. And they were situated not in Paris, but in London. Here a quotation may be useful.

This then is my general contention. That the decadence of modern painting is due to the failure of artists to search deeply into their natures, a feat which can only be accomplished if they are serious to a degree which I call religious. And that this is due to the general decadence of capitalist society which detests and fears art at its serious levels, which seeks only to escape from itself in its horrible diversions.

Graham Bell, who wrote these words in 1939, was the only one of the 'Euston Road' group who had a talent for writing; he and his friends William Coldstream, Claude Rogers and Victor Pasmore were gifted painters who in the late 1930s turned against the Ecole de Paris, or perhaps the kind of English painting which followed Paris fashions. They decided to set up a school of drawing and painting – a school which presently found its local habitation and its name in the Euston Road.

Of the earlier careers of these painters and of their later acquisition of a school, also, as one may say, of a doctrine, I know very little and that by hearsay. The first that I actually saw and heard of this remarkable enterprise was from Duncan and Vanessa. It appeared that they and Helen Anrep (Roger Fry's relict) were busy ordering donkey easels, drawing boards and other art-educational paraphernalia and at the same time persuading Virginia – who had recently been made wealthy by *The Years* – to act as a guarantor. Considering these facts, and further, that both Duncan and Vanessa agreed to teach in the new school, it would be easy to conclude that the so-called Euston Road School, considered as a place of education, was virtually a creature of Bloomsbury.

This was far from being the case. Vanessa and Duncan assisted these young men because they were serious artists and agreeable people, but the teachers at the Euston Road School had their own ideas about painting. The younger generation reacted against their seniors, which is normal; the seniors gave them material assistance, which is not. It has been said, on I don't know what authority, that someone – presumably someone with a sense of history – wrote on the walls of the Euston Road School: 'The painting of Cézanne, the drawing of Degas'. Certainly Cézanne was greatly admired by the group, but it was Degas who seemed the most potent and visible influence, and it was Sickert, the great apostle of Degas, whom they invited to lecture at the school. (I daresay his hosts were unfamiliar with that great painter's views on Cézanne.) But a more suitable inscription for those walls would have been that provided by Ingres:

'*Le dessin c'est la probité de l'art*'. Looking at Coldstream's sensitive but brutally honest drawings – or indeed at his paintings – one feels that for him it was true.

Alas, it has never been so true for me. When, sometime in the summer of 1939, at a time when I was installing a kiln in my new pottery at Charleston, I felt the need for a model – models not being available in Sussex – I made my way to the Euston Road. I was in a sense venturing into enemy territory – not that I was, in any way, made to feel this; in fact everyone was extremely kind. Even when I painted my 'portrait' head everyone – and in that school one got an enormous amount of criticism from Rogers, Pasmore and Coldstream to a point at which so much attention, gratifying though it was, seemed almost an *embarras de richesse* – everyone, I say, was most polite.

Of my painting I must say a few words, for it amounted almost to an act of defiance. The model was old and hideous, she had the face of a camel. I painted her with only the slightest preliminary use of charcoal, using a palette knife to apply an abundance of pure colour, and, as tends to happen to me whatever my intentions, I flattered the poor woman outrageously. As Duncan remarked when he saw the thing, 'Well, you *have* made her a dreaming beauty!' I suspect it was a very bad picture.

During rest periods I saw very little of the chief figures of the school for they went to another part of the building where, with a ball made of newspaper, they played violent and to me incomprehensible games of cricket. But I did make contact of a kind with the tall, strange-looking man who worked beside me. I say contact, because it can hardly be said that we conversed; he stammered badly and in doing so released such a fountain of saliva that the conversation could scarcely amount to an exchange of views. It was a brief and unsatisfactory encounter, but I was to hear a lot more from Lawrence Gowing in later years.

I got a great deal more from Claude Rogers, and from the first I felt some kind of affinity with that amiable and sensitive man. The war, which brought the school itself to an untimely end, scattered the members of the group and alas killed Graham Bell, did not quite separate me from Claude.

Two remarkable sisters (both of whom were in love with Duncan) decided that it was their mission – London being emptied of culture by the war – to establish a centre for the arts at Millers, their home in Lewes. They organized lectures and exhibitions, and showed the work of Claude Rogers. I liked it immensely and for the first time in my life wrote a fan letter. Claude replied, and presently he and Elsie Rogers came to Charleston. In those years it was only on grand occasions that one travelled in motor cars, Claude and Elsie came by bus. I met them at the end of our road where there was once a Cézanne in the hedge and where I saw a hoopoe in the wood. Claude and Elsie seemed no less remarkable; they appeared almost spherical and although they were heavy one feared, the weather being atrocious with rain and violent wind, that they might be blown away. In my mind's eye I saw our unhappy guests rolling helplessly before the gale, down our track, across the main road and far out into the weald. These fears were not dispelled as they struggled up the drive, the surface of which resembled that of the moon, it being pitted with vast craters, craters now filled with tempestuous water lashed into fury by the gale. Claude, head down but resolute, led the way while Elsie followed, crying 'Claude! Claude!' – a vocative which she pronounced as though his surname had been Lorraine. Ten years later I was to see them travelling in the same manner and with the same piteous cries as they toiled up the steps towards Marcus Aurelius on the summit of the Capitol.

But in the interval I got to know and increasingly to love them better. Claude, like many painters, had developed an interest in art history at a time when he had long ceased to be a student. More than that, enraged by some foolish remarks in the *Daily Mirror*, he had embarked upon an essay on *Tradition in Art*. He found writing difficult and asked me to help him. I was sufficiently vain to believe that I could. Claude's essay was never finished, but I think we both enjoyed the correspondence which resulted, and when I came to London in 1941 I looked forward to seeing him. But I was disappointed. I found Elsie alone; Claude was in the army.

It was something to the credit of the army that in the end it dismissed Claude and did so in the kindest manner. He returned with a fine collection of stories, one or two of which I remember.

Quite near to the beginning of his military career Claude found himself marching, as young soldiers do. On this occasion he was, I take it, on the left flank of the formation; before him was a landscape of great beauty; it claimed his attention and the further he went the more charming it appeared. Suddenly he discovered that he was alone; while he was advancing, his companions had wheeled to the right and vanished.

At another time he found himself alone beside a road which traversed a valley. His task was to excavate a slit trench; a general in a staff car would drive past, and Claude was at once to take cover in this field work. Having brought with him a copy of Clausewitz's *On War*, Claude must have realized the importance of terrain, but his commanding office was less well informed. When the slit trench was made, it at once filled with water and Claude, not wishing to throw himself into a cold bath, looked for some drier part of the valley for this trench and set to work again. The result was no better. Soon there was a whole series of little ponds beside the road. He was still at work in his search for a 'better hole' when the general appeared. Claude dropped his spade and saluted; as he did so the side of the latest trench gave way and, still at the salute, he slithered heavily into the water below.

As a boy, and perhaps as a young man, Claude was shy and afraid of making any kind of public appearance. This made his attendance at synagogue a painful affair. By some unlucky chance he was, or was supposed to be, a lineal descendant of (I think) Aaron, and this distinction meant that by taking a prominent part in the proceedings he could give the congregation some tremendous emotion. His own emotions were deeply painful and embarrassing. Saturday became for him a day of pure misery until a friendly young rabbi divined his feelings and managed to spare him. Of his actual beliefs he said nothing to me, but I fancy that in later years his only God was Cézanne.

I do not know when it became impossible to describe Claude as shy, but certainly he had overcome any kind of social timidity by the year 1951 when we went to Italy. 'We will take a loaf of bread, a jug of wine, and each of us a "thou",' he wrote to me. Claude also brought – or perhaps purchased on arrival – a wide-brimmed straw hat. This was important; not only did it shield him from the sun, it could be swept off, waved in the air, used as an adjunct or indeed a substitute for speech. To see Claude sweep off his hat with exuberant courtesy and then address some stranger in a language which he supposed to be French was a joy. The natives responded, sometimes with some bewilderment but always with sympathy and good humour. They perceived – and indeed it was obvious – that Claude had fallen in love with Italy. He perceived that his love was returned.

Although the hat seemed to be an essential property, in one of his finest performances it was discarded. We went together to the barber and I offered to translate, but he did not need me and I left him. When a little later I returned, passing in front of the big plate-glass windows of the shop, I looked over the heads of the little crowd which had gathered to observe the scene within. Claude looking calm and contented was making a self-portrait; by means of this he was able to show what needed to be done to his hair and his beard. Behind him stood a fascinated barber together with several other barbers and a number of half-sheared, half-shaved clients who, having been abandoned by their attendants, had come as spectators. Everyone seemed perfectly happy.

It was a lovely time. We not only saw those things which must been seen in Italy, we sat in cafés drawing the townscape or sometimes the many urchins who collected around us, my drawings – perhaps due to my flattering pencil – being much preferred to his. We went to innumerable churches where one was asked to contribute something 'per la fabbrica' and then Claude and Elsie would declare that they too needed something 'per la fabbrica' which usually meant buns filled with cream.

It was sad when they had to leave. We had our last supper in a restaurant which spread its tables out on to the piazza S. Ignazio in Rome. It was a good dinner, but the last course crowned the whole. A vast assortment of sweet creamy confections was wheeled out upon a trolley at the sight of which Claude, unable to contain his enthusiasm, leapt to his feet, clapped his hands, and called out 'Oh dolce, dolce! Yum, yum, yum!' 'Oh *Clode*,' wailed Elsie; there were times when she found him a little too unselfconscious. Nevertheless, she too enjoyed the Roman sweatmeats.

'It's really too shocking the way those two go off and gobble what they call "cweam buns".' It was Coldstream who, in one of our rare conversations, thus described the conduct of his friends. At the time I felt that he was a little too severe upon what seemed to me a relatively harmless vice, but he was to be proved right.

That joyous cry of 'dolce, dolce!' was in a sense Claude's swansong. We returned from Italy to find Claude in hospital suffering from diabetes, frightened to find that he was pissing blood and altogether sorry for himself. He recovered and was able to live a normal, but more frugal life.

Although I was now living in the north of England I came south to look at and write about works of art. In Claude I saw one of the few artists who remained true to his own vision and made no efforts to adjust his manners to the fashionable styles of the age.

When I was in a position to do so I brought him to Leeds to give a lecture; by this time my children were old enough to appreciate him, and when he came to our house he was faced with a banner which they had constructed bearing the words 'Welcome Claude Rogers' displayed at the top of our drive. I discovered later that he had taken it home with him.

Claude complained that he had reached an age when he would be more comfortable if he could have a Chair. I am glad to say that he got one in 1963 at the University of Reading. This had the effect of bringing us together in a new way. A committee had been set up to regulate the distribution of students' applications to universities. In the case of those students who wanted to paint pictures this presented special problems. The universities concerned set up a sub-committee, the official name of which escapes me, but Claude called it The Three Buggering Old Professors – Kenneth Rowntree (for Newcastle), Claude (for Reading) and myself for Leeds. We met for dinner and usually managed to transact some quite useful business before the first course was eaten, but thereafter Kenneth and Claude began, in a jovial way, to abuse each other, to raise their voices and to dissolve in uproarious laughter. When the other two buggering old professors finally staggered away in opposite directions they agreed that any remaining business should be dealt with by me. One of the efficient and serious-minded people who worked on the efficient and serious committee told me that the activities of our sub-committee were the only thing that made their work interesting.

My last meeting with Claude was in his studio off Haverstock Hill. Like the first it resulted from my need to work from the model. We had agreed that if I paid the girl, he would provide the rest. It was a great treat; until the last two days we worked in silence, then Claude began to talk to our model, telling her what he was doing and describing the manner in which he dealt with the most interesting parts of her anatomy. She didn't seem to mind at all and I daresay was well used to his eccentricities. It was very different from his manner when he used to teach in Euston Road.

✳

I left Lawrence Gowing, impressive but inarticulate, in the Euston Road School. During the war I saw him but once and he was still speechless. Frances Partridge had purchased a still-life of his which was eloquent and impressive. One might, if one had been more alert, have guessed that the larva of the Euston Road had begun to pupate; soon it would burst out gloriously and soar into the heavens, not a butterfly but a coleopter, its wings sheathed in armour and its tail armed with a sting.

Lawrence received some important assistance from Julia Strachey. What form it took I do not know; others are better qualified than I to write about that remarkable woman, but it seems worthwhile to offer my own contribution to the general account.

When Marjorie Strachey was teaching me to understand music I met at her doorstep a figure who left a lasting impression. The door was opened before I could ring the bell by a young and elegant lady. She seemed foreign; indeed to my eye she seemed to have something Chinese about her. (Could this have been connected in some way to the *Son of Heaven* which was then being staged?) I found her exciting, strange and overpoweringly elegant. She was quite unlike any other Strachey ladies and yet I knew that she was a Strachey. I don't think that we exchanged a word, and yet her appearance was unforgettable so that after three or four years, when I was a schoolboy engaged with other schoolboys in hiring a boat at Sonning, I became aware of a lady and a gentleman who clearly belonged to the world that I knew only through brief encounters during the holidays. I found myself staring. She stared back for an instant, and then we knew each other. It was Julia Strachey – or rather it had been, for that very day she had married the gentleman who stood beside her – the Honourable Stephen Tomlin. The circumstances were not such as to encourage more than a few cheerful remarks, but again the meeting had been unforgettable. Julia and 'Tommy' became part of the occasional furniture of my life and I came to know him rather better than I knew her.

Tommy died in 1937. I continued to see Julia from time to time –

usually at Ham Spray, the home of Ralph and Frances Partridge. But I only saw Lawrence Gowing once after I left the Euston Road School until 1952 when Lawrence and Julia came to our wedding party and were sufficiently infected by it to get married themselves. I was looking for work and found it in what was then King's College, Newcastle-upon-Tyne, first as a visiting lecturer and then on a more permanent basis. Meanwhile I was discovering the Professor of Fine Art there, who was Lawrence; he had learnt to talk more clearly, although his speech was still punctuated by distressing interruptions. His stammer had become not so much an impediment as the preparatory explosive roar which announced the discharge of a projectile. I soon learnt that he didn't in the least welcome assistance. I remember a discussion of Dutch landscape in which he found himself stuck on the letter 'r'. Thinking to be helpful I supplied the name for which I thought he had was searching: 'Jakob van Ruysdael?' He made a noise like an angry elephant in distress, and finally managed: 'Nnno, *Salomon* van Ruysdael.' He made that respectable name sound like an imprecation. But this was our honeymoon and, when he understood that I was looking for a job, he offered a choice of two: I could be an art historian, or I could teach teachers to teach art. I had the good sense to opt for art education, for although I knew even less about it than I did about art history, I realized that my colleagues would be even more ignorant. Nevertheless, when I came back to Newcastle to be interviewed I was alarmed to find five other candidates, all of them teachers with far more experience than I, and although I was aware that Lawrence had been preparing the ground with some care, I doubted, while these impressive people were being interviewed, whether my own deficiencies would not be too glaringly obvious. At the end of the day I walked back with Lawrence to his house and he said: 'Quentin, you've been s-s-s-'. He struggled manfully to complete the word. 'You've been s-s-s-'. We walked on while he continued to hiss in vain. Had I been second-rate, or selected, or just plain stupid? We must have covered at least a hundred yards before he managed to get the word out – 'successful'.

My duties at Newcastle divided me between two departments. My students were in the Department of Education; I was in the Department of Fine Art. Education was the care of Professor Tuck, a wise and amiable man. His department was democratic; at staff meetings everyone had his say and some of my colleagues said a great deal. The meetings lasted until late in the afternoon and I did not look forward to them.

The meetings of the Department of Fine Art were rather different. They took place every morning when Lawrence was not away. We would wander into his room with a cup of departmental coffee and chatter about pretty well anything. Those 'coffee mornings' were often hilarious and even frivolous and yet in a way dignified. Lawrence's first act when he took the chair had been to buy a handsome silver inkstand to give tone to the proceedings. The department was the oldest institution in the University; it dated back to before the period when William Bell Scott taught and Rossetti wasted his time at Newcastle, and as the Rector once remarked: 'It is the brightest jewel in our crown.' The students felt something of this; they were proud – 'she's a nice girl but she walks out with an architect'. Under Lawrence – and perhaps his predecessor – the department gained in academic respectability by introducing a serious course in art history and by holding historically interesting exhibitions in its gallery. In this, and indeed in most other ways, it was then very unlike a municipal art school.

Thus the 'coffee morning' acquired something of the character of a little court with Lawrence as its sovereign. He took leave of us in 1975 regretting that there would be no more coffee mornings: 'We have had a great deal of fun together' he said, adding, 'even though that fun has sometimes been rather like the fun that a cat has with a mouse.' Richard Hamilton who was present reminded us of that remark at a memorial meeting which made me think that he may have been a victim, for Lawrence could be fierce. Not that I can remember he or anyone else suffering at Lawrence's hands at a coffee morning; my work took me to distant schools so I may have missed a good deal. I must admit also that I took my external examiner Mary Hoad to one such meeting after which she said, 'Everyone except you was terrified.' (Mary was a tactful woman.)

It was true, I was not terrified; it might have been better if I had been. My fault was that I admired Lawrence too much and in consequence imitated him, which must have been irritating. When we did fall out it was over a trifle: I had absented myself from a party which he thought it my duty to attend. It was however a painless quarrel; I had few duties to keep me in the department and many which took me elsewhere; so for a time I disappeared. It was Lawrence who ended the quarrel by saying: 'I had got it into my head that you were persecuting me, but I have realized that I am persecuting you, and I will bring it to an end', which indeed he did, and we remained on good terms for the rest of his life.

The most memorable meetings were those in which Lawrence's imagination took flight and we entered a world of pure fantasy. One such was the affair of the 'shere legs'. Even now I do not know what shere legs are, but they were needed to move a piece of sculpture. A local magnate had been asked to lend a bust and had agreed, insisting however that it should be most carefully handled. Lawrence read us his letter and began to dictate his reply; then he was struck by an idea. Two of his staff had been in the Navy: Eric Dobson, a painter, had been an Able Seaman; George Knox, an art historian, had commanded a minesweeper.

'Two members of our staff are experienced naval officers; they will undertake the work of removal, bringing with them all the necessary tackle including shere legs.'

'What,' asked someone, 'are shere legs?'

'I haven't the faintest idea,' said Lawrence, and continued to dictate his letter. It seemed that an expedition carrying ropes, planks, winches, and I daresay shere legs would be sent, together with a team from the British Navy, to undertake this delicate task. And indeed a formidable party with a large lorry and vast collection of impedimenta set off to the magnate's home. When they got there the curator led them into a gallery where the bust stood on a shelf; using one hand he reached it down and gave it to one of the sailors.

Another recollection concerns a mission, composed of serious-minded and intelligent people, who felt that the importance of religion was not sufficiently understood in the University. It was a formidable body, made more formidable by the fact that it was the charming daughter of the Rector (i.e. the Vice-Chancellor) of the University, a girl who happened to be a student in the Department of Fine Art, who went to Lawrence and begged that the mission be entertained to coffee. Lawrence said that he would be delighted.*

---

*Eric Dobson is my source and I have attempted to repeat his words. I am now told that the mission was called 'Honest to God' and was led by the Revd Mick Stacey.

Other students got wind of the business; placards began to appear: 'God is coming', 'This space reserved for God', etc. The faculty meanwhile began to wonder whether Lawrence had met his match.

The group arrived; Lawrence received it with enthusiasm and then, before anyone could speak or even stutter, explained that his visitors had come at a propitious moment. He had a problem which he wanted to lay before them. Certain structural alterations were being made to the students' cloakrooms and a moral question arose. The plan, which seemed in other ways admirable, did involve a disposition of the men's cloakroom which in certain improbable, but not by any means impossible circumstances, would allow a clear view into the women's cloakroom.

Slightly baffled, the visitors suggested that perhaps it was not for them . . .

'But', objected Lawrence, 'this is a moral problem. Certainly, from a practical point of view it would be most convenient to accept the risk involved and agree to the architect's plan, but . . .'

The mission attempted to turn the conversation, but it was not easy to turn Lawrence when he was in full spate. They had rather thought that they might discuss the atom bomb; it seemed a much simpler question than the gents' lavatory. But it was no use; and they were still bogged down in questions of plumbing when the session ended.

When I arrived at Newcastle the Department of Fine Art was teaching painting very much as it had been taught at the Euston Road School: the exploration of nature and the disciplines which that imposes were generally accepted. But within a few years the 'party line' was changed. Roger de Grey left us, and he was succeeded by Victor Pasmore and Richard Hamilton. In making these appointments Lawrence was in effect creating an opposition. He seemed to have no doubt that he could govern according to his own lights, but in this he was mistaken.

The fashion in art, like all fashions, demands change and although, to me, theirs seemed a mode decidedly lacking in novelty – inasmuch as it appeared little more than a refurbished version of styles which had flourished and expired while I was still a child – to my colleagues it appeared eminently chic. Before long Lawrence himself was leading the reaction. He went to the United States and returned enthusiastic for the 'abstract expressionists'. To me it appeared a tragic waste of his enormous talent and I regretted what seemed to me a dreadful example of the modern passion for change. In another age he who had created a splendid style of his own would, like Claude Lorraine or Chardin, have gone on painting the kind of painting which so magnificently suited him. Instead he had to fiddle about with little shapes of coloured paper or to have himself strapped to a board and soused in paint by his students. I am glad that before the end of his life he returned to the kind of work for which he was so superbly fitted.

These no doubt reactionary reflections have led me away from Newcastle. Lawrence himself left us in 1958 to take command at Chelsea School of Art. Rashly I attempted to take his Chair. Fortunately I failed in this and about a year later went to head the Department of Fine Art at Leeds.

I did not apply for the post at Leeds which Maurice de Saumarez was vacating. I was asked to advise a committee which wanted to know how his work – which had been purely art-historical – should be continued. Before meeting this committee Maurice took me over the local habitation of the new department which was then being built. It was to contain amongst other things a very handsome studio capable of being used by a fair number of students. I assumed that this would not have been provided unless painting was to be taught and it was on this assumption that I spoke to the committee. The committee, it later appeared, assumed nothing of the kind, but it did offer me the department, and on that misunderstanding I accepted it.

I soon made some discoveries. The first was that I should have to live and work with an assistant who had been moving heaven and earth, or at least canvassing an enormous number of people, in the hope that he might get the job himself. He was furious and miserable and his fury must surely have been increased when he discovered that the post had been taken by an art-educationist who was not an art-historian, and indeed was without academic qualifications of any kind.

I asked him to dine with me at the Reform Club and listened patiently while he told me how much he knew about art history – he did indeed know a great deal about architecture and about Dutch painting of the seventeenth century. We parted, both I think feeling that we had a heavy but not intolerably heavy cross to bear.

I also discovered that a great many of my colleagues, not to speak of some municipal servants, were very much opposed to the idea of studio teaching in the University; after all there was already a large and distinguished art school in Leeds.

Under the circumstances it seemed best to begin in a modest way, to make influential friends in the town, to live at peace with my assistant Dr Noach, and to find an artist who was a man of probity and good sense and who could help me. Here I was supremely lucky, I found John Jones. Although I have been lucky in choosing colleagues I have never been luckier than when I enlisted him. With his assistance we made what seemed to me a right little, tight little school. The advantage of a departmental university such as Leeds is this: you may have the devil of a job getting your plans approved by Faculty and Senate but once you're through no one will come meddling with another's department; dog does not eat dog.

A time came at last when I thought that I had made a good enough start to launch my vessel and go home to Sussex. But who should succeed me? I felt that the moment had come for more audacious ventures than I had undertaken. Lawrence would be the perfect choice. He had finished recreating Chelsea and was now working at the Tate but he might be tempted back to a Department of Fine Art.

Of course it was 'no business of mine'; the outgoing Professor is not supposed to choose or in any way determine the choice of his successor. But a course in which painting is taught presents problems. If one could bring in another painter to sit on the selection committee, and if he could prevent the physicists, philosophers and chemists from getting out of hand, it might work. But as things stood, although I had some charming friends in the faculty I didn't quite trust them to see the point of Lawrence.

At any rate there could be no harm in asking Lawrence to come to Leeds and give a lecture. It was one of his miracles that, notwithstanding his stammer, he learnt to do this not merely with ease but with panache. At the same time we asked the Vice-Chancellor to dinner.

Roger Stevens was my favourite Vice-Chancellor, an approachable human being, the sort of person who might see the fun and the value of appointing Lawrence. The trouble was that Lawrence, who understood the purpose of my manoeuvres very well, did not like being manoeuvred. He regretted having to meet the Vice-

Chancellor; he was in a bad temper, and the meal started badly. After a time Lawrence began to talk about his work at Chelsea. It seemed dull enough: he discussed the plans for the canteen and the business of 'portion control' which I gathered meant the division of such things as sponge cakes and butter pats, and at this point the comic muse descended. That the scrupulous division of comestibles should, when described by anyone, provide a rich source of mirth may sound impossible. I can only say that on this occasion we became helpless with laughter and when I saw Sir Roger actually reduced to tears I knew that Lawrence could have the chair if he wanted it and guessed that perhaps he would.

Before leaving I wrote Lawrence a private letter in which I tried to give him a history of the department; I wished that Maurice de Saumarez had done as much for me. In it I described the problem of Arnold Noach, with whom I had lived on reasonably good terms. He was in many ways a likeable man; he made some good jokes, he was a kindly person, he really did know a great deal about his special subjects and I had contrived to hear some of his lectures and these were clear and instructive. But he was a problem.

He came to me to ask me for a reference for I know not what post. I agreed, and asked him for his curriculum vitae. It was a remarkable document. He was the same age as myself and had gained a doctorate at a Dutch University with a thesis on the Oude Kerk at Amsterdam. Allowing for the fact that being a Jew, he would probably have been unable to achieve anything during the German occupation, he had nonetheless had about twenty-five years in which to produce something else. All he had managed during this time was the script for some broadcast – I forget what – on the Third Programme.

I had to tell him that although I could conscientiously say that he was a man of great learning who could deliver a very good lecture, and although I did not sympathize with those scholars whose first and only question to an applicant was: 'What have you published?', I still felt that his chances were slender. In sorting out applications the first thing that academics looked for was the evidence of written work; if they could hear him lecture he might stand a better chance. But how was that possible?

The poor fellow moaned. He was always about to write a book but somehow it never got written. 'I agree with other scholars to produce a joint volume. They write, but I can't. My name is mud.'

He confirmed what I had already observed. If one went into Arnold's room one would find him reading a book, gossiping with a secretary, or fast asleep. When he was not lecturing he was useless in the Department. To remove him would be very difficult but I was beginning to think that some way of doing it would have to be found.

Then, quite unexpectedly, the situation changed. An American University asked him to come and teach for a term. He went, and they loved him. It seemed possible that he might return to them and they would give him that for which he longed – a Chair. American Chairs are more easily given than British Chairs and perhaps not quite the same thing, but he would at least be Professor Noach. It seemed the happiest solution.

This was the situation when Lawrence arrived. When he had heard of my imminent departure poor Arnold had again begun to canvas his friends in the University. I was a little surprised; had it occurred to him that he might be at a loss dealing with a painting school, and had he noticed that a Head of Department has to do a certain amount of work? Of course it did not really matter, although it was sad that he would have to face another disappointment.

In my letter to Lawrence I could not conceal the nature of the problem presented by Arnold Noach. Perhaps imprudently, I suggested a policy of masterly inactivity. The new appointment would surely convince Arnold that there was no point in his remaining in Leeds when America was ready to welcome him. Leave him alone, and he would remove himself.

I suppose it was foolish to recommend inactivity to Lawrence, and perhaps it was also a mistake to tell Arnold that with the departure of King Log he had to expect the advent of King Stork.

Lawrence was installed and, almost at once, he obtained a personal Chair for Arnold. Why did Lawrence do it? Being Lawrence it might be that he had some tremendous plan in mind; also of course it might be – and I think almost certainly was – that he was damned if he would take any advice from me. (I was in a no-win situation; if I had failed to warn him he could justly have blamed me.)

From the moment he entered the University it was as if the Chair of Fine Art had been given a three-ring circus. In no time we had a splendid library, more than double the number of students, twice as many staff, a row of terrace houses for studios, the University's own art gallery . . . a couple of promotions, and ten paradoxical remarks a day to think about. Being both artist and scholar, he exemplified the Department's ideal.*

Lawrence was having a splendid time; in the euphoria of the moment it would have seemed natural and proper to give his second in command promotion.

Arnold must have been very happy, but his happiness was brief. Indeed it was the personal Chair which led to the first contretemps. Arnold celebrated the event by ordering fresh writing paper. It was headed: *Arnold Noach, Professor of Fine Art*. Lawrence, showing his claws for the first time, reminded him that he was nothing of the kind, and the paper had to be pulped.

When I visited Leeds about two years after my departure I found that a state of open war existed in the Department; perhaps it was persecution rather than war, although I fancy that Arnold, when provoked, would not have concealed his opinion of Lawrence's book on Vermeer. He must though have been fairly miserable. His health was bad, and Lawrence when he set himself to hurt could indeed be cruel; even John Jones, whom he valued and who found him enormous fun, had sometimes to suffer at his hands. When I asked Lawrence why he gave Noach the Chair he replied: 'The biggest mistake I ever made in my life.' It was not an explanation, but it was a handsome and not at all a typical remark.

Lawrence remained in Leeds for some years and then went to the Slade. He adventured into glorious situations and into another world in which I had no place. He produced some excellent television programmes which have I hope been preserved. He had a third and very charming wife and a delightful family. But I must leave the description of those final years to some other observer.

---

*John Jones, 1994

15

Robert Medley and Mary Butts

ROBERT MEDLEY DIED on 20 October 1994. It has become possible to say things which he would not have liked to hear, although they are not at all to his discredit. He was five years my senior. When he first came to Charleston I was a schoolboy, Angelica a child, or at least young enough to believe Vanessa when she said that Mr Medley was an old gentleman with a pink beard and would expect her to greet him with a curtsey.

When I met him again I was with Duncan in the Boulevard St Germain and we were looking for a place where I could work from the model. Robert had the answer. He himself was working in a small school where Marchand taught and in which Leger and Ozenfant were supposed to teach; it was called l'Académie Moderne. Thither I went to work every day and there I usually found Robert. We were, I fancy, the only male students.

We got to know each other rather well; he was likeable and admirable. He was a very serious young painter, serious about his work that is; on other subjects he was well-informed and amusing. We would sometimes get a cheap lunch together in a restaurant which knew how to make horsemeat edible. We went to see the avant-garde films that were then appearing in Paris and I was intro-duced to his friend Rupert Doone. Rupert was at that time a young ballet dancer and, as far as I could judge, an accomplished per-former. He had been a very pretty youth but was just beginning to lose some of his beauty. He belonged to a troupe which was com-manded by Ida Rubinstein. Robert and I went to the first night of Mademoiselle Rubinstein's production; we heard Ravel's *Bolero*, a new composition which seemed, to my untutored ears, a tedious affair; possibly it was the ludicrous spectacle of La Rubinstein dancing energetically upon a table which set me against it. Another number, in which Rupert danced with two companions, was much more to Robert's taste and to mine.

But Rupert was not content to be a *ballerino*. He was writing a novel. He believed that it would be one of the great literary masterpieces of the twentieth century and he read us several chapters. I was impressed. (I wonder whether that manuscript survived and what one would think of it today.)

At first I saw but little of Rupert; he was rehearsing by day and dancing at night. When I did begin to see him and Robert together they introduced me to the writings of Laurence Sterne which were a lovely discovery and also a welcome distraction from my own instructive but arduous study of *Du Coté de Chez Swann*.

But seeing Robert and Rupert together brought instruction of another kind. That Robert was deeply in love with Rupert was obvious, but that Rupert was in love with Robert seemed less certain. I suppose in a way he was, but it was a love of a special kind or rather, as one might say, of a special unkind. They lived together as man and wife, Robert being the wife and Rupert the tyrannical husband. It may be that a husband beats his wife (or vice versa) and that, if this be done in private, it is a matter of mutual consent; but to chastise and humiliate your partner in public is, it seems to me, a different matter.

This punishment *coram publico* took place with me as a reluctant witness. Rupert's cruelty was merciless and ingenious. He knew how to bring his amiable friend to the verge of tears. He understood perfectly well how hateful it was for Robert to be savaged in my presence and how distressing it was for me to be a witness. He knew also that Robert would submit and come to heel like a whipped dog and that if I expostulated I should lose not only his, Rupert's, friendship but that of Robert as well.

It may appear that Robert was a weak character, but half the horror of the thing was that, in the ordinary transactions of everyday life, he was not. Outside 'marriage' he was self-confident and could be quietly obstinate. It was 'love', if that be the word, that unmanned him. It was this which, without ever causing an open break, led us to part company. Even after Rupert's illness and death

Robert was so much in love with his memory that one could not hurt him by saying what one thought of Rupert.

It was Robert and Rupert who took me to the Rue Montessuy to meet Mary Butts. We had already met but that had been so long ago, when Mary was consoling Roger Fry for his loss of Vanessa, that I had no memory of her. Nevertheless at this second meeting, when I was about nineteen, she greeted me enthusiastically, swearing that we were like as two peas in a pod, that Clive was probably her father, and proposing that we should exchange clothes and sally out into Parisian society, me as she and she as me. The plan was never put into effect but we got on well together. Mary was also very fond of Robert and Rupert; I was soon to have proof of this.

One of Rupert's many infuriating traits was his belief that he was far better educated than I, which was at best only half true, and that he was much better educated than almost anyone, which was false. I remember an evening when he told me and Mary and Robert about Plato. He had read the dialogues; he advised us to do likewise, we should not find them too difficult, he could especially recommend the *Symposium*. He told us a lot about it, he really thought we should study it etc. I was half irritated, half amused, but the person who suffered and suffered acutely was, as usual, Robert. Robert, so Mary said, appealed to her with a look of pathetic agony, for Robert knew that Mary had it in her power to demolish Rupert. Rupert had forgotten, if he had ever known, that Mary was a Greek scholar with – I am told – a good reputation as such. She had been very severely tempted to tell Rupert that he was a pretentious idiot and had refrained. She behaved beautifully, leaving Rupert happily conscious of his superior attainments.

When we were alone together Mary was forgiving. One had to remember that Rupert was disadvantaged. 'While we were going to school he was going round with the milk,' – she seemed to know more about Rupert's background than I ever learnt. He came from a very poor home and had to educate himself. Having done so he must be excused for thinking that he was wonderful, for after all he was, in his way. What it was that tried Mary's patience once too often we shall never know. But much later, when I asked Robert whether he had news of Mary he replied, 'I haven't spoken to her for years. She said something unpardonable to Rupert.' I still wonder what it was; there were so many things that she might have said.

I think that it was early in 1929, Robert and I having both returned to London, that Robert asked me to sit for my portrait. I had been used as a model a good deal and so I hope that it was not my fault that Robert struggled in vain. In the end he gave up in despair and went back to Paris. After that we did not see much of each other for quite a long time. He told me later of the catastrophe of the following year.

It had always been Rupert's ambition to find a place in Diaghilev's company. That year he met the great man in Paris and there had been a useful conversation which ended with a promise that Rupert would be enlisted. In August he and Rupert were at Cassis awaiting a summons from Diaghilev who was in Venice, but the summons never came. On the 19th Diaghilev was dead. It must have been a miserable disappointment.

❊

I returned to Paris and the Rue Montessuy in the summer of 1929. I saw a good deal of Mary at this time; she seemed to me a remarkable person. I read and enjoyed her books – I should hate to be examined on them now – but it was her conversation which was most enjoyable; she was tremendously good company and she helped to educate me. She told stories about her ancient family: the Butts had been big people in the time of Henry VIII and there was a family portrait, reputed to be a Holbein; another Butts had been the friend and patron of William Blake; and Mary's mother had committed unspeakable crimes, and as for Mary's brother Tony – his crimes were still worse. It was a rich and potent mixture of fact and fiction which Mary could pour out in splendid abundance when she had enjoyed a pipe or two. It should be explained that Mary's pipes were charged with opium.

Although Mary believed strongly in this drug as a means to inspiration, contending that there was hardly a single good poem in the English language which was not produced under its influence, she never – and this is rare amongst addicts I have known – attempted to 'convert' me. After all I was not intending to write poetry and was what in another context is called 'invincibly ignorant'.

Mary, like Roger, was a lover of the marvellous, but whereas his flights of fancy were inspired by the wonders of science hers were of the traditional kind, ghosts and second-sight, witches and vampires;

all were conjured up in her talk and although I do not usually feel the urge to call spirits from the vasty deep, she talked so well that for the moment I would suspend disbelief and enjoy her fantasies. Like Roger she was for a time convincing, but her credulity was even greater than his.

I saw a great deal of her in the summer of 1929 and again when I returned to Paris in the autumn. By that time she had acquired a lover, Gabriel Atkins, who had been Maynard Keynes's catamite and indeed the toast of the British Sodom. Poor Gabriel was in a sad condition; his beauty had faded and indeed he had not much else. What Mary saw in him I do not know, unless perhaps it was his misfortune. Like Rupert he was unfortunate and she pitied him; unlike Rupert he was amiable in a pathetic way. He sought comfort not only in Mary's kindness but also in religion. He had been received into the Catholic faith but he did not find happiness; he confessed to me that he was very worried, indeed terrified, because his spiritual guide had insisted that sodomy was – I think I quote correctly – 'the sin against Christ'. The unrepentant sodomite would go to hell. From this I concluded that Mary was not his only love at this time.

This was horrid for him, poor fellow, but I must confess that I was more worried by his persistent habit whenever we met of 'borrowing' money. I hadn't very much money and could not admit that Gabriel had any call upon my charity, but I was weak and I did give him a little. It was a foolish thing to do and in the end I had to tell Mary that I could not come to the Rue Montessuy when Gabriel was there. All this was a preface to the most disastrous tea party of my life.

I continued at that time to work in the *atelier* to which Robert had introduced me. Amongst other advantages it was an agreeable place in which to make friends, and it was here that I met a young woman whom I will call Monica. Monica was in every way a good girl. She was the daughter of respectable people in Eastbourne. She had been sent to live with a French family in Paris, there to study art. Why she did this I could not tell, for she was completely uninterested in the subject and had no gift for it. Instead, what she wanted to do in Paris was to 'see life'. I do not think that she knew what that commodity might be, but evidently she felt that the bevy of nice girls from the United States at the *atelier* did not constitute 'life' and in this perhaps she was right. She was equally right in thinking that I might be able to show her some; in fact she was perhaps more right than either of us knew.

Seeing that she was amiable, amusing, exceptionally beautiful and game for a certain amount of innocent dalliance, I gladly undertook to show Monica a small sample of 'life'. I must admit that I myself was vague on the subject, but I supposed that something remote from the suffocating decencies of Eastbourne or the industrious pursuit of beauty in the Atelier Moderne would fill the bill. I therefore wrote to Mary asking whether I might bring a nice young woman to see her. This was my first blunder: I should have described Monica in greater detail, not that, in the event, it would have made any difference if I had done so.

There was trouble initially at Mary's door; we could hear human noises from within, but no one answered our knock until, at our third or fourth appeal, Gabriel appeared. His voice quavered and I suspected him of being drunk or doped. It must have been fairly late in the afternoon; the outer room was very dark.

There was always a certain bohemian *sans-gêne* about Mary and her environment to which I was not unsympathetic, but on this occasion she had surpassed herself. The room was brilliantly lit and uncomfortably warmed by a multitude of candles planted in bottles, on shelves, on bookcases and on the floor which was littered with the underclothes of both sexes. The big square bed was rather like the divan of Sardanapolis as Delacroix painted it. On it sat Mary swathed in a bedspread which was, rather obviously, her only garment; beside her a great scroll reached the floor, on it were the achievements of a multitude of armigerous families. I recognized it as the Butts pedigree.

Mary spoke first, addressing herself to a rather obvious hiding place, a wardrobe from whence a rather dirty little man emerged. '*Alexandre, tu peut sortir, ce sont des amis, ce n'est pas la police.*' Alexandre, she explained, had been deported by the police but had managed to get back. 'My dears,' said Mary, 'have you had any tea? Gabriel, go and make some.'

While Gabriel attempted to make tea Alexandre was the major object of attention. He had it seemed a friend, a Monsieur Drieu de la Rochelle, who could be of service, but he had no money. In the end Mary gave him a little and sent him off. Gabriel was still failing to make tea.

Mary, who later explained that the arrival of Alexandre had quite put our visit out of her head, told us that Alexandre was a charming person but at times difficult. I think he peddled drugs. There was still no tea. I asked Mary to explain the candles. The electricity company had cut off supplies, but didn't they look charming?

The conversation became rather sticky. I perceived that the two ladies did not much care for each other. Mary told me later that my little friend was an unremarkable person and looked at the furniture 'as though she had been a female bailiff'. Also, she did not dress very well.

If Mary could be made to give one of her performances Monica might still be charmed into enjoying herself. Mary obliged: she began to talk about her father's service as a drummer-boy in the Crimea (although the dates sound impossible I believe this was true). She talked about the hardships of that terrible winter of 1854–5 and of how the Turks stole all the delicacies that had been sent from England for the boys. 'And when they opened the hamper what did the poor boys find? No marmalade, no cheese, no brandy, nothing but sand and shit, sand and shit.'

In 1929 a nicely brought up girl might well not know what the word 'shit' meant. Monica knew enough to blush and I was angry with Mary. I rose and said that we must leave (we still had no tea) and despite Mary's pleas we did so. We had already said goodbye when Mary sat up almost screaming and holding something between finger and thumb.

'Bugs!' she cried, and I believe that her horror was genuine. 'Bugs! I knew that it was a mistake letting Alexandre into the flat. He sleeps with all kinds of people in all kinds of places but I had not thought that he would bring bugs into my bed.' Mary looked at me resentfully as we made our escape. Later on, when I reproached Mary for her conduct that afternoon she affected to be, and perhaps really was, quite unconscious of her eccentricities.

Monica was also reproachful. To be sure she had wanted to see 'life' and that afternoon's entertainment had been lively enough for anyone; but it was in truth a rather strong dose of life to offer to a beginner.

I continued on good terms with both ladies and found them excellent company so long as they could be kept apart. This was not difficult and when I returned to England I had the advantage of being able to meet Monica far from the Rue Montessuy, for Monica's home in Eastbourne was within easy distance of Charleston. Monica came to Charleston and met Vanessa, who thought her eyes very beautiful. I took the bus to Eastbourne where I met Monica's mother who, without exactly approving of me, was not unfriendly; together the two of them took me to a performance of *Lilac Time* which showed a kind intention and later I was invited to tea.

This was a disappointment; I had hoped for a tête-à-tête, but I found Monica with three other friends; they were playing tennis. Even if I could have played adequately, five is an awkward number for tennis or for any game, as I discovered when the weather changed and we went indoors to play bridge. I knew even less about bridge than I did about tennis. Everyone was perfectly polite, but the conversation drifted at once into local gossip which, to me, was incomprehensible. In short I was isolated and felt ridiculous. In the end I thought it better to face the rain than the company and went home. At home I found a telegram telling me not to come to Eastbourne, it had been despatched too late.

There is a fable concerning a fox who invited a crane to dinner. The meal was served on so flat a dish that the crane could pick up no food; the crane returned the invitation, putting the food into so deep a vase that the fox could not reach it. Had Monica dealt with me as the bird did with the beast? If so she was very ingenious. Monica could hardly command the weather, which had made my situation unbearable, but neither could I have known that Mary would forget her invitation.

These disastrous occasions had their use: they showed each of us that the other lived in a world containing territories in which a stranger might perish. Monica made a good and, I hope, a happy marriage and disappeared from my life. Mary meanwhile was in difficulties. When we were both in England I had a message asking me to dine with her and her mother, Mrs Colville Hyde, who lived somewhere near Buckingham Palace. I found Mary looking younger and handsomer than I had ever seen her (I think she had come off opium). There I also saw the Butts Holbein: it was certainly authentic; and when a great deal of black paint together with the dirt of centuries had been removed, it looked splendid. I think I am correct in saying that it is now in the National Gallery at Washington DC.

With looks and health restored, and I suppose a promising financial situation, Mary should have been happy, but she was not.
Gabriel had been carried away, filched like Ganymede, the eagle
being an elderly American lady. I was invited to rescue him. I was to
approach Maynard who, I was given to understand, had some way
of redirecting Gabriel. I was loth to accept this commission but I did
approach Maynard; he seemed as puzzled as I and was able to affect
nothing. In this matter I was certainly at fault for in the end Angus
Davidson was entrusted with the same task and managed to retrieve
the fugitive.

Whether Gabriel was altogether reclaimed I do not know but I
have my doubts because in 1934 while staying in Cornwall with
Yvonne Kapp, she and I made a brief visit to Sennen Cove near St
Ives where I found Mary cultivating a garden full of poppies; quite
her old self, but no sign of Gabriel. My memories of that visit are
however scanty.

I continued to hear about Mary from two sources: from Angus
and from my aunt Virginia. Virginia was in touch with Tony Butts,
Mary's brother. He and Mary were on bad terms and his reports
were disobliging: Mary was drinking herself to death. Angus
brought more sensational news. Mary and her friends were not only
raising poppies, they were raising the devil, and by this I mean
trying actually to get in touch with Apollyon. This has always
seemed to me rather a work of supererogation. But for Mary and her
friends it was something worse or at least more dangerous.
According to Angus she took the thing very seriously and ended by
literally frightening herself to death. Gabriel attended her funeral,
caught a cold and died too.

*

I saw little of Robert Medley or of his work in the late 1930s and
nothing of him during the war. But his reputation was growing and
after the war he taught at Chelsea and the Slade. He later took over
as head of the Painting School at Camberwell which became one of
the most distinguished in the country. It was natural that Lawrence
Gowing should invite him to show his work at Newcastle and talk
to the students and not unnatural that he should come to stay with
Olivier and me. I am afraid that he found the hospitality meagre; in
those early years of marriage and parenthood, life was of necessity

frugal and we seldom drank anything stronger than cider. Naturally a bottle of wine was provided in Robert's honour, but I had forgotten that a guest also expects a glass of something before his evening meal. No drink appeared, and poor Robert grew so desperate that he sallied out in search of the nearest pub, returning for dinner in high spirits. When we were again in Sussex (and better prepared) he came to stay and read us part of the autobiography he was writing. By then Rupert had developed an incurable disease which destroys the mind before destroying the body; he described his last sad years in his book *Drawn from the Life*.

Charleston had hoped to arrange an exhibition of his work; thither he had been invited, and was to have lunched with us. The day before, we heard that he was unwell and must postpone his visit. Two days later he died.

16

Anthony Blunt

I MET HIM in Julian's rooms at Cambridge. I had that morning been to the Fitzwilliam and seen, amongst other things, a picture which perplexed me. I thought at first that it was a landscape by Constable; on closer inspection it seemed an extremely bad, indeed ugly, but exact imitation. I knew that Anthony was practically the only person in Cambridge who took an interest in painting and I asked him about it. He was indeed well-informed: it was by someone called Müller, 'exactly like Constable, but without his soul'. Julian laughed at Anthony for using the word 'soul' and the conversation drifted away to other topics.

Julian, at that time, had decided that he was a poet. He had always been interested in painting, however, or, at all events, in the aesthetic speculations of Clive and Roger, and he enjoyed making a case for abstract art. Anthony was also an advocate of 'modern art': like Roger he had a great admiration for Cézanne and for Poussin. Thus there was a similarity of taste between Julian and Anthony which I imagined started their friendship.

In Cambridge about the year 1929 the undergraduates were more interested in ethics than in politics. I don't think that Julian attempted to convert Anthony to socialism. Anthony did attempt to convert Julian to homosexuality but failed utterly.

The left-wing revival in the universities was more sensational in Oxford than in Cambridge; I remember how exciting it was for me – then a patient in a Swiss sanatorium – to hear that young Oxford had voted not to fight 'for King and country'. This was a pacifist rather than a communist gesture, and it was as a pacifist – a 'violent pacifist', that Julian distinguished himself at Cambridge. Communism became fashionable later on and was not noticed by me until after Julian's death (in 1937) when I read in his 'Notes for a Memoir': 'I think the bitterest thing about the communist hysteria at Cambridge has been the virtual death of the Society [i.e. the Apostles]; my hope is that it is only a temporary coma.'

It was this, I imagine, that made Julian so ardent and so consistent an enemy of communism. He does not mention any names but it is likely that this also caused a break with Anthony who was not, I think, amongst the friends whom he saw at the time of his return from China.

I myself only became aware of Anthony's political views through his writings. I forget when I read his book *Artistic Theory in Italy, 1450–1600*. It seemed and still seems to me clear, readable and immensely well informed. But in the 1930s Anthony was writing in what was for me a disquieting way; in common with many left-wing critics of the time he had rejected the formalist teachings of Clive and of Roger (in so far as Roger still was a formalist at the time of his death) and was insisting upon a political and 'literary' theory of art, the value of a work of art being related to its value as revolutionary propaganda. In this Anthony was following the 'party line' as drawn at the beginning of the century by Plekhanov. The latter rejected the fauves and abstract painters. Stalin and the Soviet artists had no difficulty in following Plekhanov, but Anthony could not abandon the taste of his own times and included amongst the 'progressives' a great part of the Ecole de Paris. Nevertheless this theory, which ignored a great deal of the art which most of us admire today and also the art of remote cultures and of savages, together with much applied art, seemed to me untenable. And yet it seemed a good deal less absurd than the opposing doctrine, that of the surrealists who managed to find in the detritus of the unconscious a powerful engine of social reform.

The effect of Anthony on the one hand and of Herbert Read on the other led me to feel that it was a mistake to start by accepting any theory based on aesthetic feeling. A materialist should begin by looking at the social and economic forces which determine changes in art and in its valuation. Without altogether losing sight of Plekhanov he should study Veblen; both of them talk a good deal of nonsense, but in each there are valuable truths.

At this point I am tempted to write many pages, the substance of which I have already given to the world without the world showing the faintest interest. I will therefore desist. I will merely repeat that as an historian Anthony seemed to me first rate and that as a theorist he was disappointing.

In an account of Anthony it is not irrelevant to mention his friends – or perhaps one should say accomplices. Donald Maclean and Kim Philby I did not know, but I certainly did know Guy Burgess. I must have met him when I met Anthony at Cambridge; my impression is that I did not see him again until the Second World War. Then it was at the Reform Club and he greeted me as though we had been intimate for many years. He did not talk about Anthony, but he talked a good deal about Julian.

Guy was a story-teller. I would not say that his stories were always true but they were unfailingly interesting – take for instance the following story about the great Lord Salisbury, a statesman for whom Guy had a considerable admiration. Lord Salisbury liked to go home by an early train; foreign diplomats would be invited to arrive at Hatfield later in the day. When they arrived they were ushered into a small room furnished with bookcases; here they would invariably notice a volume the title of which suggested 'very curious' contents; the diplomat could never resist the impulse to take out the volume and read it. In this he failed, the book could not be removed because it was a dummy glued into place between two others. As the unlucky diplomat struggled with the immovable volume Lord Salisbury entered the room and was able to begin the negotiation with a distinct advantage.

Guy told this story so well that one was almost obliged to suspend disbelief. I must admit that when he told me almost equally improbable stories concerning J.M. Barrie he was able to meet my incredulity by taking a volume from the shelves of our club.

On a later occasion I met him at the Reform before lunch and we had a drink together or, more precisely, we both had a gin and ginger and while I drank mine he had his glass refilled six times. I was amazed that he remained standing and coherent, or at least fairly coherent. He had just returned from Washington DC. He expressed his hatred for the Americans with great vigour and although I, too, disapproved of their policies, I was astonished by his violence and his bitterness. He ceased to convince or to amuse me and I escaped as soon as I could. I never saw him again and learned a few days later that he had fled the country with Donald Maclean.

When it became certain that they had gone to Moscow I was amazed that our government or the Soviet authorities should have employed Burgess. It seemed and still seems to me almost incredible that he should ever have been entrusted with secrets of any importance.

I did not really get to know Anthony at all well until 1959 when I found myself in charge of the Department of Fine Art in the University of Leeds. It was a pleasant but in some ways an awkward situation. 'Teachers', we are told, 'are those who, because they can't do a job, teach it'. This has been my position in academic life, and I could make a case for those who teach by learning in company with their students. But it must be allowed that the position of a head of department who knows very little of his subject and yet needs to recruit and employ colleagues who are better informed than he, is somewhat delicate. The really great scholars naturally tend to consider scholarship a necessary qualification for teaching and to be severe in their judgements. To seek their help without, as they might naturally think, fully deserving it, seemed perilous.

I had not seen Anthony for years; he may very likely have known that there were intellectual differences between us. He and Julian had parted company; all that I really had in my favour was the fact that my father-in-law, A.E. Popham, was a most respectable scholar and that my wife had been Anthony's student at the Courtauld Institute. How much importance he attached to these family connections I do not know; he never said anything to make me think that he needed reasons for his generosity. He quite simply did everything that he could to help me make a success of my job. He helped me to find a really competent and hard-working assistant in Eric Cameron; it is true that I knew him already but I had no way of knowing how good he was until Anthony informed me. Although he never mentioned it I have good reason to believe that I owe it to him that I later became Slade Professor at Oxford. I received a great deal of assistance from him when I was researching my study of Degas. He came to stay with us and to give his Poussin lecture at Leeds and he invited me to lecture at the Courtauld Institute on Ruskin. This, it must be said, was rather an awkward sort of privilege; like others I felt considerable misgivings at the prospect of addressing such a scholarly audience and he, knowing what I should feel, handed me a rather large glass of brandy before I descended to the lecture hall. In short he treated me as a friend and I was grateful.

In 1964 Sarah Whitfield, a Courtauld student, came to Charleston to make a catalogue of drawings and noticed a seventeenth-century landscape which excited her interest. Duncan had bought it in a shop in the Rue des Saints-Pères for about £40 and it had hung first in Gordon Square and later had been taken to Charleston. It looked Poussinesque and as Clive once said to a guest, 'we think that it is by one of the many artists called Millet'. Miss Whitfield thought that it might be by Poussin himself and, returning to London, mentioned the matter to Anthony. He and John Sherman immediately came to Charleston, looked at the picture and at once identified it as one of a series of three commissioned landscapes by Poussin.

Anthony admitted to me that he was a little shocked. He supposed that the picture had always been at Charleston and that, in the days when Julian used to invite him to stay, he must have looked at it repeatedly without recognizing it for what it really was. In fact it was then in Gordon Square where it was most improbable that he would ever have seen it.

Anthony was very anxious to buy it and Duncan, who needed the money, agreed to sell; the price was fixed by an outside party (Agnew). It was high enough to oblige Anthony to pay in instalments, an arrangement which suited Duncan very well at that time. Subsequently Anthony was offered a larger sum by Montreal and sold it. In his account of the transaction Richard Shone observes that 'this was an act to which Duncan referred with philosophic forbearance'. Certainly it would have been pleasant for Duncan if the first valuation had been as high as the second, although Anthony probably could then not have afforded to buy the picture. But neither Duncan, who was the least avaricious of men, nor I think most other people, would have expected to receive part of the profit on the second transaction.

*

Here I leave my very brief account of Anthony as I knew him in the years before his reputation was publicly damaged. If his subversive activities had never been made public he would I suppose have been remembered as a great scholar, a great administrator and a kindly and decent human being – occasionally malicious, as art historians can be, but an amusing and generous friend. But now we have to face the fact that he was a traitor and a spy.

Regrading the charge of treachery, I must confess that my own moral feelings are unorthodox. 'Treason doth never prosper: what's the reason? For if it prosper, none dare call it treason.' Sir John Harington, an Elizabethan, puts the matter very clearly; his epigram was well illustrated in the late seventeenth century. Monmouth raised a revolt against James II, it did not prosper and he was beheaded. William and Mary did likewise, prospered, and became King and Queen. Later on the Jacobites rose against the reigning house, they too failed and lost their heads. The majority of Englishmen are loyal to the winning side even when it is the other side that won; we do not now think of George Washington as a traitor. But over and above this we may excuse those who are traitors in what we consider a good cause, like those German generals who would have betrayed Hitler.

Political treachery is more easily excused than private treachery: there is something about Judas Iscariot that we do not like.* The cheat and the liar in private life can justly be accused of treachery and in using the word we all know what we mean. The definition seems to me much less clear when we accuse someone like Sir Roger Casement of treason for he was politically motivated. I would accuse Anthony and his accomplices not so much of betraying their country as of betraying themselves: they were converted to a religion and it was a bad religion. One may excuse them on the grounds that they were, in the beginning at all events, fighting against something as mendacious as any religion. British governments had not hesitated to tell lies, as for instance when the Soviets were accused of nationalizing women. Those of us who canvassed for the Labour Party in those years grew accustomed to the accusation that we were paid in 'red gold', but to reply to such accusations by imitating them was both wrong and foolish.

When I describe communism as a religion I mean that although like other faiths it inspired effective and at times heroic activities, it also asked of its believers that they should accept certain proposi-

---

* 'We' i.e. the agnostics. Believers must surely love Judas, for without him Christianity, as we know it, would hardly have been possible.

tions without question and be ready to turn a blind eye to certain facts. In almost every religion there is an injunction to take some things on trust and to believe 'because it is impossible'.* Thus when all the world knew that Stalin was murdering his comrades the faithful had somehow to be blind and deaf. In their enthusiasm for the cause and their impatience with social democracy young Cambridge forgot the tradition of its university and adopted a dogmatic creed.

Graham Greene writing about Kim Philby compares him to the 'many Catholics who, in the reign of Elizabeth, worked for the victory of Spain. Philby has a chilling certainty in the correctness of his judgement, the logical fanaticism of a man who, having once found a faith, is not going to lose it because of the injustices or cruelties inflicted by erring human instruments.'[†]

But the Comintern ended by asking too much of the faithful. Most of the British comrades could, and eventually did, leave the Party, thrown off by the violent changes of direction in Moscow, but for those who were seduced by the idea of espionage it was more difficult.

Whether espionage is in itself an immoral thing I do not know. King Alfred the Great, disguised as a minstrel, is said to have acquired military intelligence in the Danish camp and I do not know that this is held against him.[††] The spy risks his life for his country, but governments not unnaturally treat spies severely. I fancy that we forgive our own spies and perhaps even those who, employed by our enemies, betray them.

Reading Andrew Boyle's *The Climate of Treason* it is difficult not to feel a certain sympathy for those men who committed themselves to an arduous and dangerous double life. Here we can see how two of these communists – Philby and Burgess – attempted to disarm suspicion, Philby by joining the Spanish fascists as a journalist, Burgess by associating with those right-wing politicians who were on the friendliest terms with Hitler. To cultivate such friendships must have been a kind of torture. Also, so it seemed to me, a very serious disqualification if they were to seek employment in a nation

---

* 'Certum est quia impossibile est', Tertullian *De Carne Christi*, pt. II, C. 5
[†] Graham Greene, preface to *My Silent War* by Kim Philby, McGibbon & Kee, 1968, quoted by Andrew Boyle, *The Climate of Treason*, Hutchinson, 1982, p. 503
[††] See *Dictionary of National Biography*

at war with the fascist powers. In this I was quite mistaken; as near-fascists Burgess and Philby were it would seem quite acceptable to our intelligence services.

Anthony was never driven to such expedients, nor so far as I know did he ever attempt to conceal those left-wing sympathies to which he had given expression in his writings on art. It was not until 1940 that he found a job in intelligence; considering all the other things that he found time to do while this appointment lasted it would not seem to have been a full-time job and most of the time he would have been sending information not to an enemy but to an ally.

Margaret Thatcher, not a friend of Anthony, said that 'it was unlikely British military operations or British lives were put at risk'.* It has been suggested that Anthony may have been responsible for the death of others who were not British, but this would seem to be pure speculation.

When Burgess and Maclean decamped, Anthony helped them and I for one do not blame him for that. Philby followed them and thereafter Anthony was under suspicion. He was questioned at a series of interviews and finally accepted the offer of immunity from prosecution and from publicity in return for a complete confession. This was in 1964. In 1979 however the then Prime Minister, Mrs Thatcher, decided to ignore this undertaking; to prosecute him on the basis of his voluntary confession was not legally practicable, but he could be disgraced and arraigned before Parliament. Her conduct was applauded by the great and the good but perhaps, as a condemnation of treachery, it is not exemplary.

Anthony's knighthood was annulled; there was a considerable outcry and perhaps a certain resentment that he should have escaped punishment. It was rather humiliating that first Burgess and Maclean and then Philby had managed to make a get-away, and now the fourth of the Cambridge spies, while remaining in England, was still a free man. Nor was this all; Anthony was able to make a new confession in the *Times* offices while the journalists of the tabloid press were excluded; he had been neither assaulted or abused, he had even – horrible to relate – been given lunch.

I do not know whether he appreciated the comedy of these trans-

*See Andrew Boyle, *The Climate of Treason*, p. 215

actions but I certainly felt that he needed what little amusement he could get from his situation. Friends reported that he had aged greatly; he had in fact been struck by cancer which, though not mortal, cannot have been easy to bear. A few of his old friends and students felt that they could not desert him, but he must at that time have been the most unpopular man in England. At the very least he had been guilty of disastrous folly, and perhaps of something far less forgiveable. It was therefore with very mixed feelings that we accepted an invitation to lunch from old friends with whom Anthony was staying in Lewes.

He was old and worn but did not look the total wreck that I was expecting. In fact I was amazed by his resilience. He could sit with us and crack jokes about his fall from grace, never for a moment appearing bitter, angry, or sorry for himself. It was a most successful lunch party. If he was anxious or downcast he never let us see it; whatever else Anthony may have lacked, he did not lack courage.

APPENDIX I

A Room of One's Own and Three Guineas

WAS VIRGINIA, AS Leonard suggested, 'the least political animal that has ever been since Aristotle invented the definition'? At times, rereading *Three Guineas*, I have agreed with him. But one does not feel this so strongly when one reads *A Room of One's Own*. Here Virginia is not concerned with politics in the ordinary sense of the word. Her subject is fiction, a subject which she addresses with the greatest authority and the work itself is presented to us as fiction so that one need not regard the various little taradiddles – as for instance those concerning university regulations – with any concern, for she has already told us that she will mix fact with fancy. But although this work keeps clear of party politics it is political.

Alex Zwerdling in his admirable *Virginia Woolf and the Real World* tells us that Virginia Woolf felt anger but suppressed it: 'In place of anger we have irony; in place of sarcasm, charm.' *A Room of One's Own* is indeed a condemnation of anger. 'Anger had snatched my pencil while I dreamt. But what was anger doing there?' What indeed? For she goes on to point out that if she, the female novelist, is angry 'she will never get her genius expressed whole and entire. Her books will be deformed and twisted. She will write in a rage where she should write calmly. She will write foolishly where she should write wisely.'

Talleyrand said that politics is 'the art of the possible'. If you want to get your brother to behave sensibly – and this roughly speaking is the essence of Virginia's kind of feminism – you may attempt to coerce him but you will probably find it easier to persuade him. This was at all events the policy of those whom one may call the 'suffragists'. But it was not the policy of the suffragettes. In America we still find a devoted band of feminist critics who believe that it is a fault in Virginia's work that she did not lose her temper. She smiles and mocks when she ought to be screaming and spitting. With enviable self-assurance they assume that they know better than Virginia how her books should be written; she should have understood that 'anger is a primary source of creative energy'. These critics seem unconcerned with policy, rather they are thinking in terms of aesthetic value and there I am not qualified to comment. But it is worth considering the political implications of a literature which aims at the cultivation of violent hatred. It cannot be denied that writing of this kind can have impressive results: the denunciation of nations, of minorities, of classes and perhaps above all of races, has had an undeniably important effect upon the world and perhaps the same kind of effects might be achieved by setting sex against sex. I do not think that Virginia had any such ambition.

For what it is worth, my opinion is that *A Room of One's Own* is a masterpiece and makes a convincing case which might have been weakened by yells of hatred. It is, however, difficult to measure its effect upon society. It was an immense success and it may be that it bore political fruit, but the chief aims had already been attained. Women had won the vote, subject to an age limit, in 1918 (it is worth noting that this was not the result of window breaking, although the memory of militancy may have helped; in principle the vote was given for patriotic work by women during the First World War). Virginia was not greatly interested, nor I think did she take much notice of the 1928 Act which gave women complete political equality with men. I think it is possible, even, that Virginia forgot that this important event had taken place. The years 1928 and 1929 were for her a happy time. Her fame was growing and Europe had some reason to hope that the enmities of the past might be forgotten and that those disputes which remained might be settled. But the years which followed were years of disaster. Everywhere reaction triumphed: in the Far East, in Abyssinia, in Germany and finally in Spain, everywhere it bred war or the threat of war. Meanwhile Virginia was engaged upon *The Years*, a work which, although it was a commercial success, did not quite satisfy her. It was also horribly difficult to write and nearly led her to a nervous breakdown. Finally, in 1937, public tragedy was merged with private tragedy:

her nephew, Julian, was killed in Spain. By this time Virginia was at work on *Three Guineas*. I think it suffered from the deterioration of the political climate.

Three Guineas is a much less cheerful work than *A Room of One's Own* but I would not call it an angry book. There is a good deal of fun, witness the comic pictures of gentlemen disguised as historical monuments. There is also some fascinating and moving information concerning the achievements and tribulations of women. The book consists of three letters, the first of which is addressed to an imaginary man, a man who has been given a great many educational and other advantages and all at the expense of his sisters. This was undeniably true of a great many men, even though the division of wealth and power in 1938 was rather less extreme and less unfair than it had been. But to this she adds that men, unlike women, positively rejoice in war. 'Obviously' she writes, 'there is for you some glory, some necessity, some satisfaction in fighting which we have never felt or enjoyed.' This it seems to me is the main argument of *Three Guineas*, the assertion which gives the book its thrust and its character.

In order to explain her meaning Virginia gives examples of masculine militarism and, to be fair, one of masculine pacifism. She cites a young aristocrat who writes: 'Thank God, we are off in an hour. Such a magnificent regiment! Such men, such horses! Within ten days I hope Francis and I will be riding side by side straight at the Germans.' This surely is a period piece; it is clear that this imprudent young man knows very little about modern warfare – that is, war which was modern in 1914 – and one guesses that if his 'magnificent regiment' does ride 'straight at the Germans' it will not be magnificent for very long. It is no doubt typical of many young soldiers at that moment in history, the kind of thing one might expect from a young soldier, born in a nation which had only a very limited notion of what war was like. This romantic view of war had come to end long before 1918. If any young soldier had used such words in 1939 he would probably have been sent to a mental hospital.

The second example is of another young aristocrat who feared that 'if permanent peace were ever achieved . . . there would be no outlet for the manly qualities which fighting developed'. And yet a long period during which England had been engaged in no great war had not failed to produce those 'manly qualities' which were so evident in the courage, enthusiasm and ignorance of our first specimen.

These two rather slow-witted soldiers are hardly typical of mankind in general. The same may be said of Virginia's one non-conforming example, Wilfred Owen, who had indeed experienced war and objected to it on religious grounds. It is a remarkable fact that in the course of the past 1,500 years or so only a tiny proportion of Christians have opposed war; those who *have* done so were of both sexes. But the vast majority seem to have decided that, in preaching the Sermon on the Mount, our Saviour was talking through his halo. A rather odd example then and one that suggests that the male pacifist is a rarity. And yet, as Virginia should have remembered, there had in the last fifteen years or so been no lack of men willing, like General Sherman, to say: 'War is Hell'. Robert Graves, Richard Aldington, Edmund Blunden, Ernest Hemingway, Ford Madox Ford, Erich Maria Remarque and many others had all expressed their horror of war.

The literature of war in the period 1918–38 is very different from that of both the patriots and the pacifist quoted by Virginia; it describes the horrors, the beastliness and the boredom of the trenches. The only notable exception is T.E. Lawrence and he was not in the trenches, indeed his war seems almost to belong to another age. It reminds us that in former centuries, although the common soldiers may sometimes have been brutalized barbarians, their officers could be skilled professionals and these may indeed have enjoyed war. But they were a tiny minority of the nation; few gentlemen ever became soldiers, nor were they expected to do so. In the fearful struggle against Napoleon no one ever suggested that Frank Churchill should 'do his bit'; there were no white feathers for Mr Knightley nor, it should be added, was there an army of vociferous women baying for blood.

But if the nation under arms is a new idea in Europe and a very new idea in Great Britain, Virginia can still assert that in 1937 the great majority of men 'are today in favour of war. The Scarborough Conference of educated men, the Bournemouth Conference of working men are both agreed that to spend £300,000,000 annually upon arms is a necessity.* They are of the opinion that Wilfred

---

*It should be noticed that the defence budget of 1935 which had been £122 million was increased in 1936 to £158 million – about half Virginia Woolf's figure. See Neville Williams' *Chronology of the Modern World*, 1966, p. 552

Owen was wrong; that it is better to kill than be killed.' We may presume that 'educated' and 'working' are so to speak *noms de guerre* for Conservative and Labour and therefore the 'war makers' were representative of the great mass of the politically conscious population. But are there no politically conscious working women or conservative ladies? Obviously there are; Virginia herself had noticed the presence of women delegates at the Labour Party Conference in 1935. As for the Conservative ladies, no one who has taken part in a parliamentary election can have failed to notice them and I have yet to hear of a pacifist Conservative woman, indeed they seem sometimes more bellicose in their sentiments, more thirsty for the blood of foreigners and criminals than their menfolk; for them the gun, the rope and the birch offer a primrose path to eternal bliss.

Virginia tended to forget that she had a vote; not only did she have one, every adult woman in the country had one too. If women wanted peace and disarmament then, together with that not inconsiderable part of the male population which was of the same opinion, they could have thrown out any government which proposed to rearm the nation.

I do not think Virginia could admit that the great majority of women, if they have any political opinions, tend to share those of their brothers and husbands. She is more inclined to think that the bad treatment from which they have suffered for centuries has alienated women from the other half of society and made them, in a sense, stateless persons whose patriotism must be qualified: 'Our country still ceases to be mine if I marry a foreigner . . . in fact, as a woman, I have no country. As a woman I want no country. As a woman my country is the whole world.' But might it not be possible for a man to say the same thing? It is true that a man cannot marry his way out of his country but there are other means of escape. Virginia's friends T.S. Eliot and Henry James changed their country, while several million others have done likewise by crossing the Atlantic. I doubt whether these migrations had the effect of making the gentlemen less patriotic.

But Virginia clearly did think that in some way her sex excluded her from the full enjoyment of civil liberties. There had been woeful grievances in the past; some remained; the vote was useless, persuasion needed great wealth and clout to succeed. What then was to be done? How were women to prevent war? They were to found a society, a peculiarly unsocial society, without organization, officers or funds. If it had to have a name it could be called the 'Outsiders' Society', it was to be not only pacifist but passive. The members were not to incite their brothers to fight, but neither were they to dissuade them from fighting. They were to maintain an attitude of complete indifference. As Virginia says, the duty to which they would pledge themselves is one of 'considerable difficulty'. It is indeed. To bid a clever girl fall silent while her brothers talk nonsense is brutality worthy of a male tyrant. She is to be sure given a number of subjects upon which to meditate, she is to earn her own living and to agitate for maternity grants: for 'a wage to be paid by the State legally to the mothers of educated men'. A maternity grant to the rich alone would I think be a politically hazardous operation but to agitate for any kind of maternity grant would surely be difficult for a society with no organization.

Virginia believed that the 'Society of Outsiders' was already in being and supported her assertion with these examples: the Mayoress of Woolwich had declared that she 'would not even do as much as darn a sock to help in the war'. Miss E.R. Clarke of the Board of Education 'referred to the womens' organizations for hockey, lacrosse, netball, and cricket, and pointed out that under the rules there could be no cup or award of any kind to a successful team.' Canon F.R. Barry, vicar of St Mary the Virgin (the University church) at Oxford observed that the daughters of educated men didn't go to church.

The fact that Virginia saw in these reports evidence of a silent feminist and pacifist revolt forces us to consider them with interest and respect. Nevertheless I cannot but think that if the mothers of Madrid, hunting in the debris of their bombed-out homes for the shattered limbs of their babies, had known of this passage in *Three Guineas* they would have said: 'What on earth is there here to save us from the fury of our fascist enemies?' I will return to those murdered children, but first it is necessary to say something about Virginia's kind of pacifism.

There are, I would suggest, two kinds of pacifism, limited pacifism and total pacifism. Limited pacifism condemns any kind of aggression, it also condemns military or imperial rule without the consent of the governed, but it would not condemn armed

resistance to aggression, armed revolt against tyranny, the maintenance of armed forces for a purely defensive purpose, or the supply
of arms to the victims of aggression.

Total pacifism simply forbids any use of military force for any
purpose whatsoever. The total pacifist, it must be allowed, argues
that all aggressors can find reasons for representing their aggressions
as justifiable. Nevertheless I believe that there is a definable difference.

Now I can return to those murdered children: 'Here then on the
table before us are photographs . . . They are not pleasant photographs to look upon. They are photographs of dead bodies for the
most part. This morning's collection contains the photograph of
what might be a man's body, or a woman's; it is so mutilated that it
might, on the other hand, be the body of a pig. But those certainly
are dead children . . .' 'War . . . is an abomination; a barbarity; war
must be stopped' – such is Virginia's reaction; it is also the reaction
of her correspondent. What then is one to do? One can agitate, write
to the press and so on, sign a letter, join a society. But the emotion
caused by the photographs, 'that emotion, that very positive
emotion, demands something more positive than a name written on
a sheet of paper; an hour spent listening to speeches; a cheque
written for whatever sum we can afford – say one guinea . . . You, of
course, could once more take up arms – in Spain, as before in France
– in defence of peace. But that presumably is a method that having
tried you have rejected'. But if the reply to this barbarity has to be
something different from 'a name written on a sheet of paper' or the
use of war in defence of peace, where is the alternative? Virginia's
reply is not wholly clear, but I think that it may be not too unfairly
summarized thus: being a woman and therefore politically power-
less we can do nothing or practically nothing. It is necessary therefore that we should first change our condition and to do this we have
to create the 'Outsiders' Society'.

But, as we have seen, the achievements of that society had not
done much for the people of Madrid. In fact if we adopt the principles of the total pacifist there is practically nothing that can be
done. But was Virginia a total pacifist? Reading *Three Guineas* one
would certainly say that she was. I cannot believe, or believe that
she could believe, that in the 1930s the British Government, or
indeed the British nation, *wanted* to undertake an aggressive war.

And yet, when considering the vote of £300 million for arms Virginia makes it clear that she considered this to be a vote in favour of war. This is quite in keeping with the views of the total pacifist; the total pacifist would tell even the Swiss to disarm. Nevertheless, although the authoress of *Three Guineas* seems to have been an absolutely uncompromising pacifist, Virginia Woolf in her diaries was not.

Let us suppose that she had allowed her fictitious correspondents to say: 'I do not think that we need to make war on behalf of the Spanish republic; we need do no more than is already being done by its enemies, that is to say, to give the people of Madrid the 'planes, the anti-aircraft guns and whatever else they may need for their defence? That might at least save some innocent lives.'

Now consider Virginia's diary for 1937 when she was writing *Three Guineas*. Julian Bell, her nephew, had been killed near Madrid in July of that year. On 13 October Philip Hart, a doctor who had been with Julian, came to see her and described the circumstances in which he died: 'A nice, sensitive thin man, an enthusiast. If we allowed arms through we should save thousands of lives. And then I go upstairs and find Leonard enraged with the Labour Party which sent a deputation to the Foreign Office and was diddled by Vansittart. So we shan't let arms through: we shall sit on the fence: and the fighting will go on – But I am not a politician: obviously, can only rethink politics very slowly into my own tongue.' No, she certainly was *not* a politician, and one has to allow for the horrible and heartbreaking circumstances of that dreadful time. One may sympathize with the apparent contradiction of one who regards the desire to fight as incomprehensible and at the same time calls for the supply of arms to the victim of aggression. These are the words of a 'limited pacifist'; perhaps if one could more perfectly understand what is meant by the 'rethinking of politics' one could arrive at a truer comprehension of those hard sayings in *Three Guineas* which I find so difficult to accept.

Here perhaps I should end this attempt to examine some of the arguments in *Three Guineas*. It is only fair to say that they are weaker than those in the magnificently successful *A Room of One's Own*. Both sexes deserve justice and I feel that it would be entirely unjust to suggest that, amongst the British, either sex actually *wanted* war in 1938.

Finally I would like to say a word of thanks to the fate that ordained that Virginia should not live to see a female Prime Minister joyfully leading her country into a short but bloody war fought over 'a little patch of ground that hath in it no profit but the name.'

APPENDIX II

Maynard Keynes and His Early Beliefs

I HAVE ALREADY attempted to discuss 'My Early Beliefs' in a book on Bloomsbury published in 1968.* I return to the subject, partly because what I then said needs to be modified, partly because I now want to discuss certain passages which I think ought to be, and have not been, noticed.

First let me attempt, since I am now the only witness, to describe that first reading of the memoir in the summer of 1938. We met at Tilton – Maynard's country house. 'We' consisted of the Memoir Club, i.e. Bloomsbury together with two new recruits – Janie Bussy and myself. Maynard was, as always, charming, brilliant, impressive and very persuasive.

Here let me remind readers that the essay contains three main themes. Maynard began with a description of the meeting at Cambridge between himself and Bertrand Russell on the one hand and D.H. Lawrence on the other. It took place he thought in 1914 (actually it was 1915). The meeting left Lawrence depressed and angry, hating Maynard. These violent feelings were aroused also by Duncan Grant and Francis Birrell, who seemed to him to resemble black beetles, disgusting and obscene. Maynard suggests that Lawrence declared that we – meaning Bloomsbury – were 'done for' and at the end of his paper concludes that, with certain reservations, he thinks that Lawrence was right. [Actually it was Duncan, Francis Birrell and perhaps Maynard himself who were 'done for'.]

The greater part of the paper consists of a description of

---

*Quentin Bell, *Bloomsbury*, Weidenfeld & Nicolson, 1968

Cambridge in Maynard's youth, its charms and its failings. This description merges with a penultimate section in which Maynard considers the political morals which resulted from his arguments concerning Bloomsbury.

The central part of the memoir, that which dealt with young Cambridge around 1903, was that which naturally engaged the greatest attention of his audience, many of whom had of course shared his experiences. There was some critical comment. Desmond MacCarthy felt that Maynard had painted too gloomy a picture. Clive objected that the best years were over before 1903 when Maynard arrived and he, Clive, went down. But on the whole the memoir was well received; it had a nostalgic charm.

Janie and I were depressed. Janie expressed astonishment that our elders and betters had been so obsessed by G.E. Moore. We agreed that Maynard had become very reactionary; we were both more concerned by the immediate future than by pre-war Cambridge. The Munich crisis was drawing near.

Eleven years elapsed. In 1949 David Garnett published 'My Early Beliefs' adding some material taken from letters written to him by Lawrence.* In 1952 F.R. Leavis used Maynard's text in an effort to magnify Lawrence and belittle Bloomsbury. In my own book I pointed out that Lawrence had never attacked Bloomsbury as such, although he clearly disliked Maynard, Duncan and Francis Birrell who was close to Bloomsbury. The fault of these people lay not in any intellectual attitude but in something else – they were attractive and they attracted Bunny (David Garnett).

Lawrence regarded Bunny as his own disciple; he was a jealous prophet who could not bear that his followers should be led astray. Francis Birrell was also condemned: 'Keynes, Grant, Birrell . . . were all very delightful people. They could also be imagined, when once the demon of jealousy had taken command, as rivals, not rival intellectual influences but sexual rivals . . . Lawrence's nightmare insects were in fact . . . erotic phenomena.'†

In saying this I was looking in the right direction but I did not look far enough. I produced evidence the implications of which I should have considered; it is contained in a letter from Lawrence to Bunny.

---

* In *Two Memoirs*, ed. David Garnett, Hart-Davis, 1949
† *Bloomsbury*, pp. 75–6

> Yesterday, at Worthing, there were many soldiers. Can I ever tell you how ugly they were. 'To insects – sensual lust.' I like sensual lust – but insectwise, no – it is obscene. I like men to be beasts – but insects – one insect mounted on another – oh God! The soldiers at Worthing are like that – they remind me of lice or bugs . . .

Here no one, not even Dr Leavis, could suppose that Lawrence was talking about Bloomsbury, but also it is quite clear that he is in no way jealous; he is simply shocked.

Since the publication of my book a great deal of new information has appeared. Professor S.P. Rosenbaum has written a magisterial summary of the evidence.* It is now clear that Lawrence objected not so much because his friend Bunny was being seduced by Duncan and Francis but rather because he felt that their sexual activities were obscene. Lawrence himself had homoerotic feelings but as Rosenbaum puts it 'there can be no doubt that it was Keynes's homosexuality more than anything else that repulsed Lawrence'.

> Suddenly a door opened and K[eynes] was there blinking from sleep, standing in his pyjamas. And as he stood there gradually a knowledge passed into me, which has been like a little madness to me ever since.

Bunny was the brand that Lawrence had to save from burning; his injunction was clear: 'Go away David and try to love a woman'. Eventually Bunny complied.

All this I tried to say in 1968. I think that it is worth emendation, but since then I have realized that it is the final part of Maynard's lecture which is the most interesting and the most questionable.

'We', that is young Cambridge in the year 1902, 'were among the last of the Utopians, or meliorists as they are sometimes called, who believed in a continuing moral progress by virtue of which *the human race* [my italics] already consists of reliable, rational, decent people, influenced by truth and objective standards, who can be safely released from the outward restraints of convention and traditional standards and inflexible rules of conduct, and left, from now onwards, to their own sensible devices, pure motives and reliable intuitions of the good.'†

---

* *Cambridge Quarterly*, Vol. XI, No. 1, 1982
† *Two Memoirs*, p. 99

This is Maynard in his most cavalier mood, trying to see how much he could get away with and it must be said getting away with a great deal. Clearly he did not mean that young Cambridge in his day was worse informed than the nuns in a convent. But one may at the very least suppose than his fellow students took very little interest in politics and that the anger of the masses, the villainy and cruelty of the ruling classes was unknown to them.

But did they really lead such a sheltered life? In *Sowing*, the first volume of Leonard Woolf's autobiography, he says:

> Of course we were naïve. But age and hindsight unfairly exaggerate and distort the naïvety of youth. Living in 1900 and seeing the present with no knowledge of the future, we had some grounds for excitement and exhilaration. The long drawn out crucial test of society and politics in the Dreyfus Case had not yet ended in decisive defeat for the old régime, but the 'pardoning' of Dreyfus foreshadowed their final defeat ...

No one who took an interest in the Dreyfus affair could fail to notice the anger of the mob, a mob cozened by the villainy and cruelty of the ruling class.

The faults and follies which led to the judicial crime by which Captain Dreyfus was persecuted were confined to France, but it was not difficult for an intelligent young man to guess that other crimes – in South Africa or China – might be the work of other nations. How then were these to revere their rulers?

Now the charge that Maynard made against himself when young and by implication against Janie and me, was that we lacked reverence. 'We had no respect for traditional wisdom or the restraints of custom. We lacked reverence, as Lawrence observed and as Ludwig [Wittgenstein] with justice also used to say – for everything and everyone.'

Leonard, in the work from which I have quoted, examines this charge and, using the dictionary, he finds two meanings for the word 'reverence': on the one hand to regard as 'sacred or exalted', which seems to be the meaning of the word as used by Maynard, Wittgenstein and, presumably, D.H. Lawrence; and on the other 'deep respect and warm approbation' – what Leonard felt for G.E. Moore. The trouble about this definition is that it can too easily be stretched. If for instance Roger Fry, who never felt a great respect for Moore, had found fault with his philosophy Leonard would have argued with him, but would not have condemned him for irreverence.

This is not nearly strong enough for D.H. Lawrence, for Maynard or it may be for Wittgenstein; reverence transcends argument, it is born not in the brain, but in the solar plexus. One must bow down in the House of Rimmon and one must ask no questions, to do so would be deeply offensive to all good Rimmonites.

It would seem that the young men at Cambridge were, in this sense, irreverent: they believed in the innocence of Dreyfus, whereas if they had regarded the authorities of Church and State with proper reverence they would have thought him guilty.

Maynard continues: 'It did not occur to us to respect the extraordinary accomplishment of our predecessors in the ordering of life (as it now seems to me to have been) or the elaborate framework which they had devised to protect this order.'

I wish that Maynard had said rather more about this elaborate framework; he does not tell us who constructed it or where or when. All that we know is that he and his friends did not respect it. From this are we to conclude that he and they disregarded or disobeyed the laws of their own country? That they were, in the common sense of the word, habitual criminals I do not believe. But there was one convention which they certainly did disregard. Judged by the traditional standards and inflexible rules of conduct accepted for centuries by our predecessors, sodomy is a crime. At one time it was a capital offence. At the time with which Maynard is concerned it was still an almost unmentionable obscenity and until quite recently it was punished quite severely. What, given his earlier beliefs and his earlier love affairs, did Maynard really think and feel about homosexuality? Unfortunately we are never told. He passes on to other topics and develops his defence of unreason. 'Some of the spontaneous, irrational outbursts of human nature can have a sort of value from which our schematism was cut off. Even some of the feelings associated with wickedness can have value. And in addition to the values arising out of spontaneous, volcanic and even wicked impulses, there are many objects of valuable contemplation and communion beyond those we knew of – those concerned with the order and pattern of life amongst communities and the emotions they can inspire.'

I cannot think that Maynard intended to write an apology for those who lynch negroes or put Jewish children into gas chambers, but how easy it would have been for those who acted on 'spontaneous volcanic' impulses, those who ordered the pattern of life, teaching communities to unite in their hatred of alien races and to rejoice in murder, to quote Maynard's words and find in them a 'sort of value'?

At this point it may be useful to return to that original meeting in 1915 which started the entire paper. The third party in that discussion was Bertrand Russell; he asserts that 'Lawrence had developed the whole philosophy of fascism before the politicians had thought of it'. This, surely, is an overstatement; Lawrence was neither a nationalist nor a racialist. But he did sympathize with the idea of an authoritarian state, he trusted in the solar plexus rather than the brain, he demanded not consent but obedience. Perhaps we may say that he was not a fascist but that he was not entirely unsympathetic to fascist ideology.

Can we say the same of Maynard? Certainly one couldn't say it of Maynard in his youth; but Maynard in 1938 is a more doubtful proposition. What really were his beliefs? For the purposes of my argument I have of course neglected a great deal; in fact he had two personalities. In addition to the Squire of Tilton there was the young Mr Keynes whom Maynard later condemned but who wouldn't be silenced. Old Keynes deplored the repudiation by the young of conventional morality. Young Keynes interrupted him: 'I remain and always will remain an immoralist'. He condemned the 'religion' of Moore's disciples, only to insist that 'it was a very good religion to grow under . . . it is still my religion under the surface'. And finally, having argued with vehemence that Lawrence was in the right, he discovered that he was not so very right after all. Maynard contradicted himself and this enables me also to be equivocal. Politically Maynard's earlier beliefs make me find his later beliefs deplorable. But the survival of the young Maynard allows us to forgive the old one and to continue to love him.

Index

Aberconway, Christabel, Lady: *The Divine Gift* 136
Abyssinia 36
Acton, Lorna (*née* Bell; QB's aunt) 24–6, 60
Acton, William 25–6
Albert Hall meeting (1937) 17–19
Aldington, Richard 215
Alfred (the Great), King 209
Alfriston, Sussex 6
Angus, Peggy 16
Annan, Noel, Baron 144
Annie (cook, Gordon Square) 90–1
Anrep, Boris 89, 111
Anrep, Helen 111–12, 177
Apostles (Cambridge society) 27–8, 118, 204
Armour, G.D. 24, 28
Artists' International Association 16, 18
Asham (house) Sussex 6, 116, 137
Asolo, Italy 82–3
Astor, Nancy, Viscountess 25
Atkins, Gabriel 88, 197–8, 201
Attlee, Clement 38–9, 146
Auden, W.H. 124
Austen, Jane: QB reviews Cecil's book on 133; *Emma* 80–1
Austria: annexed 36

Bagenal, Barbara (*née* Hiles) 39–42, 97
Bagenal, Judith (daughter of N. and B.) 40
Bagenal, Nicholas 40
Balzac, Honoré de 64
Bam (Blanche's paramour) 91
Baring, Maurice 174
Barocchi, Randolfo 92
Barrie, Sir James Matthew 205
Barry, Canon F.R. 217
Beerbohm, Sir Max 138–9

Bell family 22–6
Bell, Anne Olivier (QB's wife): at Hilton 82
Bell, Clive (QB's father): at Gordon Square 7, 90; at Trinity College, Cambridge 27–8; Blunt rejects 204; changed political views 35–9; corrects Lady Aberconway's book 136; Duncan Grant lives with after Vanessa's death 70; eye trouble 36; fails to rebuke Duncan Grant 61; flirtation with Molly MacCarthy 132; in France 11, 34, 49–50; friendship with Desmond MacCarthy 138; infidelities 51; on Keynes's view of Cambridge 222; and Lydia Lopokova 91–2, 101; marriage 29–30, 51, 54–5, 118; meets Vanessa 49–50; pursues Virginia 30, 51, 118; QB admires 120; and QB's schooling 9; radicalism 2, 30; relations with Angelica 34, 37–8; relations with children 55; relations with Leonard Woolf 118–19; relations with Maynard Keynes 88, 97; relations with parents 22; and Roger Fry's credulity 109–10; romances and mistresses 11, 28–9, 33, 35–6, 39, 41–2; on 'significant form' 31; theories of art 31, 119; and Vanessa's financial losses 93; and Vanessa's reaction to Julian's death 56–7; views on First World War 32–4; visits Sandhurst 89; wartime work 4, 33; *Art* 30; *Civilization* 35; *On British Freedom* 33; *Peace at Once* 32–3
Bell, Lieut.-Col. Cory (QB's uncle) 24–6, 34
Bell, Graham 177–8
Bell, Hannah (QB's grandmother) 22, 26
Bell, Julian (QB's brother): at Seend 24; auctions pictures 64; birth 30; childhood 4; death in Spanish Civil War 14, 19, 56,

125, 214, 219; friendship with Janie Bussy 154; hostility to Communism 14–15, 204; learns from Pinault in France 34; and Leonard Woolf 119–20; openness 55–6; post in China 12–13; relations with Blunt 203–4, 206; relations with father 34–5; relations with mother 56; on Roger Fry 107; schooling 2, 8, 90; socialism 8, 10, 120, 203–4; Vanessa helps with Latin 47; visits Garsington 164; 'Notes for a Memoir' 204

Bell, Michael (QB's cousin) 149

Bell, Peggy (QB's cousin) 149

Bell, Quentin: appearance as boy 152; at Seend 24; auctions pictures 64; begins painting 10; birth 2; and David Garnett's courting of Angelica 74–7; and Ethel Smyth 171–5; farm work 101–4; flirtation with Rachel MacCarthy 131–2; illnesses 134; Keynes and Lydia Lopokova treat 94–6; literary endeavours 120; marriage and children 39, 82; musical education 152–3; and Ottoline Morrell 163–5; political convictions 14–15, 38–9, 120; in Political Warfare Executive 77; practises pottery in Five Towns 13–14; relations with father 54–5; scars leg 4; schooling 7–8, 10, 90; sets up pottery 178; sits for Robert Medley 196; taught by governesses 6–7, 90, 151; taught by Pinault in France 9–10, 34; teaching and university posts 153, 184, 188–9, 206; tuberculosis 11–12, 203

Bell, Vanessa (*née* Stephen; QB's mother): affair with Roger Fry 33, 52–3, 107; attachment to Jack Hills 48–9; and Barbara Bagenal 40; birth and family background 44; character and temperament 52, 57; and Clive's Degas reproduction at Cambridge 28; on David Garnett and Angelica 75–6; death 70; defends Forster's clothes 144; devotion to children 55–6; early remoteness from modern art 49–50; education 47–8, 50; Ethel Smyth's friendship with 173–5; and Euston Road group 177; in First World War 4; friendship with Keynes 65, 88, 92–3, 96; and George Bergen 54, 65; and George Duckworth 45–6; in Gordon Square 2; indifference to politics 37; infidelities 51–2, 57; intercepts letters 76; and John Lehmann 123; and Julian's death 19, 56–7, 125; and Keyneses' visits to Charleston 96–7; loses money 93; and Lydia Lopokova 92; marriage 29–30, 33, 51, 54–5, 118; meets Clive in Paris 49–50; moral values 57–8; on Ottoline Morrell 164; painting 63; praises Marjorie

Strachey 154; reconciliation with Angelica 80; relates dream 49; relations with Duncan Grant 33, 52–4, 65–6; relations with parents 22; relations with Virginia Woolf 120; responsibilities as girl 45; restores Shannon portrait 24; and Roger Fry's credulity 108–9; sexual attitudes 51; visits Picasso in Paris 16–17; visits Sandhurst 89

Bell, William Heward (QB's grandfather) 22, 24–6

Berenson, Bernard 21, 93

Bergen, George 54, 65–6

Berwick, Sussex 5

Birrell, Francis 221–3

Black, Mischa 16

Blanche (parlourmaid) 90–1

Bloomsbury group; beginnings 50; membership and composition 30, 118, 150; and Ottoline Morrell 162; under temporary cloud 70; *see also* Gordon Square

Blunden, Edmund 215

Blunt, Anthony 14; artistic theories 204–5; at Cambridge 203–4; buys and sells Duncan Grant's Poussin 207; helps QB 206; political views 204; treason and downfall 207–8, 210–11; *Artistic Theory in Italy, 1450–1600* 204

Blunt, Wilfrid Scawen 138

Bosham 85

Boyle, Andrew: *The Climate of Treason* 209, 210n

Brereton, Mrs (governess) 6

Browning, Robert 150

Burgess, Guy 14, 205–6, 209–10

Burslem School of Art 14

Bussy, Dorothy (*née* Strachey) 147, 149, 151, 154–6; death 160; *Olivia* 147

Bussy, Jane Simone (Janie) 17, 149–52, 154–6, 158–60, 221–2, 224

Bussy, Simon 147–50, 156, 158, 160; portrait of Ottoline Morrell 161

Butts, Anthony (Mary's brother) 196

Butts, Mary; death 201; and Gabriel Atkins 88, 197–8, 201; in Paris 195–6, 198–200; and Robert Medley 195

Calder, Ritchie (Baron Ritchie-Calder) 84

Cambridge University 27, 222–4

Cameron, Eric 206

Cameron, Julia Margaret 44

Cannan, Gilbert 163

Carrington, Dora 39

Casement, Sir Roger 208

Cassel, Sir Ernest 93

Cecil, Lord David 132–3

Cecil, Lady David (*née* Rachel MacCarthy)

Index

130–3, 135

Cecil, Hugh and Mirabel: *Clever Hearts* 130 & n

Ceylon: Leonard Woolf in 117–18, 127

Cézanne, Paul: admired by Euston Road group 177, 180; Bloomsbury admires 118; Blunt admires 203; Bussy studies 148; in Luxembourg gallery 50

Chalmers, Dr Frederick 11

Chamberlain, Neville 20, 37, 125

Charleston (house), Sussex: Bell family move to 4–5, 85; fire at 144; garden 121; rivalry with Monks House 120–2

Chatto & Windus (publishers) 127

Chinese art 31

Cholmeley, Robert Francis 151

Churchill (Keynes's gamekeeper) 100

Churchill, Sir Winston S.: Clive's view of 37; and India 146

Clarke, Miss E.R. 217

Cleeve House *see* Seend, Wiltshire

'Click', the 90–1

Clifton College 47

Coldstream, Sir William 177–8, 181

Coliseum theatre, London 94

Colville Hyde, Mary 200

communism 14–15, 21, 204, 208–9

Cook, Ebenezer 47

Cope (headmaster) 48

Coué, Emile 110

Courtauld Institute, London 206

Covent Garden Opera House, London 94

Cranium Club, Soho 67

Cromwell, Anna: tomb 151–2

Crossman, Richard 38

Czechoslovakia: annexed 36

Davidson, Angus 65, 123, 201

Degas, Edgar 28, 148, 177, 206

de Grey, Roger 187

Delacroix, Eugène 69

de la Mare, Walter 168

de Saumarez, Maurice 188, 190

Diaghilev, Sergei Pavlovich 196

Dobson, Eric 83, 186

Doone, Rupert 193–7, 202

Dreyfus affair 9, 147, 224–5

Driberg, Tom (*later* Baron Bradwell) 14

Duckworth, George 29, 37, 44; relations with half-sisters 45–6, 48

Duckworth, Gerald 44, 46

Duckworth, Herbert 44

Eleanor (house), West Wittering 85

Eliot, T.S. 108–9, 216

Engels, Friedrich 155

'Euston Road' group (of painters) 177–8

Evelyns preparatory school, London 47

Evening Standard 85

Fabian Society 120

Fawcett, Millicent 170

Firle, Sussex 6

Fitzroy Square, Bloomsbury 51

Five Towns (potteries) 13–14

Forain, Jean Louis 28–9

Ford, Ford Madox 215

Forster, Edward Morgan: contributes to Julian Bell memorial volume 19; dress 144; friendship with Charles Mauron 113; on Leonard Woolf 128; and Ottoline Morrell 162; QB meets 140–2, 144–5; on Virginia Woolf 145; visits Woolfs 141, 143; *Howards End* 142, 151; *The Longest Journey* 142–3; *A Passage to India* 113, 142, 145–6

Forsyth, Gordon 14

France: QB in 9–10, 34, 69; *see also* Paris

Franco, General Francisco 17

Friday Club, The 50, 52

Front Populaire (France) 13

Fry, Julian 108

Fry, Roger: in Bloomsbury group 51; Blunt rejects 204; on Clive's art criticism 31; credulity and eccentric beliefs 108–110, 196; death 115; energy 112; fondness for France 112–14; and G.E. Moore 224; influence on Clive 30; and Mary Butts 195; motoring and cycling 114; as paternal figure for QB 55; qualities and charm 106–8; relations with Helen Anrep 111–12; reputation 110–11; Vanessa's affair with 33, 52–3, 107

Furse, Charles 51

Gage, Henry Rainald Gage, 6th Viscount 100, 104, 140

Gargilesse, France 10

Garnett, Angelica (QB's sister): 21st birthday party 21; at Hilton 81; attends party with Duncan Grant 67–8; as daughter of Duncan Grant 8, 63, 65; David Garnett courts 75–6; David Garnett prophesies marriage to 73; and Ethel Smyth 174–5; illness 75; in Italy with QB 12; and Julian's death 56; lives in Paris 12–13; marriage and children 56, 80; mimics Ottoline Morrell 165; painting 75; political indifference 37–8; QB's childhood jealousy of 7–8; relations with Clive 34, 37–8; and Robert Medley 193; *Deceived with Kindness* 12, 116

Garnett, David ('Bunny'): aeroplane 114; angling 74–5; attitude to Russia 78–80; bee-keeping 72; character and appearance 71–2; contributes to Julian Bell memorial volume 19; courts Angelica 75–6; and D.H. Lawrence 222–3; disturbs Woolfs 116; enthusiasms 73–4; farm work in First World War 4, 62; friendship with Vanessa 65; holiday in Asolo 82–3; homosexuality 65; marriage and children 80–1; as paternal figure for QB 55; in Political Warfare Executive in World War II 77, 79; prophesies marriage to Angelica 73; publishes Keynes's 'My Early Beliefs' 222; reputation and recognition 83–4; in World War I 71–2; *Lady into Fox* 73, 83; *Pocahontas* 83

Garnett, William (David's son) 82

Garsington, Oxfordshire 4, 54, 164; *see also* Morrell, Lady Ottoline

Gaunt, John of 8–9

Germany, Grace 13, 91–2, 94

Gide, André 62, 147, 149, 155

Gimond, Marcel 144

Gladstone, William Ewart 137

Gordon Square, Bloomsbury 2, 6–7, 29, 51–2, 90–1, 150–1

Gowing, Julia (*née* Strachey; *then* Tomlin) 183–4

Gowing, Lawrence: at Leeds 189–92; at Newcastle 184–8; embraces 'abstract expressionism' 188; in Euston Road group 178, 183; invites Medley to Newcastle 201; marriage 184; moves to Chelsea School of Art 188; moves to Slade 192; speech 183–4

Grace (Charleston servant) *see* Germany, Grace

Grant, Duncan: as Angelica's father 8, 33, 63, 65; at Charleston 62–3, 70; attends party with Angelica 67–8; attitude to money 69–70, 207; in Bloomsbury group 30, 51, 61; charm 60–1, 68; and David Garnett's courting of Angelica 75; D.H. Lawrence dislikes 221–3; driving 67; early remoteness from Impressionism 50; Ethel Smyth's friendship with 173–4; and Euston Road group 177; farm work in First World War 4, 62; in France 69, 193; friendship with Keynes 92–3, 96; homosexual lovers 54, 57, 59, 65, 67; and Keyneses' visits to Charleston 97; knowledge and innocence 63–4; mistaken for Keynes 21, 93; musical interests 64, 68; owns and sells Poussin 207; painting 60, 63; paints Lydia Lopokova 95; on QB's portrait of model 178; relations with QB and Julian 55; relations with Vanessa 33, 52–4, 65–6; reputation 70; role-playing 64; in Rome 165–7; saves harvest mouse 63; supports Ottoline Morrell 163; tastes 68–9; and Vanessa's

reaction to Julian's death 56; visits Italy 88; visits Picasso in Paris 16–17; visits Sandhurst 89; weeps at Vanessa's death 70

Grant, Ethel (Duncan's mother) 151

Graves, Robert 215

Greece: Vanessa and Clive visit 50–1

Greene, Graham 209

Ham Spray (house), Wiltshire 184

Hamilton, Richard 185, 187

Hanoteaux, Gabriel 12

Harington, Sir John 208

Hart, Philip 219

Hecks (Sussex farmer) 62

Hemingway, Ernest 215

Hills, Jack W. 45, 46, 48

Hills, Stella (*née* Duckworth; Vanessa's half-sister) 44–5, 48

Hilton, Huntingdon 73, 81–2

Hitler-Stalin pact (1939) 20

Hoad, Mary 185

Hogarth House, Richmond 6, 117

Hogarth Press 39, 123–4, 127, 150

Holroyd, Michael: biography of Strachey 59

Honey, Dorothy (*née* Bell; QB's aunt) 24, 26–7

Honey, Henry 26–7

Hutchinson, Mary: at Gordon Square 7, 90; Clive's love affair with 33, 35–6; visits Sandhurst 89

Huxley, Aldous 163

Hyde, Mrs Colville *see* Colville Hyde, Mary

Hyde Park Gate, London 44–5, 49

Impressionism: unknown to English artists 50

India: British in 145–6

Ingres, Jean Auguste Dominique 176–7

Isherwood, Christopher 124

Italy 11–12, 180–1; *see also* Rome

I Tatti (Italy) 93

Jackson, Dr John (Vanessa's maternal grandfather) 43

Jackson, Maria (*née* Pattle; Vanessa's maternal grandmother) 43

James, Henry 216

Jenkins, Roy, Baron 33

Jews 38–9

Joachim, Joseph 150

John, Augustus: visits Sandhurst 89; *Pyramus* (painting) 51

Jones, John 189, 192

Jowett, Lesley 89

Judas Iscariot 208 & n

Kapp, Yvonne: and Elizabeth Watson 16; friendship with QB 11–12, 155–6, 201
Kennington, Eric 141
Keynes, Geoffrey 67
Keynes, Mrs Geoffrey 68
Keynes, John Maynard, Baron: at Gordon Square 7; in Bloomsbury group 30, 51; on Cambridge 222–4; champions Ottoline Morrell 163; contributes to Julian Bell memorial volume 19; converted to heterosexuality 60; death 104; D.H. Lawrence dislikes 221–3; escorts QB and Lydia 94–5; farming 98, 101–3; financial speculation 93; and First World War 32–4; and François Walther's plans 13; friendship with Vanessa and Duncan Grant 65, 92–3, 96; gives Bonfire party 103–4; homosexuality and boy friends 51, 59, 65, 88–9, 223, 225; inadequate French 92; marriage to Lydia 95–6, 98, 101; mistaken for Duncan Grant 21, 93; overwork 99–100; peerage 97–8; political involvement 86–7; political views 101; prophesies defeat of Bolsheviks 78; relations with Clive 88, 97; shooting 99; social and moral values 221–6; and Stracheys 150; teaches QB 9, 101; on trip to Sandhurst 89–90; visits to Charleston 85–6, 88, 100–1; 'My Early Beliefs' 20, 221–6; *The Economic Consequences of the Peace* 32, 60, 88
Keynes, Lydia, Lady *see* Lopokova, Lydia
Kipling, Rudyard 145
Knox, George 186
Kokoschka, Oskar 107

Labour Party (British): 1935 Conference 216; 1945 government 38; QB's membership of 14; and war threat 13
Lansbury, George 13
Lansdowne, Henry Charles Keith Petty-Fitzmaurice, 5th Marquess of 32–3
Lawrence, D.H. 61–2, 163, 221–6
Lawrence, T.E. 141, 215; *The Seven Pillars of Wisdom* 142
Leavis, F.R. 222–3
le Bas, Edward 65
Lee, Hugh: *A Cézanne in the Hedge and Other Memories of Charleston and Bloomsbury* 86n
Leeds University 188–92, 206
Lehmann, John: and Hogarth Press 123–4, 127
Lehmann, Rosamond 123
Leighton Park school, Reading 8, 10
Lenin, V.I. 35
Lewes, Sussex: Bonfire celebrations 103;

QB visits in childhood 6
Lewis, Wyndham 61–2
Lintott, Sir Henry 14
Loesers (neighbours of Berensons) 93
Lopokova, Lydia (Lady Keynes): at Gordon Square 91–2, 94; ballet dancing 94; cares for Maynard 99–100; conversation 100–1; dances at Angelica's 21st birthday 21; death 105; dress and undress 100; friendship with Logan Thomson 102; invites QB after Keynes's death 104; marriage to Keynes 95–6; in nursing home 105; outburst at Covent Garden 95; painted by Duncan Grant 95–6; teaches Russian to QB 101; visits to Charleston 97, 100–1
Lusitania, SS 3
Lycée Louis Le Grand, Paris 9

Mabel (servant) 91
MacCarthy, Dermod 130, 133–5
MacCarthy, Desmond: appearance 136–7; and Beerbohm 138–9; in Bloomsbury group 30, 39, 51; champions Ottoline Morrell 163; conversation 129–30, 139; corrects Lady Aberconway's book 136; friendship with Clive Bell 138; infidelities 132; on Keynes's view of Cambridge 222; literary ambitions 129–30; political sympathies 137–8; QB meets 135; on Roger Fry's credulity 108; shooting 138; sits for portrait 60, 136; on Virginia Woolf's reputation 169
MacCarthy, Marie (Dermod's wife) 134
MacCarthy, Michael 130, 133, 135–6
MacCarthy, Molly: in Bloomsbury group 30, 39; and children 130–1, 134; deafness 135; on Desmond's appearance 136–7; flirtation with Clive Bell 131–2; founds and runs Memoir Club 135, 137; qualities 137
MacDonald, Ramsay 8, 98
Maclean, Donald 205–6, 210
Manning, Cardinal Henry Edward 62
Marlborough College 27–8
Marshall, Frances *see* Partridge, Frances
Marx, Karl 155
Massine, Leonid 94
Matisse, Henri: Barbara Bagenal visits 42; driving 159; friendship with Simon Bussy 148; QB meets 156–9; QB secures signature for Albert Hall meeting 17–18; reputation 176
Mauclair, Camille 49
Mauron, Alice (Charles's second wife) 115
Mauron, Charles 19, 113–15, 142–3
Mauron, Marie (*née* Roumanille; Charles's first wife) 113, 115

Mayor, Beatrice (*née* Meinertzhagen) 29

Mayor, Freddie 96

Medley, Robert: attempts portrait of QB 196; death 193, 202; later career 201–2; in Paris 193–4; relations with Rupert Doone 193–5; *Drawn from the Life* 202

Meek (Seend parlourmaid) 25

Meinertzhagen, Beatrice *see* Mayor, Beatrice

Memoir Club 20–1, 135, 137, 221

Millers (house), Lewes, Sussex 179

Mitz (Leonard Woolf's marmoset) 125

Monaco 12

'Monica' 197–200

Monks House, Rodmell (Sussex) 120–2, 143

Monteverdi, Claudio 112

Moore, G.E. 27, 118, 222, 224, 226

Moravia, Alberto 165

Moreau, Gustave 148

Morrell, Lady Ottoline: appearance and dress 161, 164, 167; and Bloomsbury group 30, 162–3; Bussy portrait of 161; Clive Bell works for 4, 33; in Rome 165–8

Morrell, Philip ('Pipsy') 33, 165–7

Morris, Peter 65

Mortimer, Raymond 49, 143–4, 150

'Mud Hut, The' (house), near Haslemere 131

Müller, William 203

Munich 10

Munich agreement (1938) 20

Mussolini, Benito 35–6

Naples 11

Napoleon III, Emperor of France 153

National Union of Women's Suffrage Societies ('Suffragists') 170

New Statesman (journal) 77, 79

New Yorker (magazine) 169

Newcastle under Lyme 15

Newcastle-upon-Tyne 82–3, 184–8

Nicolson, Vita, Lady *see* Sackville-West, Vita

Noach, Arnold 188–92

Norton, Harry 7, 90

Ovens (Seend chauffeur) 24

Owen, Wilfred 215–16

Owen's School, Islington 8, 151

Oxford Movement 14

pacifism *see* war and pacifism

Palestine post-war settlement 38–9

Paley, G.A. 135

Pankhurst, Christabel 170

Pankhurst, Emmeline 170–1

Paris: QB in 10, 96, 176, 193, 197–8; Vanessa in 49–50

Paris Exhibition, 1937 ('Expo 37') 16, 18

Parliament Bill (1911) 30

Parsons, Trekkie (*née* Ritchie) 126–7

Partridge, Frances (*née* Marshall): acquires Gowing still-life 183; at Ham Spray 184; on Barbara Bagenal 41; and Cecils 132; invites QB to Spain 131; relations with Clive Bell 36; speaking voice 151

Partridge, Ralph: at Ham Spray 184; at Hogarth Press 123; Duncan Grant dislikes 62; visit to Spain 131

Pasmore, Victor 177–8, 187

Paul, Rose 7, 90, 151

Peterborough Lodge (school), London 8

Philby, Kim 205, 209–10; *My Silent War* 209n

Picasso, Pablo: Barbara Bagenal meets 42; Lydia Lopokova meets 96; Matisse on 157; QB meets 34; QB secures signature 16–19; reputation 176

Pinault, Henri 9–10, 34, 96

Pinault, Madame Henri 96

Playfair, Sir Edward 14, 17, 165

Plekhanov, Georgy Valentinovich 204

Plomer, William 109

Poland: Chamberlain's guarantee to 20

Popham, A.E. 206

Post-Impressionist Exhibition, Second (1912) 30

Poussin, Nicholas 166, 203, 207

Prinsep, Val (Vanessa's cousin) 44

Rapallo 138

Ravel, Maurice: *Bolero* 193–4

Raven-Hill, Annie (*née* Rogers) 28–9

Raven-Hill, Leonard 28

Read, Herbert 204

Remarque, Erich Maria 215

Renoir, Auguste 31

Renoir, Jean (Auguste's nephew) 9–10

Richardson, Marion 110

Ritchie, Trekkie *see* Parsons, Trekkie

Roaf, Dr 8

Robey, George 94–5

Rodin, Auguste 50

Rogers, Claude 177–82; *Tradition in Art* 179

Rogers, Elsie 179, 181

Rome 11–12, 165–8, 181

Rosenbaum, S.R. 223

Rossetti, Dante Gabriel 185

Rouault, Georges 148

Rowntree, Kenneth 182

Royal Academy Schools 48, 50

Rubinstein, Ida 193–4

Ruskin, John: influence 106–7; QB lectures on 206; *Elements of Drawing* 47; *Modern Painters* 106; *Praeterita* 106
Russell, Bertrand 221, 226
Rutherford, Dr Raymond 125
Rylands, George (Dadie) 123

Sackville-West, Edward 112
Sackville-West, Vita (Lady Nicolson) 12, 119
St Denis, Michel 73
St Ives: Talland House 45
St Tropez, France 7
Salisbury, Robert Arthur Talbot Gascoyne-Cecil, 3rd Marquess of 205
Sand, George 10
Sandhurst 89
Sargant-Florence Alix 39
Sargent, John Singer 48–9, 148
Savage, Sir George 46
Scala, La (Charlotte Street opera house, London) 142
Scott, William Bell 185
Seend, Wiltshire: Cleeve House 22–6, 60
Selwood, Mabel 3
Sevigné, Marie de Rabutin-Chantal, Marquise de 54
Seymour, Miranda: *Ottoline Morrell* 161–3, 165
Shannon, Sir James Jebusa 24
Shaw, George Bernard: *The Intelligent Woman's Guide to Socialism and Capitalism* 172
Sheehan, James 165–6
Sheppard, Sir John T. 7, 90
Sherman, John 207
Sherman, General William Tecumseh 215
Shone, Richard 70, 207
Shove, Fredegond (Vanessa's cousin) 46
Shove, Gerald 30
Sickert, Walter: on Duncan Grant 53; and Euston Road group 177
Skidelsky, Robert, Baron 41n, 93
Smith, Logan Pearsall 62
Smyth, Dame Ethel: attachment to Virginia Woolf 171, 173–5; music 173–4; and QB 171–2, 175
Snowden, Marjery 50
Sophy (cook) 45
Spalding, Frances 59
Spanish Civil War: Julian Bell killed in 14, 19, 56, 125, 214, 219
Spender, Sir Stephen 124
Sprott, Sebastian (Jack) 88–9
Stacey, Revd Nick 186n
Stalin, Josef V. 37, 209
Stalingrad, Battle of 80
Standen, Becket 104

Stein, Gertrude 158
Stephen family 43–4
Stephen, Adrian (Vanessa's brother) 44, 47, 65, 150
Stephen, Julia, Lady: death 48; marriages 43–4; relations with Vanessa 45
Stephen, Karin (QB's aunt) 150
Stephen, Laura (Leslie's daughter by Minny) 43–4
Stephen, Sir Leslie: on bores 41; and children's education 47–8; death 49; marriages 43; moral values 57; and Vanessa's dream 49
Stephen, Minny (*née* Thackeray; Leslie's first wife) 43
Stephen, Thoby (Vanessa's brother): and art 50; at Cambridge 27, 29, 47, 50, 117; born 44; death 29, 51, 118; schooling 47
Sterne, Laurence 194
Stevens, Sir Roger 100, 189–90
Stoke on Trent 14
Strachey, Alix (James's wife) 20, 150
Strachey, James 20, 150
Strachey, Jane, Lady 147, 149–52
Strachey, John 154–5
Strachey, Julia *see* Gowing, Julia
Strachey, Lytton: appearance 149, 166; at Cambridge 27–8, 50, 117; at Gordon Square 29, 150; Dorothy cares for 147; friendship with Vanessa 50, 65; homosexuality 51, 59, 65; in Naples 166; *Eminent Victorians* 3.60, 149
Strachey, Marjorie 21, 152–4, 162, 183
Strachey, Ray 131
Strachey, Sir Richard 147
suffrage, women's 170–1
Surrealists 176, 204
Sydney-Turner, Saxon: at Trinity College, Cambridge 27–9; and Barbara Bagenal 40; and Ottoline Morrell 162; Vanessa meets 50

Talleyrand, Charles Maurice de Périgord, Prince de 212
Tate, Harry 94
Taylor, Ann and Jane 80
Teed, Lt.-Colonel A.S.H. 10
Thackeray, Isabella (Mrs W.M. Thackeray) 44
Thatcher, Margaret, Baroness 210, 220
Thomson, Logan 101–3, 105
Tilton, Sussex (Keyneses' home) 96, 97–8, 101–5
Times, The 18
Toklas, Alice B. 158
Tomlin, Stephen 183
treason 208
Trinity College, Cambridge 27, 117–18

Index

Trotsky, Leon 155
Tuck, Professor John Philip 184
Turner, J.M.W. 60, 106, 164

USSR: attitude of English intellectuals to 36–7; campaign in 80; invaded 21, 77–8

Vansittart, Sir Robert 219
Vasari, Giorgio 111
Vaughan Williams, Ralph 67
Veblen, Thorstein 204
Venice 49
Verdi, Giuseppe 112

Walther, François ('Pierre Gerôme') 13, 17, 38
war and pacifism 214–18
Watson, Elizabeth 16–18
Watts, George Frederic 44
Wedgwood, Colonel Josiah Clement (later 1st Baron) 15
Weller, Edgar 98–9
Weller, Ruby 98
Wells, H.G. 8
Westminster School 47
Whitfield, Sarah 207
Williams, Neville: Chronology of the Modern World 215n
Wilson, Field Marshal Sir Henry 90
Wissett Lodge, Suffolk 4, 62, 71, 149, 163–4
Wittgenstein, Ludwig 224–5
women's movement 170–1, 213, 216–17
Women's Social and Political Union ('Suffragettes') 170
Woolf, Leonard: amused by Duncan Grant 64; at Monks House 120–2; at Trinity College, Cambridge 27, 117–18; in Bloomsbury group 118, 150; certainties 109; in Ceylon 117–18, 127–8; dislikes QB's childhood noise 3; entertains Bell children 117; essay on Erasmus 35; and Ethel Smyth 172–3; gardening 121, 141; and Hogarth Press 123–4; Julian Bell admires 119–20; keeps marmoset 124–5; and Keynes' peerage 97–8; marriage 118; motoring 114; plays bowls 122; political views and activities 120, 219; protects Virginia 117, 119, 125; QB visits at

Asham 116–17; relations with Clive Bell 118–19; and Roger Fry's ideas 109; in Tavistock Square 150; travel in later years 127; and Trekkie Parsons 126–7; and Virginia's death 126; on Virginia's lack of interest in politics 212; visits QB at Charleston 13; and women 122; Sowing 224
Woolf, Virginia (née Stephen; QB's aunt); amused by Duncan Grant 64; at Seend 23; attitude to father 49; avoids QB's childhood noise 3; and Barbara Bagenal 39–40; birth 44; childhood 45; on Clive's Civilization 35; criticises Desmond MacCarthy's clothes 137; death 126, 169; and Desmond MacCarthy 129; disapproves of Clive as Vanessa's suitor 29; education 47–8; esteem for Forster 141; and Euston Road School of painters 177; and feminism 170–1, 213, 216–17; on John Lehmann 123; and Julian Bell's death 56, 214, 219; Leonard protects 117, 119, 125; marriage 118; and Mary Butts 201; motoring 114; nervous fragility 117, 119, 125, 213; on Ottoline Morrell 162–3, 165; and outbreak of war 125; plays bowls 122; and politics 37, 212–20; pursued by Clive 30, 51, 118; and QB's visits 116–17; relations with Ethel Smyth 171–5; relations with half-brothers 46; relations with Julian Bell 120; reputation 169; on Roger Fry 106; in Tavistock Square 150; tooth trouble 117; and Vanessa's love for Duncan Grant 52; visits QB at Charleston 13; A Room of One's Own 170–1, 212–20; Three Guineas 19, 212, 214, 217–19; The Waves 125; The Years 177, 213
World War I: Clive's views on 32–3
World War II: Clive in 37; Duncan Grant in 37; effect on Virginia Woolf 125–6

You'd Be Surprised (revue) 94–5
Yourcenar, Marguerite 142

Zeller (Bloomsbury baker) 3
Zola, Emile 32
Zwerdling, Alex: Virginia Woolf and the Real World 212

Illustration Credits

1. The author at Charleston by Duncan Grant, 1922, © Henrietta Garnett (photo courtesy of the Charleston Trust)
2. Clive Bell by Henry Lamb, 1911 (photo courtesy of the Charleston Trust/Fitzwilliam Museum)
3. Vanessa Bell, a self-portrait, c. 1958, © Angelica Garnett (photo courtesy of the Charleston Trust)
4. Duncan Grant, a self-portrait, c. 1926, © Henrietta Garnett
5. Maynard and Lydia Keynes by William Roberts, c. 1932
6. Julian Bell and Roger Fry playing chess by Vanessa Bell, c. 1930. Study of a picture at King's College, Cambridge
7. Leonard Woolf by Vanessa Bell, 1940, © National Portrait Gallery
8. Desmond McCarthy by Duncan Grant, c. 1942, © Henrietta Garnett (photo courtesy of the National Portrait Gallery)
9. E. M. Forster by Vanessa Bell, 1940, private collection
10. Lytton Strachey by Vanessa Bell, 1912, private collection
11. Lady Ottoline Morrell by Simon Bussy, c. 1920, © Tate Gallery
12. Ethel Smyth by Quentin Bell
13. Claude Rogers, a self-portrait, 1975, Crispin Rogers (photo courtesy of the Belgrave Gallery)
14. Lawrence Gowing, an undated self-portrait, © Lady Gowing
15. Robert Medley, a self-portrait, 1977, private collection, © the Trustees of the Robert Medley Estate (photo courtesy of the Museum of Modern Art, Oxford)
16. Anthony Blunt by Peter Foldes, 1947, © Courtauld Institute Galleries, London
17. Charleston (photo courtesy of Richard Shone)
18. 46 Gordon Square (photo courtesy of John Moore)

The author and publishers thank Richard Shone for his help in assembling the illustrations.